"Want to hang out your dotcom shingle? It doesn't matter whether you're a man or woman—read this and learn what's in store. Any aspiring entrepreneur can benefit from these compelling tales of imagination, resolve, and bottom-line acumen."

—Don Tapscott, Chair of Digital 4Sight and coauthor of
Digital Capital: Harnessing the Power of Business Webs

"A truly inspiring book filled with great advice from thoughtful business leaders and trailblazing role models. A must-read for any aspiring entrepreneur. It's about time someone wrote about the many amazing women leading the dotcom revolution."

—Denise Brosseau, President and cofounder,
Forum for Women Entrepreneurs and Springboard 2000

"Don't let the title fool you! Dotcom divas aren't cranky singers–they're focused, resourceful, smart, and on the way to revolutionizing the Net. Entrepreneurs like Rosalind Resnick are the cream of the Internet crop . . . we need a lot more like them. Read this book and find out how they're changing the face of e-business."

—Seth Godin,
author of *Unleashing the Ideavirus*

"I have been delighted to see an increasing number of bright young women entrepreneurs who are succeeding in bringing their business ideas into the market. UC Berkeley alumna Elizabeth Carlassare and Haas alumna Kim Fisher of AudioBasket are just two examples of a new breed of enterprising women challenging the myth that entrepreneurship is a male sport. This book tells the inspiring stories of some of these women."

—Laura Tyson, Dean,
Haas School of Business, University of California, Berkeley

"*Dotcom Divas* truly delivers! Real-life drama, inspirational ideas, business blow-by-blows, sound advice . . . this is the fuel for any aspiring or existing entrepreneur. If this doesn't motivate women to start e-businesses in droves, nothing will. You go, grrls!"

—Aliza Sherman, author of *Cybergrrl @ Work* and founder,
Cybergrrl, Inc. and Webgrrls International

Dotcom Divas

Dotcom Divas

E-Business Insights from the Visionary Women Founders of 20 Net Ventures

Elizabeth Carlassare

MCGRAW-HILL

NEW YORK   SAN FRANCISCO   WASHINGTON, D.C.   AUCKLAND   BOGOTÁ
CARACAS   LISBON   LONDON   MADRID   MEXICO CITY   MILAN
MONTREAL   NEW DELHI   SAN JUAN   SINGAPORE
SYDNEY   TOKYO   TORONTO

—To my partner in life and love, Jon

Library of Congress Cataloging-in-Publication Data

Carlassare, Elizabeth.
 Dotcom divas: E-business insights from the visionary women founders of 20 net ventures
 / Elizabeth Carlassare.
   p. cm.
 Includes index.
 ISBN 0-07-136242-8 (cloth)
  1. Electronic commerce—United States. 2. Businesswomen—United States.
  3. Women-owned business enterprises—United States. I. Title
 HF5548.325.U6 C37 2001
 658.8'4—dc21   00-059458
                                                              CIP

McGraw-Hill
A Division of The McGraw-Hill Companies

1 2 3 4 5 6 7 8 9 0   DOC/DOC   0 9 8 7 6 5 4 3 2 1 0

ISBN 0-07-136242-8

This book was set in Clearface & Trade Gothic.
Book design by Michael Mendelsohn at MM Design 2000, Inc.

Printed and bound by R. R. Donnelley & Sons Company.

McGraw-Hill books are available at special quantity discounts to use as
premiums and sales promotions, or for use in corporate training programs.
For more information, please write to the Director of Special Sales, McGraw-Hill,
Two Penn Plaza, New York, NY 10121-2298. Or contact your local bookstore.

 This book is printed on recycled, acid-free paper
containing a minimum of 50% recycled, de-inked fiber.

Contents

The *Dotcom Divas* email list is a discussion forum for women Internet entrepreneurs and anyone interested in the topic of women's entrepreneurship and the Internet. To subscribe, send a blank email to dotcomdivas-subscribe@egroups.com.

Also visit www.dotcomdivas.net. The site provides resources for Internet entrepreneurs as well as information about this book.

Foreword

As someone who has worked for 22 years in information technology and, more recently, as a leading e-business consultant, I was flattered when Elizabeth asked me to preview her book. It's great to read so many fascinating stories about gutsy women who have risen to the challenge of this vibrant new economy.

The dotcom businesses you're about to discover range from financial disclosures to astrology, pet supplies to B2B e-markets, email marketing services to online communities, and Web applications to Net infrastructure. Twenty different businesses, with almost as many different business models. Each one took an amazing amount of chutzpah, some luck, and a lot of hard work.

What impressed me most about the stories you're about to read is the variety of creative ideas these women brought to life, and the dedication and passion with which they pursued them. I found it refreshing to learn how these women—spread out across three continents—balanced their work and personal lives. This is a dimension that's usually left out when you read about male entrepreneurs and their triumphs and tribulations. Some of them partnered with other people, but each was a key driving force behind her company's success. Many raised money while they were pregnant, launched new products as they were giving birth, and kept up the blistering pace required to nurture a new company into adolescence while balancing home and family.

How did these dotcom divas fund their businesses? You'll learn about a wide variety of successful approaches. Some of these brave souls bootstrapped their startups, drawing on their own resources—credit cards, second mortgages, life savings. Others convinced private investors and "angels" to help them get off the ground. Many went the venture capital route. (It's encouraging to note that venture money was available to these women entrepreneurs, although it took imagination and guts to land it.) A few have already taken their companies public. And as the founder and owner of a successful, 15-year-old privately held consulting firm, I was delighted to see that several of the entrepreneurs opted to keep their companies private—a satisfying choice that is too often overlooked in the traditional business press.

How successful have these entrepreneurs been in recruiting top talent? Very. And, as you'll soon learn, the techniques they used to pursue the key players they wanted on their team were imaginative and persistent. For example, iVillage's Candice Carpenter and Linda Evans repeatedly wined and dined one reluctant recruit until she finally saw the light. When another candidate slipped through their net and took a job at a different firm, they intercepted him in a rented car after his first day at work and pitched him again all the way to his home. The seduction worked. Whether they were recruiting software developers or marketing professionals, these women used the most persuasive recruiting tool on the planet—their personal enthusiasm and passion for their burgeoning businesses.

One of the things that's particularly perverse about launching and shepherding an e-business to success is the constant morphing process. Internet businesses are notoriously slippery beasts. You start out with a focused product or service and a business model that seems to make sense, and, in the space of 12 months, you find that you've changed your product design three times and your business model at least twice. As one young but seasoned business executive explained to me after he'd embarked on his first dotcom, "Every time I think I know what to do, I realize that I can no longer trust my business instincts and judgment. Instead, I have to let go, and let my customers design my business."

How have the savvy women profiled in *Dotcom Divas* evolved their Internet businesses? With great agility. All the stories you're about to read are packed with dead ends and new beginnings, transformations and acquisitions, and shifts in focus. For example, Rosalind Resnick's NetCreations began life as a company developing Websites, then morphed to offer a service that let Webmasters register their sites with popular search engines, and then transformed again into a very successful permission-based email marketing company. Veronica Allende Serra's Brazilian auction site, Superbid.com.br, quickly evolved from consumer auctions offering good deals on home appliances and computers to a business-to-business infrastructure platform for a variety of vertical marketplaces. And these are just two of many examples. You're about to read story after story of changing business models and directions. But notice that, in each case, as these dedicated women followed their dreams, they let their customers lead the way.

Patricia B. Seybold
Author, *Customers.com*
CEO and Founder, The Patricia Seybold Group

Acknowledgments

I have so many people to thank for their assistance, encouragement, and support throughout all phases of this project that it's hard to know where to start. But here goes.

First I'd like to thank the incredible women entrepreneurs profiled in this book. Your enthusiasm, candidness, willingness to answer umpteen questions, and share your stories despite all the demands on your schedules are greatly appreciated. You are all inspiring, exceptional role models and are paving the way for more women to start Internet businesses and pursue leadership roles in technology.

My deep thanks to Patricia B. Seybold, author and e-business consultant extraordinaire, for writing the Foreword to this book. I'd also like to thank Denise Brosseau, Heidi Roizen, Courtney Pulitzer, Ken Morse, Tenny Frost, Ann Winblad, Tom Eisenmann, Myra Hart, Nader Tavassoli, Terry Blum, Ester Dyson, Willa Seldon, Christine Comaford, Bill Schatz, and the many others who suggested women-founded companies to me.

Loel McPhee's belief in my idea for this project was instrumental in opening the door at McGraw-Hill that would later lead to its publication (thanks for being my champion, Loel!). Brad Bunnin's advice helped me navigate through the fine print on the book contract. Tanya Wendling and Jim Stephens generously let me take several months off from the e-business team at Adobe Systems to write this book. Special thanks to Pierre Khawand for his enthusiasm for this project and, later, for encouraging me to become a "dotcom diva" myself by joining him at MyWebtivity, Inc. as a member of the founding team.

I'd also like to thank my "beta testers" who reviewed chapters as I finished them and gave me their frank feedback: Catherine Dee, Ilan Ivory, Natasha Carlitz, Cameron Brown, Karen Hoffman, and my mom, Cynthia Conant. In addition, Catherine Dee carefully edited each chapter, making this book a much smoother read than it would otherwise be.

The team at McGraw-Hill that took my manuscript and turned it into a book did a wonderful job: my editor, Mary Glenn (thanks, Mary, for taking a chance on me); editing supervisor, Janice Race; copyeditor, Peter Weissman; production supervisor, Elizabeth J. Strange; marketing director,

Lynda Luppino; associate marketing manager, Eileen Lamadore; and publicist, SallyAnne McCartin. Thanks to everyone who brainstormed title ideas and to Tony Cook for helping come up with the final title.

A sincere thank-you to Vanessa Richardson for assisting with interviews and preparing material for several of the profiles. Thanks too to Priscilla Patterson Amend for her help assembling the "Resources for Entrepreneurs" appendix, and to Leslie Brokaw and Phillip "Flip" Russell.

I'd like to thank my family and all my friends and colleagues who took an interest in this project and helped along the way. Finally, a big hug to my life partner, Jon Gimpel, for his unflagging encouragement throughout the entire book-writing process.

Introduction

Internet business books are being published as frequently as new Net ventures are going public. After reading many of these books, I was sometimes left with the feeling that they were science fiction novels set in an alternate universe where there weren't any women. There still seems to be a mass perception that the builders of the information economy are solely men—the Steve Jobses, Bill Gateses, and Jim Clarks of the world. And yet, as someone working in the Silicon Valley for the past 11 years and the Web arena since 1995, I know there's no dearth of talented, visionary women who are movers and shakers in the new economy. While some women leaders are getting more coverage in business and Internet industry trade magazines than ever before, it's my belief that women Internet entrepreneurs haven't necessarily received their fair share of recognition.

So the focus of this book is on them—successful women who are creating real, thriving Web companies from visions that were initially just twinkles in their eyes. While there are many accomplished, prominent women hired as chief executives in the Net sector, their stories aren't told here. This book is first and foremost about women founders.

As you read the stories of these 20 Net ventures and their visionary founders, you'll learn how these successful women:

- Came up with their winning business idea
- Got funding
- Built their team
- Overcame challenges
- Grew and marketed their businesses

The profiles offer in-depth, behind-the-scenes views of how these 20 companies have achieved their successes. Each profile also discusses specific strategies each company has employed and offers tips for entrepreneurs from each founder, based on what she learned from her Web startup experience—invaluable insight for soon-to-be and experienced entrepreneurs alike.

HOW THE TWENTY COMPANIES WERE SELECTED

When I started doing preliminary research for this book, I expected the pool of eligible women-founded Web businesses to be around 40 or 50, and that narrowing this number down to 20 would be a piece of cake. Little did I imagine the flood of email I would receive after putting out the word that I was looking for promising Web companies with women founders. My email box was clogged with messages from women eager to tell me about their own Web business or the business of a colleague or friend. The selection process was clearly going to be more involved than I expected. I spent weeks brainstorming about how to narrow the pool and zero in on the 20 companies to profile in this book.

I decided to first limit the universe of women-founded Web companies by considering only "pure play" Web companies—those offering their content, services, or goods over the Web, or selling a Web-based technology. Brick-and-mortar operations with online components were excluded from consideration, as were Web design shops, consulting firms, and hardware companies. I also limited the field to companies with large market opportunities. I excluded those whose ability to scale seemed dubious and those that weren't experiencing high growth in revenue, traffic, or customers. After applying these criteria, I still had more than 200 companies from which to choose the 20—a loud and clear signal that women entrepreneurs are key players in the Net economy.

In further narrowing down the universe of eligible companies, I didn't limit the pool to the most profitable ones. Let's face it: With Internet companies burning through cash on big media campaigns in hopes of building their brand and grabbing market share faster than their competition, traditional metrics like profit can prove a futile way to evaluate the viability of a company. Counter to intuition, some Web companies that are posting profits could be doing so at the expense of investing in marketing and advertising that would help their longer-term prospects. In cases like this, profit, while important, is not necessarily the best and only indicator of the success and staying power of a company.

I considered filtering companies on the basis of their valuation or market capitalization, but most prepublic companies choose to keep this information confidential. Moreover, valuation for startups is fuzzy and somewhat arbitrary. According to Joanna Strober of Bessemer Ventures Partners, "Valuation really depends on supply and demand—on how many VCs are interested in a particular deal. If an entrepreneur can create a lot of hype and excitement around their deal, they can create a higher valuation. There are very few 'real' metrics."

I also considered ranking the 200 companies by revenue and going with the top 20. But this worked to favor more established ones and exclude promising fledglings. Moreover, revenue data wasn't available for several of the companies that seemed to deserve a place in this book.

After considering these options, I became wary of going with a straight quantitative measure since this approach wouldn't guarantee a complementary and varied mix of companies. I wanted the 20 companies to highlight the various sectors of the new economy and the diversity of achievements by women Web entrepreneurs.

To narrow down the list of 200, I excluded companies with male cofounders unless the woman cofounder was at the helm in the role of CEO, chairman, or president. I then grouped the companies into four categories that roughly map the terrain of the Web economy:

- Web portal, content, and community
- Web-based services
- e-commerce
- e-business applications and Web technology

From there I selected a mix of companies using both quantitative metrics (revenue, traffic, and transaction volume, for instance) as well as my subjective sense of the company's promise. Maximizing variety and choosing inspiring stories were my final filters when selecting the 20 companies.

THE TWENTY NET VENTURES

The 20 promising Net ventures profiled in this book are diverse. While many Internet startups go belly up and success in the space can be fleeting and is by no means guaranteed, the women entrepreneurs who started these companies all share a mix of courage, boldness, smarts, good timing, optimism, and some luck that was instrumental in getting their companies off the ground and achieving their successes. Six of the companies fall into the Web portal, content, and community category; four into the Web-based services category; six are e-commerce firms; and four are Web technology companies. Six of the 20 are business-to-business (B2B), ten are business-to-consumer (B2C), and four cross the boundary between the two categories.

The businesses are also varied in terms of the source of their funding, the level of their funding, and their stage. Reflecting the growth in women's access to capital resources, and the fact that large capital infusions are usually a prerequisite for growing a major Net company, most of the profiled companies are funded by venture capitalists (VCs) or angels (high-net-worth individuals who invest in startups). Desktop.com, EDGAR Online, NetCreations, CoVia, eCommerce Industries, and Marimba are examples of companies whose founders initially opted to bootstrap their businesses (biz speak for self-fund). The other companies had outside investments from an early stage. There's also a wide range in the level of investment these businesses received. Some received relatively small amounts of seed capital and were able to build their businesses from there. Others received larger investments, some in the hundreds of millions of dollars.

These profiles were written between January and June 2000, an especially volatile time for Internet stocks. The Nasdaq fell from a high of more than 5000 in March 2000 to under 3300 in May, dampening investor enthusiasm for Internet IPOs and making VCs more cautious than in preceding months. VCs even coined yet another new three-character Internet acronym, "P2P," for "path to profitability," reflecting their increased emphasis on ensuring that their portfolio companies move steadily and swiftly toward profitability. At that time six of the 20 profiled ventures were post-IPO, one had been acquired, and another one merged with a competitor as I was writing the book. Seven of the companies were at an early stage, having received seed, first, or second rounds of funding. The remaining ones were in later funding rounds. By the time you read this, however, some of the private companies are likely to have gone public or been merged or acquired.

Although the number of profiled companies is too small to be statistically meaningful, the geographical locations of the 20 companies' headquarters give an indication of where Web companies are tending to cluster. Reflecting the San Francisco Bay Area's dominance in the new economy, three of the companies are based in Silicon Valley, one is in the East Bay, and eight are in San Francisco's Media Gulch. But not all things cyber emanate from points west. Five of the companies are based on the East Coast—two in Connecticut and three in New York's Silicon Alley. One is in Virginia. Two overseas Web ventures are also included—one in Tokyo and the other in São Paulo.

Because the Web economy operates on Web time (just like dog time, seven Web years equals a calendar year), the fate of the 20 profiled companies will be determined quickly. While I selected them because of their promising businesses, some will continue to obtain greater and greater market share while others will undoubtedly fall to the wayside as the Web years fly by.

OPPORTUNITIES ABOUND FOR WEB-SAVVY ENTREPRENEURS

As the 20 companies profiled in this book illustrate, Web-savvy women entrepreneurs are seizing the vast opportunities made possible by the Internet by starting and growing successful online businesses. Moreover, seasoned executive women are increasingly leaving their traditional, brick-and-mortar corporate positions to head up Web startups. Some of the most successful Internet companies—from eBay to Exodus Communications—are led by hired women CEOs. Considering how few women are to be found in the executive ranks of technology companies and the corporate sector overall,* the proliferation of Net startups with women founders and CEOs is astonishing.

Are you interested in starting your own online business? The explosive growth in e-commerce means that there will continue to be precedent-shattering opportunities for entrepreneurs to enter new markets in the

---

*Women comprise only 11.9 percent of corporate officers in the Fortune 500 according to a 1999 study by the research firm Catalyst.

months and years ahead. Stories abound about both mom-and-pop and venture-backed operations setting up shop on the Web and exploding into thriving e-businesses whose greatest challenge is scaling operations quickly enough to keep up with their swelling customer base.

The emergence and rapid growth of e-commerce since the release of the Mosaic Web browser in February 1993 is a sea change that is revolutionizing the business world. Forrester Research sees the consumer "e-tail" market hitting $184 billion by 2004. This represents more than seven percent of all retail sales and an increase of more than 800 percent from the 1999 level of $20 billion. And the B2C market pales in comparison to the growth forecast for the B2B market: By 2003 it's expected to zoom to a whopping $1.3 trillion, or 9.4 percent of all business sales, from its 1998 level of $43 billion—an annual growth rate of nearly 100 percent.

The high number of women Web entrepreneurs is consistent with the huge growth in the number of all types of female-founded businesses. Women in the United States are starting businesses at a rate twice that of the national average. In 1999 the number of women-founded ventures topped nine million. This represents 38 percent of all U.S. businesses and more than double the number of women-owned businesses that existed in 1987. Moreover, 30 percent of women-owned businesses launched in 1999 were in the technology sector.

Although you wouldn't know it from reading the U.S. press, women-founded Web ventures are also springing up globally. The two overseas companies profiled in this book—eSampo.com in Tokyo and SuperVertical in São Paulo—point to the emergence of women-founded Web ventures abroad. The growth in the number of women-led companies overseas is especially inspiring since the barriers that women entrepreneurs in other countries must overcome are usually considerably greater than those faced by their counterparts in the entrepreneur-loving United States.

The Internet is enabling unprecedented entrepreneurship and presents a huge opportunity for motivated, smart businesswomen. "Within the past year, women entrepreneurs have started looking at the Internet and technology as the answer to their prayers," says Amy Millman, executive director of the National Women's Business Council. "The Internet represents the biggest untapped market for businesswomen."

NET DOORS ARE OPENING FOR WOMEN

Why are women striking out on their own in cyberspace in ever-increasing numbers? Some say women thrive on the Internet's no-rules mantra. As a very new industry, the Internet space isn't tied to traditional ways of working and entrenched power structures. This explains why women and young entrepreneurs—groups that have traditionally run into barriers while striving to build businesses—are experiencing increased success in Internet ventures. "The Web gives women new opportunities to pursue their dreams. It gives women a voice and a platform for demonstrating innovation and resourcefulness," says Joline Godfrey, author of *Our Wildest Dreams* and CEO of Independent Means Inc., a business that offers entrepreneurial "startup camps" for girls, as well as other services to empower girls financially.

But the Web's freedom from the restrictions of traditional business is only a small part of the story. Nine key trends are all simultaneously responsible for the burgeoning number of women Web entrepreneurs. These trends include:

1. More abundant capital resources than ever before
2. Women's increased access to these resources
3. More role models for women in business and technology
4. More executive women joining Internet startups
5. More female venture capitalists
6. More support organizations for women entrepreneurs and women in technology
7. Successful IPOs by several women-led Internet companies
8. More media attention for women entrepreneurs and executives
9. Increased recognition of the purchasing power of women online

TREND 1: MORE ABUNDANT CAPITAL RESOURCES THAN EVER BEFORE

Far more venture capital is available to entrepreneurs now than ever before. According to Silicon Valley investment-research firm VentureOne, more than $36.5 billion of venture capital was invested in 1999—exceeding the combined amount invested the three previous years. And entrepreneurs, including women entrepreneurs, are reaping the benefits. Capital resources for technology entrepreneurs have never been more plentiful—and it's a good thing since technology and most Internet businesses require large up-front investments to succeed. The cost of developing a new technology product, creating a major Website, or building a new brand faster than the competition can be extremely high. But investments made in Net companies have been yielding staggeringly high returns in certain cases as they go public.

Successful investments in the Internet space and other sectors have ballooned venture capital funds and the portfolios of angel investors. Much of this newly created wealth is being folded back into funding new Internet startups. In 1999, Internet companies received $25 billion in venture capital—more than two-thirds of all the venture capital invested that year and more than four times as much as in 1998. And, in the first half of 2000, 85 percent of the $35.4 billion in venture capital invested went to Internet companies. Women's increasing access to capital is due partly to the abundant supply of venture capital and angel funding. Because venture capital is pouring into Internet companies at record rates, women's success at landing funding for their Web ventures is on the rise.

TREND 2: WOMEN'S INCREASED ACCESS TO THESE RESOURCES

The proliferation of women-founded Web businesses is especially impressive considering that women receive far less of the venture capital pie than men. Internet startups with women CEOs represented only six percent of the companies receiving venture capital funding in 1999.

Even if they have a solid business plan and a great team, women entrepreneurs often don't have the thick Rolodex, powerful mentors, and knowledge that are critical to landing equity financing. The venture capital arena has one of the chummiest buddy networks around and women simply haven't been as plugged in to it as men. And VCs and angel investors like to bet on winning horses; they usually favor entrepreneurs with track records. As newer entrants to the technology arena, women have had limited access to capital because of this bias toward proven entrepreneurs.

The good news is that brighter days are ahead for women-led startups and their access to venture capital. With venture funds swelling and a shortage of people working in the technology sector, venture capitalists are increasingly funding women-led startups. Even though only six percent of the Internet startups funded in 1999 had women CEOs, this is off the charts compared to the number of women CEOs in the Fortune 500. There are only three: Carly Fiorina of Hewlett-Packard, Andrea Jung of Avon, and Marion Sandler of Golden West Financial Corporation. Moreover, the percent of women-led Internet startups receiving funding has been inching upward. Eight percent of the Internet companies landing venture capital in the second quarter of 2000 were women-led, and just five percent of them were in 1998.

More Internet startups where women play key roles in top management are also securing funding (see Figure I-1). In the second quarter of 2000, 48 percent of the Internet startups funded had women in top-tier management positions, a higher percentage than ever before.

Moreover, it seems that the Internet sector is unusually female friendly. VC-backed, non-Internet startups have a lower percentage of women CEOs and fewer women in top management (see Figure I-2).

The reason for the relatively high percentage of Internet startups with women in top-tier management positions could be because there simply weren't enough qualified men to fill the glut of new management positions that emerged with the Internet boom of the late nineties. Moreover, within

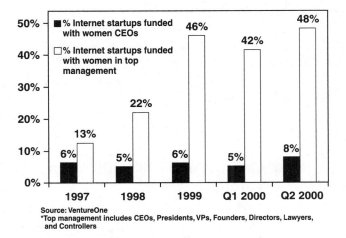

Figure I-1. Internet Startups: A Net Gain for Women

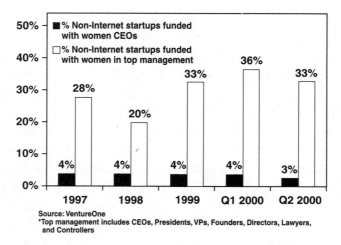

Figure I-2. Non-Internet Startups

the last few years, new titles that describe positions that women may have held for some time (such as chief marketing officer) have recently turned up on the management map.

TREND 3: MORE ROLE MODELS FOR WOMEN IN BUSINESS AND TECHNOLOGY

Female technology executives and entrepreneurs, a novelty just a few years ago, are becoming more commonplace. More women are breaking into the top ranks of technology companies and serving as high-profile, influential role models for younger women. Carly Fiorina is one example. Appointed as HP's CEO in 1999, she is the first woman in history to head one of the 30 companies that comprise the Dow Jones Industrial Average. And many trailblazing women in technology are not only serving as role models, but devoting time and energy to actively mentoring and inspiring younger women to pursue career paths as technology professionals and entrepreneurs.

TREND 4: MORE EXECUTIVE WOMEN JOINING INTERNET STARTUPS

Although women Web leaders are emerging from diverse walks of life, many of them fall into one of two categories: young, newly minted MBAs and seasoned corporate veterans. Twenty-something female MBAs are starting Web companies and obtaining venture capital like never before. Not content to spend their careers climbing the corporate ladder in hopes of someday getting the keys to an executive corner office, they're appointing themselves CEO, going after funding, and launching their own companies. Venture capital doors are swinging open for young entrepreneurs with a viable Internet business plan in one hand and an MBA from Stanford, Harvard, Wharton, or the like in the other. When compared with their senior counterparts, who've likely run into more barriers during their careers, this younger set of women entrepreneurs seems to be relatively unencumbered by notions of a glass ceiling and gender bias—an indication that the business climate is now more woman-friendly.

But more experienced women leaders are joining Net companies too. Women have been in technology and related fields long enough now to work their way into powerful positions in corporations and other organizations, such as VC, accounting, and law firms. Many women from this generation of seasoned executives are in the leadership pipeline and being wooed away from their traditional corporate jobs by the wild ride proffered by Internet startups. They're leaving corporate America and migrating to startups with increasing regularity. Meg Whitman of eBay, Julie Wainwright of Pets.com, Anne Perlman of Moai Technologies, and Radha Ramaswami Basu of Support.com are just a handful of examples of CEOs who have joined Internet companies as proven executive managers.

TREND 5: MORE FEMALE VENTURE CAPITALISTS

A growing number of women are starting venture capital funds of their own or joining venture capital firms as partners. "In the last five years, there has been significant growth in the number of women VCs," says Denise Brosseau, executive director of the Forum for Women Entrepreneurs. "In 1994, there were only six women in venture capital in the San Francisco Bay Area. Now, I'm aware of over 75 of them. Not all of these women are yet partners in their funds, but this is still a great improvement." Women VCs are helping to bridge the gap between women entrepreneurs and a male-dominated VC network.

Moreover, within the past few years, several venture capital firms that specialize in funding women-run companies have opened, including:

- *Women's Growth Capital Fund* (www.womensgrowthcapital.com). Based in Washington, D.C., and founded in 1997, this fund invests in an array of companies that serve or are led by women.

- *Viridian Capital* (www.viridiancapital.com). This San Francisco-based fund, established in 1997, invests in health care and technology companies founded or cofounded by women.

- *New Vista Capital* (www.nvcap.com). Based in Silicon Valley, this fund invests in early-stage information technology companies led by women and minority entrepreneurs.

- *Isabella Capital* (www.fundisabella.com). This fund in Cincinnati invests in Internet, health care, and consumer-oriented companies. It opened in 2000.

These funds make investments that typically range from $200,000 to $2 million. Inroads Capital Partners, another women-oriented fund, invests larger sums, typically $1 million to $15 million. These new funds are helping to increase the visibility of women-led firms and are making other investors aware of the many promising businesses started by women.

"Since women VCs are likely to have extensive networks that include a good portion of successful women, they're more likely to tap these successful women for leadership positions in companies they fund," says Brosseau. "People fund people they know. Having women VCs at the table opens the door to more women getting their business plans reviewed and funded."

TREND 6: MORE SUPPORT ORGANIZATIONS FOR WOMEN ENTREPRENEURS AND WOMEN IN TECHNOLOGY

A new girls' network is here. Women are starting support organizations for women-led technology businesses. Groups range from formal membership organizations to informal groups like Systers (www.systers.org; a networking group for women in computing) and Babes in Boyland (a group of women technology CEOs who meet to share ideas, support, and insights).

Three pioneering organizations include the Women's Technology Cluster, the Forum for Women Entrepreneurs, and Women in Technology International.

- *The Women's Technology Cluster* (www.womenstechcluster.org) is the first business incubator for women technology and Internet entrepreneurs. Started in San Francisco in February 1999 by Catherine Muther, a former senior marketing officer at Cisco Systems, it's a nonprofit incubator providing shared office space, equipment, mentoring, support, and networking opportunities to startups where women hold a major equity stake. The Women's Technology Cluster has space for approximately 20 startups. Competition to join the cluster is stiff: Less than five percent of applicants are admitted.

  The Cluster is funded by the Three Guineas Fund, a grant-making organization Muther founded and named after Virginia Woolf's "Three Guineas," an essay about philanthropy. Part of the Cluster's mission is to instill philanthropic values in the businesses it incubates. While the high-tech industry has historically come up short when it comes to philanthropy, the Cluster's entrepreneurs must agree to contribute a two percent equity stake to a philanthropy fund. Income from the fund is used to sustain the Cluster and support nonprofit programs that address social and economic change. "We're increasing women's access to capital and we've been able to achieve demonstrable results," says Margarita Quihuis, the Cluster's director. "We've helped 70 percent of our companies raise $15 million in capital in less than a year. It really shows that women are starting hot companies and that they are fundable."

- *The Forum for Women Entrepreneurs* (FWE; www.fwe.org) is the leading networking organization for women building and leading high-growth technology companies. Founded in 1993 and based in Seattle and the San Francisco Bay Area, the FWE offers women entrepreneurs advice, support, networking opportunities with other entrepreneurs, innovative programs, and access to top-tier funding sources.

The FWE has been instrumental in helping women raise capital for their Internet and technology startups. The FWE jointly organized Springboard 2000, the first venture capital forum for women entrepreneurs. Held in January 2000 at Oracle Corporation in Silicon Valley, this event was an opportunity for selected women entrepreneurs to pitch their businesses to more than 200 VCs from top firms such as Kleiner Perkins Caufield & Byers, Softbank Venture Capital, and Draper Fisher Jurvetson. This event was cohosted by the National Women's Business Council (NWBC) and sponsored by the Three Guineas Fund, among others. The NWBC is organizing more VC forums for women-led businesses in the months and years ahead.

- *Women in Technology International* (WITI; www.witi.org) is dedicated to helping women advance their careers in technology. Founded in 1989, the organization works to increase the number of women executives in technology companies and encourages young women to choose technical careers. WITI also brings women to the attention of companies, organizations, and boards looking for the best high-tech talent.

These organizations, as well as others listed in the "Resources for Entrepreneurs" appendix at the end of this book, are helping women break into the networks and build the relationships they need to get funded, grow their businesses, and succeed as entrepreneurs and executives.

TREND 7: SUCCESSFUL IPOS BY SEVERAL WOMEN-LED INTERNET COMPANIES

Successful initial public offerings of high-profile, women-led technology and Internet companies such as Vitria, eBay, Exodus Communications, Digital Island, and Pilot Network Services are making it easier for women entrepreneurs to raise money. In 1999 more women took their companies public than ever before. As more women-led companies experience successful IPOs, their founders are helping other women break into the boys' network that links venture firms with the companies they help build. As a result, VCs and angels are more inclined to fund other promising women entrepreneurs.

TREND 8: MORE MEDIA ATTENTION FOR WOMEN ENTRE-PRENEURS AND EXECUTIVES

Successful women entrepreneurs and execs are also garnering increased recognition in the media. *Fortune, The Wall Street Journal, Upside, Fast Company*, and other business publications are running articles about women business leaders with increasing regularity. Further boosting recognition for women Web entrepreneurs are:

- "The Top 25 Women on the Web" awards, given annually since 1998 by San Francisco Women on the Web (www.sfwow.org) to leaders in the Internet and new media industries.
- The FWE's annual Entrepreneurial Achievement Award, most recently awarded to Donna Dubinsky, CEO and cofounder of Handspring.

TREND 9: INCREASED RECOGNITION OF THE PURCHASING POWER OF WOMEN ONLINE

As women have flocked online, they have contributed significantly to the growth of e-commerce. The online gender gap in the United States has almost disappeared: Jupiter Communications forecasts that women will comprise 52 percent of the U.S. online population by 2002. And, according to a demographic study conducted by CommerceNet and Nielsen Media Research, the number of online purchases made by female users increased 80 percent over the nine-month period from June 1998 to April 1999. Women made 50 percent of all online purchases during the 1999 holiday shopping season, up from 39 percent in 1998.

It's no surprise that women are driving consumer e-commerce revenue—after all, they control or influence 80 percent of personal and household goods spending in the brick-and-mortar world. As women bring their purchasing power online, Web content providers and e-tailers are increasingly molding their Websites and wares to better appeal to women. Women constitute a major online consumer force for everything from cosmetics, cars, and clothing to online news and financial information. This female online buying power is not lost on VCs and angels. They are increasingly funding consumer-oriented e-commerce companies led by and targeted to women.

Given these nine key trends, it's no wonder that the number of women Web entrepreneurs is burgeoning. There's never been a better time for a woman entrepreneur to start a new business, especially in the Net space. So if you're thinking about starting your own Web venture, what are you waiting for? Go to it!

WHO SHOULD READ THIS BOOK

Dotcom Divas will appeal most to present and would-be Internet entrepreneurs. The inside look at these 20 companies and their women founders or cofounders provides invaluable insight into tactics and strategies that have worked, as well as practical advice and key take-aways. The book will also appeal to technology professionals, businesswomen, investors in Internet companies, business professors, college students brainstorming about their future, and anyone considering embarking on an entrepreneurial path.

The chapters can be read in any order. If you want to learn about a certain type of business, you can read the chapters grouped under your area of interest. The chapters are divided into four categories: portal, content, and community; Web-based services; e-commerce; and e-business applications and Web technology.

If you're reading this book because you want to start your own Web business, be sure to check out the "Resources for Entrepreneurs" appendix, as well as the book's companion Website at www.dotcomdivas.net. They both provide pointers to organizations, capital sources, Websites, and other resources for entrepreneurs that will help get you on your way. If you want to tell me about a successful woman-founded Web company, a nifty resource for Net entrepreneurs, or a successful strategy you've employed at your own Internet company, email me at elizabeth@dotcomdivas.net.

My ultimate hope is that, in demonstrating the variety and success of women's Web ventures, this book will inspire and empower other women to form their own businesses, work for cutting-edge Internet companies, start technology careers, or just think more like entrepreneurs in their chosen fields.

Part

I

PORTAL, CONTENT, AND COMMUNITY VENTURES

VITAL STATS

- Founder: Eugenie Diserio ("Genie Easy")
- URL: www.astronet.com
- Stock: WOMN (now part of Women.com Networks)
- Founded: 1995
- Headquarters: New Canaan, CT

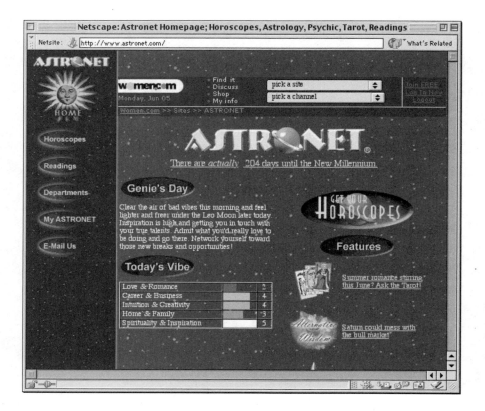

1

Astronet

Publishing the Ultimate Addictive Content

"You never know what makes a hit. You can build your company, make a product, and spend a lot of money marketing it, but ultimately the public decides what hits their raw nerve."

—Eugenie Diserio

A ROCKY START

There's an age-old saying that when a door closes a window opens. This adage is especially true for the eclectic, arty Eugenie Diserio. She founded Astronet, the most highly trafficked astrology Website anywhere, which today is part of Women.com Networks. Astronet offers cosmic counsel on love, relationships, money, careers, and even issues important to teens. Known online as "Genie Easy," Diserio is a wizard at transforming setbacks into new possibilities and opportunities. In fact, Astronet would never have come to be if Diserio hadn't faced one particularly difficult situation.

In 1992, after the breakup of a five-year relationship, Diserio returned home to New Canaan, Connecticut, with her four-year-old son, Jake, and moved back in with her mom and dad. She was down on her luck and depressed. Recalling this period of her life, she says: "I'm someone who's graduated from the school of hard knocks with a definite Ph.D." In an effort to survive financially, she started a new job as an executive assistant (or as she puts it, a "glorified schlepper") at a company called New Sub Services started by Jay Walker—now notorious for the wild success of his current company, Priceline.com. Corporate culture was completely foreign to Diserio, who had spent the bulk of her career as a singer, song-writer, and recording artist pioneering New Wave music in the early and mid-eighties. She had been in two bands—Model Citizens and The Dance—which toured internationally and regularly played at popular Manhattan dance clubs such as CBGB, which helped launch alternative groups like the Talking Heads, Television, and Blondie. But after Jake was born in 1989, Diserio left the music business—the late nights and the chaos of a performer's life didn't mesh well with motherhood.

So, at New Sub Services, Diserio felt like a fish out of water working nine-to-five for a paycheck to support herself and her son. But a staid corporate career wasn't in the stars for her. After only 18 months on the job, she was laid off when her division was unexpectedly downsized. Diserio began collecting unemployment compensation and looking for a new corporate job, but her efforts didn't result in any offers. "With my creative, performance-oriented background, I didn't fit in anywhere and I felt too old to climb the corporate ladder," remembers the 46-year-old entrepreneur.

A FATEFUL READING

One of Diserio's lifelong passions was astrology. "I was in graduate school when I had my first chart done by a professional," she says. "It was $75, and I thought that was so expensive then. But I remember thinking the insight it gave me into myself was cool!" Seeking guidance after the layoff, she ran her own astrological chart (she's a Libra with Aquarius rising). Despite her difficulty finding employment, the planets were aligning favorably in her career house. Encouraged, Diserio decided to capitalize on this positive force and began brainstorming business ideas. Determined to craft a successful venture and survive financially, she read about how to start a business and met with seasoned entrepreneurs through her local Chamber of Commerce to learn the ropes, all the while keeping her eyes peeled for an unfilled niche.

Before Diserio left New Sub Services, a coworker with an AOL account introduced her to the Internet. Now, as a budding entrepreneur, Diserio decided it was high time to learn more about the new world emerging online and scope out the possibilities. She bought herself a 14.4-baud modem, plugged it into her Mac SE, and got her own account on AOL using the handle "Genie Easy." She recalls: "I wanted Genie of Love—the title of one of my favorite self-penned songs—but it was already taken, so I signed up as Genie Easy and it stuck."

During several early online romps, Diserio made a discovery that would soon change the course of her life: "The Internet at that time was a virgin idea and truly the Wild West. Using free trial accounts on Delphi, GEnie, and CompuServe, I went out on the Internet and discovered that many, many people in online forums were interested in astrology." It was this realization that inspired her to create a Web-based astrology business with the intention of building it into the premier astrology brand online. Given Diserio's longstanding fascination with astrology, her entertaining charisma, and her talent for giving advice, a Website about astrology was the perfect fit.

Convinced that she had the right stuff to build an online astrology business, Diserio crafted a business plan and presented her idea to several East Coast angel investors and venture capitalists. But this was 1994 and VCs weren't accustomed to hearing about businesses built around horoscopes and metaphysical consultations. Moreover, most equity investors at that time viewed the Internet with uncertainty. Diserio boldly made her unconventional pitch time and time again with no bites. She says, "Venture capitalists were like, 'An Internet business about astrology by a woman? Hello!'"

INCUBATION IN THE "GREENHOUSE"

While it was clear that her cyberastrology vision was ahead of its time, Diserio's instincts and the planets told her that the business would succeed if she kept at it. Undaunted by her unsuccessful efforts to secure funding, she turned to the America Online Greenhouse, AOL's business incubator, which made small equity investments in the ventures of Web "infopreneurs" willing to develop content for the AOL service.

Diserio's decision to approach AOL was right on the mark. "I relentlessly pursued Ted Leonsis [AOL's longtime marketing magician and president of AOL's Interactive Properties Group] and after many pitches to the Greenhouse team I was chosen as one of the first ten entrepreneurs they funded out of more than 2000 applicants," she explains with pride. As part of the AOL Greenhouse, Astronet was in excellent company: BetterHealth (now part of iVillage); NetNoir, a highly trafficked destination site for African Americans; and the popular Motley Fool are just a handful of the successful businesses initially incubated by the Greenhouse.

Astronet was funded in the nick of time: Diserio received a seed investment of $150,000 in May 1995 just as her unemployment money was running out. Her credit cards were maxed out and she was prepared to accept an entry-level position at Prodigy if the money for Astronet didn't come through.

A COSMIC COUNSELOR IS BORN

Encouraged by AOL's vote of confidence, Diserio set up shop in her parents' basement. She bought computers and office equipment, and hired an assistant and Web producer who knew Rainman, the proprietary language used to build Web pages on AOL. She sought out the best astrologers from around the nation, bringing editors of top astrology magazines, the owners of astrology software companies, and celebrity astrologers—such as the Cosmic Muffin (well-known for his Boston-based radio show)—into the Astronet fold. "I like to think of Astronet like Woodstock—you put all of these different people up on stage and watched it come together," says Diserio.

She hung out in AOL chat rooms to recruit a herd of volunteer chat hosts willing to work in exchange for free AOL accounts. For employees on the payroll, there were other perks. Even during these humble beginnings, Diserio ran the business as a true Web company, awarding employees stock options as part of their compensation packages. It wasn't long before she had five part-time employees working in the basement.

Managing a startup was new territory for Diserio, who had earned an MFA from Columbia University in the late seventies. But her father, an attorney and businessman, offered solid financial and management advice, as well as encouragement, as she built the business to the point where she could hire a chief operating officer. "My dad helped me do my books and gave me great advice on people and strategy," she says. Does she feel that her lack of an MBA held her back? Not at all: "Good instincts matter more. A lot of the entrepreneurs who are making it in the Internet world don't have a traditional business background because so much of it is about rule breaking."

Six months after the business was funded, Astronet first launched under the sign of Scorpio on November 13, 1995. (Astronet's astrological chart hangs on the wall near Diserio's desk, next to hers and her son's.) At its launch, the Astronet site on AOL (keyword "astronet") offered a variety of specialized horoscopes including ones focused on love, career, money, and eros, as well as psychic, tarot, and astrology readings offered either online or by phone.

SUCCESS WAS IN THE STARS

Soon after Astronet's AOL launch it was clear that the site was a hit. Astronet had hoped to have AOL users spend 25,000 hours in the Astronet area within the first few months after the launch, but the company achieved this goal within its first 30 days. "We didn't even promote Astronet that much," says Diserio. "We simply provided something people really enjoyed." Astronet's traffic continued to top itself month after month, and the site twice received the AOL Member's Choice award.

In the summer of 1996, with Astronet's monthly traffic growth rate in the double digits, AOL further fueled the site's meteoric rise in popularity with a second-round investment of $750,000. Diserio used this infusion to hire an executive staff and move Astronet into a building in downtown New Canaan. This second investment brought AOL's equity stake in Astronet up to 33 percent. How did Diserio feel about handing out such a large chunk of her company's equity to AOL? "It was fine by me since it was their investment and support that got my business off the ground at such an opportune time in the Net's history," she says.

Diserio was well aware that the online world extended far beyond AOL. To reach a broader audience and establish an Internet presence early on, the company launched its own stand-alone Website at Astronet.com in January 1997. The site began selling ad space and services. And soon after the launch, Astronet.com landed major content sponsors: Godiva Chocolates paid to have their brand on Astronet-created "passionscopes," while Avon backed custom "beautyscopes."

Astronet.com was the first major astrology site to be launched on the Internet. There were no immediate competitors, and even today the site faces little serious competition. The closest contender is Astrology.com (now part of iVillage), which doesn't have Astronet's breadth of offerings. So Astronet.com remains the largest, most popular astrology site in the world. As of March 2000, it was among the top 200 most highly trafficked information and entertainment Websites and was receiving nearly one million unique visitors a month according to Media Metrix.

IDEALLY SUITED FOR CYBERSPACE

Diserio's instinct to take astrological services online proved a direct hit partly because of the nature of the content. Horoscopes are one of the Web's ultimate "sticky" (or addictive) and personalized forms of content, driving loyal, repeat traffic and creating a daily habit among Web users. In the United States, more than one out of three people read their horoscope regularly or have consulted astrologers for private readings.

Horoscopes have become a fixture in the online landscape: Almost all the major portal sites—including Yahoo!, Excite, Lycos, the GO Network, and LookSmart—now offer horoscopes as part of their personalized content. "AOL had some qualms about the Astronet business concept at first," says Diserio. However, these concerns were quickly put to rest by the volumes of visitors repeatedly frequenting Astronet's horoscopes.

HEARST CATCHES A RISING STAR . . .

Astronet's strong first-mover advantage enabled it to become the dominant player in its niche, and by late 1998 large media enterprises on the lookout for promising acquisition targets in the Web space began to take note of the site's popularity. Astronet was approached by several suitors—including the mothership, AOL—and in January 1998, Diserio decided to sell it for an undisclosed amount. The buyer? Hearst New Media and Technology, a unit of Hearst Corp. and creator of the HomeArts.com women's online network.

Hearst New Media bought Astronet in part because of its high level of traffic and its women-dominated demographic. But the media giant was also attracted to the financials: Astronet was breaking even by the time it was acquired. "We never really operated like an Internet company financially," says Diserio. "We ran lean and mean, and didn't burn cash on big marketing campaigns."

As part of Hearst New Media, Astronet became the horoscope and astrology channel on HomeArts.com, a site that was also using content from Hearst magazines such as *Good Housekeeping*, *Cosmopolitan*, *Redbook*, and *Harper's Bazaar*. Astronet brought HomeArts.com a massive new traffic stream of more than 45 million pageviews per month. At the time of the acquisition, it accounted for a whopping 28 percent of Home-Arts.com's 2.3 million unique monthly visitors.

...AND HANDS IT OFF TO WOMEN.COM

In the Web space, major changes happen in the blink of an eye. Just weeks after Astronet was acquired, Hearst New Media merged with Women.com—a leading destination Website founded by Ellen Pack and soon joined by CEO Marleen McDaniel, two early Internet visionaries who were among the first people to foresee that women would grow into a huge online force. The two companies formed Women.com Networks, which has since gone public. "I was very excited when Women.com Networks went public, since I had been anticipating this step when Hearst New Media acquired Astronet earlier," says Diserio.

As a unit of Women.com Networks, Astronet continues a partnership with AOL and is still its leading astrology and horoscope provider. In fact, according to Diserio, by 1998 Astronet had become AOL's second-largest content area behind Love@AOL. And while Women.com doesn't break out its traffic numbers, it's safe to say that its horoscope channel drives a significant percentage.

Although Women.com Networks is based in San Mateo, California, Diserio and her team of 15 full-time employees remain in New Canaan, working from their pleasant offices that belie the company's basement beginnings. The atmosphere at Astronet's headquarters is cozy and casual. The staff is almost like a family, celebrating birthdays, births, weddings, and holidays together.

THE BUSINESS MODEL

How did Astronet capitalize on America's fascination with astrology to generate revenue? Its business model incorporated four main revenue streams: royalties from AOL, content syndication, advertising sales, and e-commerce transactions.

AOL Royalties

From Astronet's inception until the end of 1998, when the company was acquired, it earned royalties based on the amount of time AOL subscribers spent in the Astronet area. This created a strong cash flow, accounting for approximately 70 percent of the revenue from AOL. The remaining 30 percent of AOL revenue came from ad sales as well as live, email-based, and phone-based astrological readings.

Things have changed dramatically since the early days when AOL paid royalties for content. Today many content publishers *pay* millions of dollars to distribute their material through major distribution channels such as AOL. Content may be king, but distribution is divine. When AOL axed its hourly subscriber fee in 1996 and switched to a flat monthly fee for unlimited usage, the online behemoth stopped paying royalties to many content providers. But Astronet was smart— it had negotiated a contract that guaranteed continuing remuneration.

Content Syndication

Astronet syndicates daily and weekly horoscopes and other astrology-related content through United Media and portal sites, including Yahoo! and Snap, as well as a slew of smaller sites. The company earns royalties through many of its syndication deals.

Ad Sales

The demographic of Astronet's user base is attractive to advertisers, even though some companies have reservations about being associated with astrology. Women comprise 67 percent of Astronet.com's traffic, and a large percentage of these customers are affluent and highly educated: 40 percent have household incomes between $50,000 and $100,000, and 66 percent have college degrees.

Because many advertisers are eager to market to this demographic group, ad space on Astronet.com sells at a respectable rate of $30 per thousand page impressions. Astronet sold ads at this CPM (cost per thousand) rate before being acquired, and the site continues to earn the same rate in its new home at Women.com Networks.

E-Commerce

Astronet's bread and butter is e-commerce. Its sales of computer-generated astrology charts and a wide range of readings, including personalized psychic and tarot consultations, have always been strong. When the company was acquired, e-commerce transactions accounted for approximately 60 percent of the company's revenue. As part of Women.com Networks, Astronet collects a large portion of the money earned from these readings, which cost $25 to $90 each and are supplied by Astronet's national network of more than 50 metaphysical advisers.

PERFECT TIMING

Diserio believes that building her company during the Web's formative years was critical to Astronet's success. Since then, the cost of starting up a successful Web-based brand has headed toward the moon. "Building an online brand today costs at least $25 million," she says. "But we were able to build the entire company for $900,000." Her success turning an old media standby into a staple on the Web hasn't gone unnoticed. In February 1998 she was selected as one of the top 10 finalists for the prestigious Harvard Business Club of New York's "Entrepreneur of the Year" award, along with such Net notables as James Cramer, founder of TheStreet.com, and Fernando Espuelas, CEO of StarMedia.

While she thanks her lucky stars that she was able to develop a successful Net business with a small up-front investment and sell it to a major media company, the acquisition experience wasn't all smooth sailing. "Being acquired has been bittersweet," muses Diserio. "It was initially hard to relinquish control of something I built and shepherded into a successful business, but in order to grow I believed merging or being acquired by a larger media or content company was the best exit strategy for Astronet."

THE SKY'S THE LIMIT

Regardless of who owns Astronet, Diserio remains its heart and soul. Although she ceased being CEO when it became a wholly owned unit of Women.com Networks, she continues as creative director, evangelist, and chief online personality. And she has no shortage of things to do. "Working on the web is very 24/7—I work all the time," says Diserio, noting that she personally answers wagonloads of business and fan email, does radio and TV spots, and publishes several regular columns (including "Genie's Week" and an "Ask Genie" advice column).

At the end of 2000, Diserio's equity in Women.com Networks vested, unlocking her proverbial golden handcuffs. So what's in store for her next? Enjoying family life with her new husband and child, and further building her trademarked Genie Easy persona. She's also toying with the idea of getting back into entertainment, this time as a television talk show host à la Rosie or Oprah. She plans to write a book of practical wisdom based on her own experiences, tentatively titled "Road Blocks on the Highway of Life: How to Overcome Obstacles and Get What You Want." And, with the demand for veteran Web entrepreneurs so high, she's not ruling out the option of getting involved with another Web business. But before determining which opportunity to pursue next, Diserio will first consult the stars.

Eugenie Diserio's
TOP THREE LESSONS LEARNED

1. *"Focus!* Locate a niche that needs to be filled and create a focus. Remain disciplined and totally focused on your mission. Don't let anyone or anything let you waver."

2. *"Endure!* Confront obstacles as opportunities for problem solving and for constantly pushing yourself to new levels. Follow your own gut instincts over anyone else's."

3. *"Act!* Timing is everything. Procrastination is very damaging in this type of fast-moving industry. If ya snooze, ya lose."

Astronet: KEY STRATEGIC TAKE-AWAYS

- Find an unfilled niche, even if it's an unconventional one. Your business's chances of success are higher if you are the first to identify a new market opportunity.

- If your business is content-centric, focus on publishing material that is refreshed frequently and grabs and sustains visitors' attention. Astronet owes its success to the addictive quality of horoscopes.

- Seek out key distribution channels for your content. Partner with larger businesses and brands for wider distribution. Astronet's early partnership with AOL helped launch the business.

- Personalization works. Provide your audience with content that's intelligently tailored to their specific profiles and preferences.

- Develop a celebrity persona or other distinctive gimmick to help build a large and loyal following. Astronet publicized Diserio's Genie Easy persona through print, radio, and TV spots.

- Use email newsletters as traffic drivers. Astronet distributes an astrology newsletter with links back to Astronet.com to more than 20,000 registered AOL and Women.com users.

- Finally, a word from Astronet's "dotcom divascopes": Don't sign deals when Mercury is in retrograde! According to Diserio, "Deals signed during a retrograde of Mercury often fail."

VITAL STATS

- Cofounder: Kim Fisher, CEO
- URL: www.audiobasket.com
- Stock: Private
- Founded: 1999
- Headquarters: San Francisco

2

AudioBasket

Delivering Personalized Audio Content on Demand

"Get out there, show your face, and talk about your company to everyone. I found great contacts and business partners in the most unexpected places—in cafés and through speaking engagements, for instance."

—Kim Fisher

THREE STRIKES, YOU'RE IN

For Kim Fisher, the third time she ran a business was the charm. She had already cofounded two vastly different enterprises—a fitness center in New York City and an Internet portal in Lithuania—and wanted the third company she headed to be a Silicon Valley high-tech startup. Her chance for a home run came in spring 1999, when her brother, Brian, called to ask if she'd help write the business plan and raise capital for a new high-tech company he and two friends planned to start.

Seven years her junior, Brian, a former computer programmer, had dropped out of a Ph.D. program in mathematics at the University of Chicago to join his friends Andrew Edelson and James Goldstein in turning a novel idea into a groundbreaking company. The venture would focus on a technology they had just filed patents on that allowed the transmission of customized audio to all types of Internet-connected devices—PCs, cell phones, MP3 players, and personal digital assistants, for example. When Fisher met with them and heard the details, she was convinced that the venture would be a success. "I wanted to be involved full-time and do more than just write the business plan," she says. Realizing that, of all of them, she had the most experience running companies, the three men unanimously agreed to make her a cofounder and CEO.

Fisher and her partners immediately got to work devising AudioBasket's strategy. "There are more magazines, newspapers, Websites, and other news sources than most people can absorb," she reasoned. "People don't need more information, they need a way to obtain relevant information." There were already ways to receive personalized content in text format, such as newspaper clipping services and personalized Websites, but no such application existed for audio and radio. AudioBasket would be the first to provide it, supplying custom audio news from well-known providers such as Bloomberg Radio, the Associated Press, CNET Radio, and the BBC World Service.

AudioBasket enables anyone to use the Internet to custom-tailor audio content. It searches audio files and gathers all broadcasts covering user-specified topics. For example, you can create a personalized profile at the AudioBasket Website (or a partner Website) to listen to all news about Intel's stock, an upcoming Super Bowl game, and tropical locales to consider for your next vacation. You select your preferred topics, the length of time for your personalized broadcast, and the time of day you want to hear it. You can then download your customized audio clips from the Web to your desktop computer or any type of wireless playback device you specify, and listen to them at your convenience. Best of all, the service is free.

"Listening to audio is a great way for people to absorb content at times when they're unable to read, like when they're driving in a car during rush hour," explains Fisher. People are working longer hours and driving further on their commutes, and AudioBasket offers them many more aural choices than typical radio fare.

AN ENTREPRENEUR FROM THE START

A 32-year-old serial entrepreneur, Fisher counts herself among the busy professionals that comprise AudioBasket's target market. The oldest of four siblings, she moved with her family to Paris at age 14, when her father, a lifelong IBM employee, was transferred there. She stayed in Europe until college. "Being an 'expat' helped me become a business-woman because it taught me how to be flexible, adapt to new situations, and quickly build connections with people," she says.

Fisher returned to the United States to earn degrees in both psychology and economics from the University of Pennsylvania, and then started a fitness center in New York City with a business partner after graduation. She helped raise $1 million in seed funding for the business and discovered that running companies suited her. "I loved the ability to be involved in all aspects of the business, from financing and marketing to training clients and even greeting people at the reception desk," she says.

Two years later she went back to school for an MBA from UC Berkeley's Haas School of Business. She then signed on for the school's "MBA Enterprise Corps," which sends new grads to developing countries for a year to assist local businesses. Fisher landed in Lithuania in 1994. Although there was no Internet presence there at the time, buzz about the Net had reached the country, so she decided to help start a Web venture. She and her business partner had no HTML experience, but after viewing the code of existing Websites, they were able to create Lithuania's first Internet portal, www.inyourpocket.com, which features guides to Eastern European cities. After the year-long program ended, Fisher stayed on to continue helping other Lithuanian ventures. She started and ran the marketing department for a Motorola joint venture that became Lithuania's largest Internet and wireless service provider. "The opportunity to start any type of business in Lithuania was vast," she says, "and I wanted to leverage my knowledge of the people, the language, and the culture." Ultimately, though, she couldn't stand a fourth below-freezing winter in Eastern Europe, so she returned to California to continue learning about business on the Net.

Fisher's next gig was a position as director of strategic business for Synacom, a wireless networking startup in San Jose that was partially funded by Cisco Systems. Her boss, Stu Jeffery (AudioBasket's first investor and adviser) was a major influence. "I learned the fine art of schmoozing from him," she notes. "He was constantly on the phone, calling people he didn't know and whose connections to Synacom were sometimes thin, but he was always expanding his network and looking for synergies with his company."

THE NEW GIRLS' NETWORK

When she started AudioBasket with her cofounders in May 1999, Fisher used the networking tactics she had learned from Jeffery and her international moves as a teen to help put the company on the map. Her strategy was to approach organizations committed to helping startups get off the ground. To test out the AudioBasket concept, she entered an international business plan competition in England called *Venturefest* (www.venturefest.com). When AudioBasket was selected and the founders were offered a trip to England, they decided it would be a great way to test the merits of their idea. AudioBasket placed third among hundreds of entries and generated interest from angel investors who jointly invested seed funding of half a million dollars in exchange for a 10 percent stake in the company. This early success validated Fisher's belief that the business idea held tremendous promise.

Another organization she approached was the Women's Technology Cluster, a business incubator in San Francisco for women-founded technology startups that she heard about through a friend. For a two percent stake in the new company, which would be used to support future women entrepreneurs, the Cluster provided Fisher and her cofounders with office space, equipment, and mentoring. Through the organization, Fisher participated in Springboard 2000, a conference the Cluster cosponsored with the Forum for Women Entrepreneurs. The event, designed to kick open VC doors for more women, provided selected women entrepreneurs a chance to pitch their businesses to 225 leading venture capitalists. Fisher was picked from over 300 applicants as one of 27 presenters for the January 2000 event and lucked out with a key time slot—right after the keynote speech by Oracle CEO Larry Ellison. The auditorium was packed as people waited for Ellison to show, but since he was running late, Fisher went first. The response was incredible. Her phone started ringing as investors took an interest in the business. By June 2000 she'd closed a $12 million second round of funding with

DotCom Ventures and venture capitalists she'd met through Springboard 2000, including Isabella Capital (a fund that invests in women-led startups) and Panasonic Ventures.

Times have certainly changed for Fisher since she pitched to investors about her first business venture more than a decade ago. "When I was raising money for the fitness center in New York, investors rarely looked at me," she reports. "Even though I was the finance person, they would always direct their questions to my male partner. That doesn't happen anymore. Although my partners are all still male, investors today know that I'm in charge and look directly at me when they ask questions."

A SWEET-SOUNDING MARKET

Fisher believes she's found an enormous market opportunity in serving people who are looking for ways to use their time efficiently and cut through information overload. According to an Arbitron Internet listening study, AudioBasket's target market—busy professionals who listen to audio news online—will consist of more than 10 million people by 2004. The company plans to capture a quarter of this market by initially focusing on three especially info-hungry groups: media professionals, high-tech marketing professionals, and financial analysts. AudioBasket is reaching them through targeted marketing efforts and focusing on signing up partners that provide streaming audio content that's of interest to them.

AudioBasket enables any Website from Schwab.com to Excite to provide its users with access to AudioBasket's service with premade profiles called *QuickStart AudioBaskets*. For example, a finance site can host a QuickStart AudioBasket containing investment tips and news that appeal to the site's audience. Users can further personalize a profile to their tastes by adding, say, quotes for stocks they own or local weather. High-traffic Websites have been eager to add AudioBasket's service to their offerings. "They all realize it's a sticky service that keeps users on their site longer and keeps them coming back," Fisher explains.

Ironically, content providers were one of the toughest group to convince of AudioBasket's benefits. Old media organizations have not always been receptive to putting free content online. So Fisher hired Thierry d'Allant, a former photojournalist, magazine editor, and media consultant to court content providers. "We were talking to big organizations like ABCNews.com and Bloomberg that were skeptical at first," says Fisher. "They became more interested when they saw our prototype, but it still took anywhere from one to five months to hammer out agreements. We've had to learn to go slowly."

The Associated Press and Bloomberg signed on, followed by the BBC World Service, ABCNews.com, and *Financial Times*. After AudioBasket officially launched its online service in April 2000 at the Internet World conference in Los Angeles, interest shot up, and *The Wall Street Journal* signed on shortly afterward. Now AudioBasket is talking to droves of other content providers. But the emphasis is on quality, not quantity. "We won't provide just any audio content," explains Fisher. "We screen through every program to make sure we're not just giving our users fodder."

THE BUSINESS MODEL

AudioBasket is generating revenue from a new form of advertising: targeted audio commercials. The company has devised an ad server that delivers ads tailored to specific types of listeners. Advertisers pay AudioBasket an average rate of $60 per thousand ads, which are delivered to users along with their daily doses of personalized audio content, and AudioBasket's content partners receive a share of ad revenue. "We offer a lot less advertising than what's on the radio, but it's much more effective because it's more highly targeted," says Fisher. (While AudioBasket's service is free to end users, they can pay a $10 monthly fee to receive commercial-free content if they prefer.) The company also generates revenue through licensing its technology to other Websites.

While revenues were negligible in 1999 (the year the company was founded), Fisher expects AudioBasket's combined revenue sources to put the company in the black with $17 million in profits in 2002. "I think this is actually a conservative projection," she estimates. "We'll be able to do what we say we'll do." One reason she expects profitability so quickly is that AudioBasket's user base (and therefore its advertising revenue) is growing so fast. The company is acquiring customers quickly through partnerships with Websites that have large user bases. Others are being exposed to the service through "word of mouse": "A marketing manager in the travel industry could set up her AudioBasket to get news about other travel companies, travel alerts, and vacationing trends," explains Fisher. "She can then email her profile to her staff and other employees who need to keep on top of the same news, and they, in turn, may decide to sign up for their own AudioBaskets."

AudioBasket has four patents pending on proprietary aspects of its technology related to content customization, targeted audio ads, and the ability to deliver streaming audio content to any type of Internet appliance, regardless of the supported audio formats. Fisher believes the patents will help protect the company from would-be competitors. "If a much larger company comes along and shows interest in our technology, our intellectual property can help us defend ourselves," she says. "But to raise barriers to entry, we need to keep innovating and forming partnerships with portals and content providers so that we are the first to capture users."

Beyond AudioBasket's wealth of partnerships and proprietary technology, Fisher says her company has additional advantages over current competitors such as Audible, Voquette, and Command Audio. For one, AudioBasket content can download to any type of playback device. Second, while other sites require the user to download audio selections individually, AudioBasket users can download their audioclips together and play their personalized audio Webcast with a single mouse click. They can also receive automatic daily downloads. Most important, AudioBasket touts its customization factor: Users receive only selected content. What's more, as AudioBasket learns about a particular user's preferences through audio downloads, it makes program recommendations. "Our service caters to an audience of one," says Fisher. In contrast, competing services only allow content to be chosen from broad, generic categories such as "national news," "sports," or "technology."

THE RIGHT PITCH, TEMPO, AND BALANCE

In its first 10 months, AudioBasket jumped from four people to more than 40 and outgrew its digs at the Women's Technology Cluster, moving into two floors of a renovated San Francisco warehouse with sweeping views of the bay. Fisher has arranged the seating chart to maximize each group's comfort and performance. The second-floor suite is noticeably quiet: Workers sit at workstations with headphones, further developing the company's technology and screening the daily supply of audio content to ensure that it's high quality. On the third floor the ambience is more hectic, with members of the sales and business development teams rushing between the conference room and their desks, slapping high-fives as new deals are closed.

To get the current staff, Fisher and her cofounders asked people they went to school with for references. The net then widened to friends, acquaintances, and former coworkers. To encourage staff to refer friends, employees earn points in a lottery for a special prize—such as a three-day getaway to Cabo San Lucas—each time they refer a candidate. If a prospect is hired, the referring employee receives shares of stock. "This has proven to be a great way to recruit trustworthy people," says Fisher. "'A' people bring in 'A' people."

Like many other startups, AudioBasket has a hardworking culture, but Fisher takes pains to ensure that the office doesn't become a second home for employees. She prefers not to offer perks such as free in-house dinners and game rooms that encourage staff to work round the clock. Instead, the company gives out free passes to local health clubs so employees have an incentive to get out of the office, work out, and stay healthy.

MAKING NOISE ABOUT AUDIOBASKET

As CEO and cofounder of a promising Net startup, Fisher has less time to indulge one of her other main passions—weight training. She speaks highly of her strong management team—the seven vice presidents who help her run the company. However, that doesn't mean she's relaxing; she's getting out the word about AudioBasket by talking to current and prospective investors, networking at events, and speaking at conferences.

What's next for Fisher? She wants to spend more time sharing her experience and skills with up-and-coming women entrepreneurs both in the United States and abroad. She envisions advising entrepreneurs on a grander scale once AudioBasket successfully goes public. "Starting incubators similar to the Women's Technology Cluster in less developed regions of the world is my ultimate goal," she says. In the meantime, she's preparing herself for this mission. She now serves on the Cluster's advisory board, and was asked by the U.S. State Department to take a two-week trip to the Baltic States to advise on ways to help stimulate the development of women-run technology businesses in Eastern Europe. "That will probably be my two-week vacation this year!" she says, laughing.

Kim Fisher's
TOP THREE LESSONS LEARNED

1. *"Always plan as if you know you'll succeed.* If you believe you will succeed, those around you will too and they'll invest in and join your company. In addition, you'll be prepared for your future success."

2. *"Hire smart people that you like,* even if they don't have the exact background for the job you're looking to fill. Don't worry about hiring friends and family. It's wonderful to work with people you already know and trust."

3. *"Don't change your strategy based on the whims of the market.* In late 1999 some VCs told me that branding, having a dotcom on our name, and not ever being profitable was what we should show in our business plan. Now they advise me to subsume our

brand to our partners' and take the dotcom off our name. Ignore these whims. Do what works to build a good, sustainable, profitable business."

AudioBasket: KEY STRATEGIC TAKE-AWAYS

- If you have savings, consider investing some of it in your company. This can signify to investors that you believe in the future of the venture, which can help convince them to commit.

- Take advantage of programs available to women entrepreneurs. Fisher incubated AudioBasket at the Women's Technology Cluster and made connections with venture capitalists through Springboard 2000. The Cluster accepts promising young businesses with at least one woman founder who holds a significant equity stake.

- Develop incentive programs to encourage employees to refer job candidates. Employee referrals are one of the best ways to locate qualified, quality employees. AudioBasket provides prizes and stock option rewards to employees who refer others to the company.

- Be careful about providing perks that may inadvertently make employees overwork and burn out. Fisher provides perks that encourage a balanced lifestyle and stays away from ones that reward employees for working long hours.

- Look for innovative ways to distribute your content or service to users because aggregating traffic at a Website is usually very expensive. There are often better ways to attract users than big media campaigns. AudioBasket provides customized audio news to other sites, wireless service providers, and device manufacturers, sharing ad revenue with them.

- Recruit industry insiders if it will help in negotiations with partners. AudioBasket initially had a hard time getting in the doors of large media companies, so Fisher hired a media veteran who could address content partners' concerns in terms that were meaningful to them and show them how the company's technology could benefit them.

VITAL STATS

- Founder: Meiko ("Mae") Towada, CEO
- URL: www.esampo.com
- Stock: Private
- Founded: 1999
- Headquarters: Tokyo

3

eSampo.com

Creating an Online Community for Japanese Women

"I started my company to give women in Japan access to online information that I'd looked for myself but hadn't been able to find. I also wanted to provide a supportive network for Japanese women trying to find balance in their lives."

—Mae Towada

IT'S A WOMAN THING

Women.com, iVillage, and Oxygen may be battling it out for the potentially massive "mainstream women's community" market in the United States, but they're hardly alone in their quest for women's online attention. All across the Web, sites are popping up to create similarly broad-in-scope online women's communities in different languages, countries, and cultures. Cadamujer.com, for instance, for Spanish- and Portuguese-speaking Latin American women, was launched in March 2000 by megaplayer StarMedia Network in a marketing partnership with L'Oréal cosmetics. Sweden's Kvinnor.net ("Women.net") was started by that country's leading women's magazines. At sites both big and mainstream as well as small and alternative, women's online communities are springing up around money advice, career networking, relationship talk, and online shopping.

Just a few steps behind in Asia, a crop of both Asian-based and U.S.-led ventures is vying for the Japanese woman's online loyalty. With the feminization of the Internet in Japan (current estimates put Japan one

43

year behind the United States in terms of closing the gender gap of its online population), Japanese women are a leading driver of the country's consumer e-commerce growth. The sites catering to them are relatively new even by Internet standards—all founded in 1999 or 2000—which puts them side by side at the starting gate.

Who will emerge as the star in this niche? Don't bet against Mae Towada, a 31-year-old former Disney exec who started plotting out a women's community site in August 1999, launched eSampo.com just three months later, and landed $5 million in venture capital three months after that. Though eSampo.com (which means "take a stroll" in Japanese) may sport a Hello Kitty look and feel, it also has a solid base of visitors, an equally solid war chest of cash, and a clear vision of how to serve Japanese women.

REACH OUT AND TOUCH . . . THE KEYBOARD

It may sound like an oxymoron, but Japanese culture's traditional reticence toward touchy-feely sharing presents a huge opportunity for community Web ventures such as eSampo.com. "Here in Japan, there are few support groups compared with the States," explains Towada. "It's just not part of our culture to talk about personal problems. People think it's shameful. But everybody everywhere has problems, so when you *do* open a space where they can talk anonymously, there are a lot of people willing to join the conversation." She points to the popularity of the country's telephone hotlines, which began emerging in the mid-nineties, as evidence of people's strong desire for anonymous, safe havens to discuss problems, share feelings, and get support.

And, as a nascent feminism continues to emerge in a country where more women are trying to stay in professional careers after having children, Japanese women are increasingly grappling with issues surrounding balancing career with family. "In the past, they would get married, quit their jobs, and stay home," says Towada. "Building a career wasn't really an issue. But nowadays, many Japanese women are deciding that, even if they do get married and have children, they'd like to continue working." Unfortunately, gender inequality, combined with little infra-structure for working mothers, makes juggling a career and family difficult for women in Japan. Because the number of nursery schools and day-care centers is limited, securing day care is very tough. These issues and more form the social bonds connecting the women of eSampo.com's online community.

AN ENTREPRENEUR FOR THE DIGITAL AGE

Raised in Japan and schooled in the United States, Towada is an eclectic cultural mix that defies easy generalization. She's fluent in three languages (Japanese, English, and Mandarin), fluid in crossing international borders for work and love, and equally at home in large corporate environments and her own dotcom. Well-versed in Japanese customs, she's also steeped in unabashed American capitalism. "My grandmother had her own business," says Towada. "She's Chinese, and started the first English school in Taiwan. And my father has always had his own business. So when I was thinking of doing something on the Internet, it felt natural to do it on my own."

Towada grew up in Tokyo and, after her undergraduate years, worked for the Boston Consulting Group in Japan. She earned an MBA at Northwestern University and married Chinese-American Michael Hsueh. They moved to Hong Kong in 1996, where Towada landed a management position at Walt Disney Television Asia Pacific, marketing Disney TV and the company's satellite and cable business in Asia. "I got the idea of starting an Internet business while I was working for Disney," she says. "The Internet wave was really hitting the United States, but Disney's Asian business units seemed several steps behind." With firsthand knowledge of how slow large corporations could be when it came to retooling themselves for the new economy, Towada saw big opportunities in Asia for nimble Net startups.

In 1998, when she and Hsueh left Hong Kong for Japan, her break from the corporate fast track began. Although she was offered a job at a large Japanese entertainment company as director of business development, a position she considered her dream job, she realized that it was the optimal time to risk starting her own business. "I knew that if I took a good, stable, high-paying job at a large company, it would be very hard to give it up," she recalls. "My husband and I also wanted to start our family, and I felt that running my own company would give me more flexibility."

So she turned down the biz dev position and instead got hands-on entrepreneurial experience at her father's frozen dim sum manufacturing business. She helped streamline operations, oversaw the company's move to a new office, and managed relationships with clients. All the while, though, the gears were turning in her head about the women's Website she wanted to start.

Towada's idea for the site sprang from the reverse culture shock she experienced when she returned to Japan after living in Hong Kong and the United States. "At this turning point in my life, I came to realize that Japanese society is not very supportive to women wanting to balance their professional and family lives," she explains. It was her desire to help address this problem that would soon lead to the launch of eSampo.com.

A UNIQUE TARGET: COMPUTER-LITERATE HOUSEWIVES

Towada read women's magazines voraciously, looking closely at the ways they catered to different narrow audiences. "Just like in the States, there are a lot of magazines for all sorts of segments of the market," she says, noting that she believes the percentage of women who read women's magazines in Japan is higher than in the United States. But the feasibility of enticing those women to the Web for similar kinds of news and entertainment was less certain—Japan, for all its innovation in electronics manufacturing, lags behind the United States in embracing the Net. "It was only very recently that major universities started giving out email addresses to students," says Towada. In fact, by late 1998, while the e-commerce boom was sweeping through the United States in full force, only 13 percent of Japan's population was online, the result, in part, of an economic downturn in Asia. But estimates forecast that the number of

Internet users in Japan will swell to more than 60 million by 2003, from 19 million in 1999.

Since many women Internet users in Japan were starting to surf from home, Towada decided her online women's community would initially target them. "A lot of homes have Internet access," she says. "And women are increasingly using the Net from home because the infrastructure is already in place." Surveys bear this out: According to a March 2000 Nielsen/NetRatings survey, half of the households in Japan with PCs have Internet access, despite high connectivity charges (the rate for a local call is about $25 an hour, roughly the same cost as an ISDN connection). And 26 percent of women Internet users in the country classify their primary occupation as "homemaker."

LET'S DO LAUNCH

After Towada had crystallized her vision for eSampo.com, the first thing she did was look for like-minded people to join the venture. "I needed to find outgoing women willing to take big risks—not especially easy traits to find in Japan," she says. "I looked for people with Internet, publishing, business development, and marketing experience. I also looked for people with the ability to change and adapt quickly." She tapped her network of former colleagues from Disney and the Boston Consulting Group, and by October 1999 she had hired four women. "They weren't sure how the Internet was going to work out here, but they wanted to go through the experience with me," she says.

The small team got to work creating original content for the site, designing its look, and securing e-commerce partnerships. Designing the site in Japanese, a language with one of the most complex writing systems in the world, was a major challenge. "Japanese characters aren't screen friendly," says Towada. "There aren't many fonts to choose from. Our solution was to use relatively small amounts of text on each page and not shy away from graphics."

Towada initially funded the company with all of her personal savings —about $60,000—and convinced some angel investors in Chicago she met through an acquaintance to put up another $300,000. In November

1999 the site launched with stories and information covering family, health, career, fashion, and money issues. The message boards were initially seeded with 50 questions to get conversations rolling. Since then, child-care topics have proven most popular, along with conversations about pregnancy and Japanese soap operas.

The site even included a cooking channel where visitors could learn to cook everything from minestrone soup to traditional Japanese dishes by viewing images of each stage of the preparation process as they read a recipe (the recipes are provided by a chef trained at Cordon Bleu in London). After the launch, traffic ramped up quickly as word spread, and it wasn't long before more than 5000 people were visiting every day.

LOTS OF WOMEN, LOTS OF COMPETITION

One litmus test for judging the viability of a given business concept is the level of competition. Because the Japanese online women's market is lucrative and ramping quickly, it's no surprise that competitors are flocking to the scene. eSampo.com faces competition from sites in Japan as well as U.S.-based Net companies that want to grab a piece of the women's market in the world's second-largest economy.

U.S.-based Women.com Networks, for example, has jumped into the Japanese market in a content licensing agreement with Sankei Living Shimbun, Inc.'s "Living Ladies Community" site (www.lcomi.ne.jp). San Francisco-based Onnanet.com (with financing from Israeli backers) is also rolling out sites for women audiences in Japan and other Asian countries.

According to Towada, Japanese publishers of women's magazines, such as *Magazine House* and *Kodansha*, have been slow to move their content online because of uncertainties about how to take to the Web without cannibalizing their existing businesses. As a result, she isn't viewing them as competitors, at least for now. "Because of their resources and manpower, the biggest threat to us are the larger players like So-net, BiGlobe, and other Japanese portal sites," she says.

What's Towada's competitive strategy? First, she's partnering with potential competitors when possible. Like any savvy Internet entrepreneur, she's aware that cooperating with competitors can be a win-win strategy, so she's exploring potential synergies, including cross promotions, with cafeglobe.com (a locally grown Website for Japanese women) and others. Second, she's going broad, not narrow, with eSampo.com's offerings, organizing the site's content by life stages. "Even if you have friends you can talk to, that doesn't necessarily mean you're at the same life stage—they might not be pregnant or dealing with aging parents," she explains. The goal of this strategy is to spark vibrant, ever-widening communities of support that will result in growing streams of traffic.

LET THE GAMES BEGIN

Towada is promoting the site through games, quizzes, and lotteries that encourage visitors to return regularly. "In one of our first promotions, visitors searched the site for hidden numbers to win a free stay for two at the Westin Hotel in Tokyo," she says. The site also offers free Web-based email, personalization, and other tried-and-true sticky features that are boosting traffic and attracting new visitors.

With traffic and ad revenue on the rise, eSampo.com closed a $5 million first round from the venture capital arm of the Singapore Economic Development Board and Incubate Capital Partners (a Japanese venture fund) in February 2000. Towada, who now has 25 employees, is using $1.5 million of this investment for marketing, including the purchase of advertising space on Japanese portal sites and a direct-mail campaign aimed at Japanese women who are already using the Internet.

The company is syndicating its editorial content to other sites to build its brand where Japanese women Net users regularly surf. "The market is starting to recognize the quality of our content, and now we have a deal with Yahoo! Japan to place some of our content on their site, which will direct more traffic to ours," Towada explains. In addition, she's working with a Japanese wireless phone company to offer eSampo.com's content to its customer base in a wireless format. "We're constantly thinking of new incentive programs, community-related tools to add to the site, and new partners to go after," she says.

THE BUSINESS MODEL

While eSampo.com is reeling in revenues from three sources that are staples among community Websites—advertising, sponsorships, and e-commerce—the company also earns money syndicating content and conducting market research on behalf of clients marketing products to women.

Advertising

Advertising and sponsorships account for 50 percent of the company's revenues. The site garners ad rates of $50 to $60 for every 1000 pageviews delivered to eSampo.com visitors. Sponsors pay $6000 to $10,000 per month to sponsor a specific area of the site. Advertisers have included Kodak, TV Tokyo, Virgin Atlantic Airways, and Morningstar, as well as other multinational and Japanese companies.

E-Commerce

Commissions from e-commerce sales make up 20 percent of revenues. Towada has partnered with vendors in the Tokyo area— they sell their products including cosmetics, clothing, and tickets on the eSampo.com site, and eSampo.com earns 10 to 20 percent commissions on sales.

Market Research

The remaining 30 percent of revenues is derived from doing custom market research for clients market-testing new products. In return for answering online product marketing surveys, eSampo.com gives visitors free products or points that can be used to purchase items on the site. Towada has found that fully 80 percent of those who register are willing to act as virtual focus-group participants for the companies doing research.

Content Syndication to Mobile Phones

The company is also expanding into a new area: delivering eSampo.com's content in a wireless-compatible format to mobile phones. In exchange for receiving this content, users pay access fees.

KEEPING HER EYE ON THE FINANCIAL FUTURE

Towada expects her business to turn a profit by 2003 and has set a longer-term financial goal of taking the company public on one of two new Japanese stock markets: Nasdaq-Japan or Tokyo Stock Exchange's MOTHERS market, a securities market that makes it easier for Internet startups in Japan to list their shares publicly. (MOTHERS is an acronym for "Market of the High-Growth and Emerging Stocks," not an exchange for mother-run Internet companies, although that would certainly be fitting: Towada gave birth to a baby girl just weeks after launching eSampo.com!) The advantages of these new exchanges include the ability to offer employees stock options and take a company public at an early stage, things that were previously difficult to do in Japan.

Towada says the legal aspects of setting up a company in Japan were far more challenging than she expected. Japanese law requires that money from investors be put into escrow initially. This ties up the funds, which can be a problem for young companies with tight cash flow. Stock options are also a relatively new concept in Japan (they've only been allowed since 1997), and they're catching on fast, especially since offering them has become more feasible because of MOTHERS. There are also many licenses required to start a business in Japan, which cost money and can involve a lot of paperwork and hassle. "Commercial code here is a little backward," she admits. "It doesn't allow companies a lot of freedom, especially startups. It's hard to set up a structure to allow the company to accept outside investments."

Towada is doing her part to alert Japanese businesswomen and entrepreneurs to all the red tape and potential regulatory stumbling blocks. eSampo.com provides practical advice for women starting ventures, from bakeries and flower shops to ambitious Internet operations. "As more women in Japan start their own companies, we're providing them with the information they need," says Towada.

As for the future, the eSampo.com team has visions of offering variations of the site in Chinese and even English (for English-speaking women in Asia). A multilanguage venture in Japanese, Chinese, and English? Sounds like something her grandmother would have approved of. "My grandmother told me that it's important to be independent and do your own thing," Towada reflects. "Deep down, I look to her as my role model. She's the person I most want to be like."

Mae Towada's
TOP THREE LESSONS LEARNED

1. *"Be clear about your mission.* It can be really easy to lose your direction and focus as your company grows because there are so many options."

2. *"Be flexible enough to change* when a particular strategy isn't working. While you need to stick to your direction, at the same time you need to let go of strategies that don't work out."

3. *"Have fun and be creative.* All the people who joined this company wanted to do something different and work at a startup. We're excited about creating a new Internet community."

eSampo.com: KEY STRATEGIC TAKE-AWAYS

- Work with an experienced lawyer and a seasoned accountant. This is especially important in countries with tricky startup laws, stock rules, and tax regulations.

- Reach out to other founders, CEOs, and executives for support and advice. "It's very easy for CEOs and top people to feel isolated," says Towada, who regularly talks with former business school classmates who are now in senior positions in companies.

- Develop a unique angle or offering, especially if there's a lot of competition. Towada targeted women at home initially because a high percentage of them were online, and other women's sites were more focused on serving women at work.

- Partnering with competitors makes sense if the relationship helps you both. Towada is pursuing partnerships with other Japanese women's sites to promote eSampo.com.

- Content syndication can be a good traffic driver. If you produce original editorial content, consider syndicating it to other sites to build your brand and drive traffic back to your site.

VITAL STATS

- Founders: Candice Carpenter, chairwoman, and Nancy Evans, editor-in-chief
- URL: www.ivillage.com
- Stock: IVIL
- Founded: 1995
- Headquarters: New York

Netscape:iVil... Sharing solutions and advice

Netsite: http://www.ivillage.co... What's Related

JOIN FREE · email · chat · boards · experts · games NEW · feedback · membercenter

Sparks.com
a better card store
Visit us now and get your first card FREE!
Real Cards-Any Occasion
Shop Now!
iBaby.com

iVillage.com
THE WOMEN'S NETWORK
SOLUTIONS FOR YOUR LIFE

Welcome Back!
Click here to get even more out of iVillage!

new today in iVillage: **Monday, June 5, 2000**

diet right
Find out what iVillagers are saying about the Atkins Diet and the Zone. Then find the right diet for you in Diets A-to-Z.

today: **save money**
Did you overspend a little this weekend? Learn easy ways to save money:
¥ Quit clipping. Get grocery coupons online.
¥ Learn how to print your own business cards.
¥ Check out these 25 easy ways to save.
¥ Read iVillagers' Top 10 Saving Tips.

21st century solutions
365 ANSWERS TO WOMEN'S EVERYDAY PROBLEMS
#157: Seven quick and healthy breakfast recipes.

FIND IT
go
● on iVillage.com
○ on snap

CHANNELS
allhealth
astrology.com
beauty
click! computing
diet & fitness
election 2000
food
garden NEW!
moneylife
parent soup'
parentsplace℠
pets
readers & writers
relationships

DAILY CHECK
Email
Horoscopes
News & Stocks
Joke of the Day
Freebies &Discounts
Today at iVillage
Recipe of the Day
Daily Crossword NEW!
Sweepstakes NEW!

Shopping Central
Special products and values for iVillagers

products
Free ThermaSilk hair care set with 1st purchase.
Save 20% on select Summer products at iBaby.com!
Shampoo & Conditioner: Buy one get one free
20% off everything for your garden

stores
gloss.com for beauty
planetRx.com
NORDSTROM.com
PlusBoutique.com

4

iVillage

Pioneering a Virtual Women's Community

"Carefully consider whether it's the right time for your business idea. You have to pick one that's appropriate to the moment."
—Candice Carpenter

"Starting a business is a commitment of time and energy beyond anything you've ever done. You're going to be tired, you're going to lose touch with friends, and niceties to yourself, like those bubble baths you're supposed to take, will fall to the wayside. But if you're realizing a dream, it's worth it."
—Nancy Evans

NEW MEDIA TRAILBLAZERS

When Candice Carpenter and Nancy Evans met at a business meeting in 1994, they knew they were birds of a feather. Carpenter was president of Q2—the upscale QVC shopping channel started by Barry Diller (now CEO of USA Networks). Evans was running *Family Life* magazine, which she started and published through a partnership with Jann Wenner, creator of the empire that includes *Rolling Stone*, *Us*, and *Men's Journal*. "At that meeting we were, as we both had been most of our business lives, the only women at the table," recalls Evans, who was instantly drawn to Carpenter's drive and smarts. "When you meet someone you 'get' like that, you need to make a move." Which is exactly what she did, writing a note to Carpenter, suggesting that they get to know each other. "Had I not written that note—which was a rare act for me since I was consumed by my startup and had little time for friends—iVillage might never have happened."

In early 1995, Carpenter and Evans, now fast friends, were sitting on the floor at Carpenter's home, brainstorming their life paths. They were both at critical junctures: Carpenter had recently left Q2 and Evans was in the process of selling *Family Life*. During their heart-to-heart conversation, they had a mutual realization: "We'd both worked with major media builders, but we weren't major media builders *ourselves*," says Evans.

To buy herself some time before committing to a big career move, Carpenter, who was a new mother at the time, took an e-commerce consulting job at AOL that offered her a flexible schedule. As soon as she was exposed to the online world, the former Time Warner television-and-video exec knew the Web was going to be *the* next big thing. Excited, she called Evans and asked her to check out AOL. Evans signed up and started surfing. "I spotted intelligent life in the Motley Fool, but didn't find a lot else that was really worthwhile," she recalls. "Candice and I began to see that the Internet was like TV in the early fifties: primitive, but with huge potential. Our ideas started to percolate."

And percolate they did. Today, Carpenter and Evans are cofounders of iVillage, a publicly traded company and women's Website that's a top 20 in terms of brand strength. The company is 420 employees strong (not counting its 2200 volunteer chat hosts) and growing. With 16 "channels" focused on different issues, the site's robust online community includes message boards, chats, instant messaging, and a personalized My iVillage page. It offers more than 90 experts and countless practical tools, such as a baby-name finder and an interactive menu maker. By spring 2000 the community had 4.9 million members, up 218 percent from the previous year. The site was receiving more than 150 million pageviews per month and boasted a reach of more than nine percent, placing it ahead of rivals Women.com Networks and Oxygen Media. Moreover, iVillage's emphasis on building a virtual community sets it apart. Women.com slants its offerings toward editorial content and, at least for now, Oxygen Media's primary focus is television, a form of media iVillage doesn't plan to pursue.

IT'S A WOMAN'S WORLD WIDE WEB

When Carpenter and Evans first began iVillage in June 1995, they didn't know what Internet companies were like. As "old media" execs, they were experts at building brands, selling advertising, and increasing viewership and readership, but they were novices on the Net. Looking for a little insight, they called the folks at the Motley Fool and arranged a visit. "What we saw was one big room full of people sitting at computers," remembers Evans. "When we asked the Fools about their advertising model, they just shrugged and laughed. Advertising on the Net hadn't really entered the picture yet."

With the online terrain wide open, Carpenter and Evans decided they would stake their claim. Their intention? To humanize cyberspace. "We wanted to transform the Web so that it would contain stuff people really cared about," says Evans. "We also wanted to make it intuitive—so people would know what to click on and where they'd go if they did." Although these ideas seem like old hat now, they were groundbreaking in the days when the Web was primarily a noncommercial environment made chiefly by and for computer-savvy people.

As timing would have it, AOL had just learned that its female user population was rising fast and tending to congregate in online communities—bulletin board and chat areas organized around demographic segments (seniors, parents, and lesbians, for example) and shared interests. But the pickings were slim when it came to content slanted toward women on AOL. So in September 1995, AOL Interactive Properties President Ted Leonsis backed Carpenter with $2 million in seed funding to create a Web media enterprise that would develop original female-friendly content for AOL. Carpenter quickly invited Evans to be cofounder—her consumer publishing background made her an ideal person to help develop this type of content for the future media giant. And that's how iVillage was born.

THE SECRET SAUCE IN PARENT SOUP

Carpenter and Evans's vision was to create a constellation of Websites under the iVillage brand that focused on parenting, health, and work. In

January 1996 their flagship site, Parent Soup (www.parentsoup.com), was launched simultaneously on AOL and under its own domain. "We picked an initial focus on parenting because it capitalized on my experience at *Family Life*, which meant we could get it to market faster," says Evans, who worked out of her home to launch the site, as did Carpenter.

The pair commissioned celebrated Web designer Roger Black to create a prototype of Parent Soup, which they then used to woo potential sponsors. Because of Carpenter and Evans's solid media backgrounds and the high quality of the prototype, blue-chip companies were willing to sign up as sponsors on Parent Soup even before the site existed for the opportunity to market specifically to women. "This was a *big* deal at the time," recalls Evans. "We sold advertisers in before we launched, just like you do with magazines, which wasn't industry practice."

This wasn't the only smart, unconventional business decision Carpenter and Evans made. They believed sponsorships would provide a more consumer-friendly experience than traditional banner ads. "The first time I ever clicked on a banner ad was on AOL," recalls Evans. "I clicked a box at the top of the page, went zooming off to another site, and then didn't know how to get back. I was confused and frustrated." So they initially sold *only* sponsorships.

They also believed that creating a network of key brand-name sponsors was critical to iVillage's long-term success. "We took an unproven road very early because we believed in developing deep multiyear relationships with our advertising partners," says Carpenter. They created custom, sponsored areas and worked collaboratively with the sponsoring companies. The result: When a user clicked on a banner on Parent Soup, they wouldn't be thrown off the site. Instead, they'd jump over to a sponsored area offering a service within the site. Charter six-month sponsorships on Parent Soup were priced at $150,000 apiece. "Our goal was to sell six and that's what we did before the site launched," says Carpenter. Nissan and Polaroid were among the six companies that signed up.

After the launch, awareness of iVillage grew fast as as a steady stream of people—chiefly AOL subscribers at first—visited the site. In iVillage's first year, AOL accounted for 76 percent of its traffic. Since then iVillage has developed its own traffic streams to its network of branded communities, which offer women Web surfers a kind of cyber retreat: virtual places they can go to get and offer advice on everything from diaper rash to infertility issues to intercultural adoptions. (iVillage uses input from its visitors to hone its content offerings.)

REFUSING TO TAKE NO FOR AN ANSWER

When it came to recruiting top executives, Carpenter and Evans stopped at nothing. Their messianic passion for what they were doing attracted an early team of go-getters who wanted to pioneer building a whole new consumer medium. Their earliest significant hire was Elaine Rubin, who successfully led 1-800-FLOWERS onto the Internet. "Candice and I took Elaine out to dinner again and again," remembers Evans. "We talked her ear off on the sidewalk at midnight. We talked about a place where she could invent commerce from the bottom up, a place where she would be a star, a place where we'd understand when she needed to go home to her kids. We got Elaine."

Carpenter and Evans still celebrate recruiting John Glascott as senior vice president of sponsorships—a position that's absolutely critical given iVillage's sponsorship-oriented business model. Glascott had worked both in startup and corporate environments, so he had an ideal mix of experience for iVillage. But wining and dining him didn't work, and he accepted a position with another startup. Undeterred, the duo had one of their assistants stand at his office building and wait for him to get off the elevator after his first day at work. Her mission was to convince him to get in the car Carpenter and Evans had sent. Figuring he'd at least get to avoid a subway commute, Glascott got in.

But the car first stopped at iVillage, where Carpenter and Evans jumped in and their assistant jumped out. "We spent the hour ride to his house pitching. When we got there, we met his wife—who thought we were insane—and his kids—I told them there'd be big money for them if they convinced their dad to come with us," recalls Evans. When the women got back in the car, the driver, who had been silent the entire ride, said, "I think you've got him."

GROWING PAINS AND PLEASURES

In March 1997, Carpenter and Evans experienced one of the most anxious moments an entrepreneur can face: not being able to make payroll. "We'd run out of our first money, we didn't yet have a bridge loan, and there were people who were depending on us to pay their rents," says Evans. "I spent the day going to every bank account I had and taking every penny out. Candice chipped in what she had too." They scraped together their personal savings, and iVillage's employees got their paychecks just as they always had, never realizing how close the founders had come to running out of cash.

Since then, adequate cash hasn't been an issue. Carpenter has been amazingly successful raising large rounds of financing from both VCs and strategic partners. Unlike many other early entrepreneurs to enter the Internet space, she understood that brand building is very expensive, so she didn't wait long to reel in big investments. Investors wanting to test the Web's waters and invest in an Internet startup were reassured by the fact that the cofounders were middle-aged media vets, not twenty-something Internet entrepreneurs working out of their parents' garage. By the time iVillage went public in March 1999, Carpenter had raised $110 million in five rounds from top firms such as Kleiner Perkins Caufield & Byers and Technology Crossover Ventures—a high level of financing for any dotcom startup, and especially so for one whose core business rests on sponsorship sales.

The process of starting iVillage wasn't without challenges, however. The company has had three CFOs, one of whom accused it of fishy accounting practices just before its IPO in March 1999 (iVillage denied the allegation, and the SEC and PricewaterhouseCoopers, who reviewed the company's financials before the IPO, gave them a clean bill of health). And, in its early days, the company had its fair share of employee turnover. The unpredictability and breakneck pace at early-stage Net companies, as well as an extremely tight market for Web-savvy talent, makes high turnover a common problem at dotcom startups. "Burnout was a really big issue in the early days of the company because you couldn't rest. There was so much to do in such a short amount of time," says Carpenter. "I pulled all-nighters every week for the first two years."

But these days such long hours are rare, and work life is saner. The company is maturing, and employees and founders alike can now take more time for their nonwork lives. Carpenter, who was an Outward Bound instructor for eight years before getting a Harvard MBA, takes occasional time off to kayak, snowboard, mountain bike, and rock climb—she was one of the first women to scale Yosemite's Half Dome. As a single mom, she spends as much time as possible on outdoor adventures with her two young daughters. But the life of a dotcom CEO isn't always marked by balance. "If you commit to something big, you can't expect to be able to go to the gym every day," she acknowledges.

PLAYING BY NET RULES

In March 1999, iVillage's stock went public at $24 per share and closed its first day at $85.25—an increase of 233 percent. Carpenter and Evans were instantly two of the wealthiest women Internet entrepreneurs (at least on paper). Although the stock has headed southward since then, the company has successfully used money raised from the IPO to acquire other businesses to expand iVillage's online offerings. In 1999 it acquired Lamaze Publishing for approximately $90 million, securing not only the goodwill associated with the Lamaze name, but the premium price advertisers are willing to pay to appear in Lamaze publications. Other acquisitions include Online Psych (www.onlinepsych.com)—one of the largest online health communities—which iVillage also bought in 1999 for $25 million.

You could say that iVillage is a prime example of a dotcom company that doesn't subscribe to traditional business rules. At this stage, the company is squarely focused on "grabbing eyeballs." Spending heavily on marketing campaigns and acquisitions to boost traffic is a strategy Carpenter is fully convinced will pay off: "With a media business, you spend a lot up front to build brand and then your revenue starts scaling past that." Carpenter sees winning mindshare now as the thing that's going to ensure iVillage's position as the leading women's online network in the future. And it looks as if she's right: 1999 revenues for the company were $44.5 million, and analysts are predicting profitability for 2001.

THE BUSINESS MODEL

Like other major content and community Websites, iVillage makes money through advertising, sponsorships, and e-commerce. A sponsorship-centric strategy is key to the company's success. Eighty-five percent of revenue comes from sponsorships (which are sold for a specific duration of time) and advertising (which is sold based on the number of times the Web page with the ad is viewed). The remaining 15 percent comes from e-commerce. Statistics are part of the reason iVillage is so successful when it comes to landing large sponsorship deals: According to *Advertising Age,* women control or influence more than 80 percent of purchasing decisions. As a result, advertisers scramble to gain presence where women congregate online. Charles Schwab, Procter & Gamble, and Kimberly-Clark are among iVillage's many brand-name sponsors that pay millions of dollars for exclusive rights to advertise in certain areas on the Website.

iVillage works with its sponsors in extremely innovative ways. For example, Carpenter and Evans provided statistics to Ford Motor Company showing that women make the vast majority of car purchasing decisions, yet dread going to a car dealership second only to going to a dentist. Seeing something wrong with this picture, Ford entered a two-year, $5 million sponsorship agreement with iVillage in 1999. The result was the iVillager, a prototype car based on the thousands of submissions received from iVillage members when asked what they wanted in a dream car. Ford is now taking the items women asked for—among them improved safety features and adjustable foot pedals—and designing them into some future models. "Now that's a win-win," says Evans. "A win for Ford and a win for women."

While iVillage has no plans to move away from its focus on sponsorships, the company is expanding its e-commerce offerings. With women rapidly becoming a big consumer spending force online, iVillage has plans to offer more e-commerce choices to busy working women and mothers who don't have time to shop in real-world stores. The company is developing new commerce areas beyond its current online shops, which include iMaternity and Shopping Solutions (a medley of iVillage cobranded stores from retailers such as the Gap, Macy's, and Petopia).

In addition, part of iVillage's business model includes partnering with major media companies for promotion and new traffic streams. The company has key strategic partnerships with highly trafficked Web properties that distribute iVillage-branded content, increasing awareness of the brand and driving traffic back to the site. AOL Time Warner, which owns eight percent of the company, promotes it on AOL. NBC, which took a six percent equity stake in iVillage in 1998, promotes it both on TV and online at NBC.com and Snap. In exchange, iVillage produces original programming for NBC's online properties. Among iVillage's other strategic partners are Excite@Home, AT&T, Cox Interactive Media, and the GO Network.

A GLOBAL IVILLAGE

What lies ahead for iVillage? Global expansion. Approximately 20 percent of the site's traffic originates overseas, and the company has plans to create versions of its site for Japan, the United Kingdom, and several other European countries. And the company is continuing to sign up partners and sponsors at a rapid clip. With major partners such as NBC on board, and the trend of consolidation between old and new media companies going strong, iVillage may not remain an independent entity for long.

And what's ahead for the dynamic Carpenter-Evans duo? Carpenter wants to work on behalf of women for as long as she can. But for a future chapter of her life, the charismatic, down-to-earth entrepreneur is fantasizing about going to Yale Divinity School and becoming a minister. For her part, Evans wants to help increase the number of women entrepreneurs on the planet and hopes someday to create an organization to "turbocharge the process." With their entrepreneurial creativity and experience guiding them, their futures are wide open.

Candice Carpenter's
TOP THREE LESSONS LEARNED

1. "Pick your initial business partners with an eye toward maximizing the diversity of their skills and experience."

2. "Let criticism roll off your back. Any time you're a pioneer, you stick your neck out and get your head chopped right off."

3. "Help your employees navigate the roller coaster of a startup."

Nancy Evans's
TOP THREE LESSONS LEARNED

1. "Never take no for an answer."

2. "Keep your eye on the prize and stay focused."

3. "Stay true to the founding mission of the business."

iVillage: KEY STRATEGIC TAKE-AWAYS

- If you're launching a consumer business, develop your brand with care from day one. "You don't build a business and then tack on a brand—be obsessed with building it from the beginning," says Carpenter.

- Focus on a demographic that's attractive to advertisers: iVillage's success revolves around its focus on women, a group that advertisers covet because of their control over household spending.

- Evaluate what sources of revenue will be the most lucrative. If your Web business is supported by advertising, test the market to determine what mix of sponsorships and banner advertising works best.

- If possible, enlist a technology person as a member of your founding team. Because Carpenter and Evans considered iVillage a media company, they recruited a technology person later in the game than they wish they had.

- Consider hiring a seasoned human resources professional very early. In retrospect, Carpenter and Evans wish they'd done this sooner, since being successful in the Internet space depends on hiring and retaining good employees.

VITAL STATS

- Cofounder: Tracey Ellery, president
- URL: www.looksmart.com
- Stock: LOOK
- Founded: 1995
- Headquarters: San Francisco

Travel Deals Online   NetZero Free ISP   Buy & Sell At eBay   Hear It At Redband

looksmart categories

Home | Email | Help

Search the Web [   ] [Search]   Need traffic fast? List with LookSmart!

Entertainment
Arts	Humor
Celebrities	Movies/TV
Games	Music

Shopping
Auctions	Classifieds
Buying Guides	Online Stores
Cards/Gifts	Product Search

Connecting
Chat	Forums
Email	Homepages
Find People	Personals

Lifestyle
Auto	Food/Wine
Books	Hobbies
Fashion	Sports

Library
Education	Sciences
Humanities	Social Science
Reference	Society

Work & Money
Business	Industries
Companies	Jobs
Finance	Professions

Computing
Computer Sci	Internet
Design	Sales
Hardware	Software

Lookup
Businesses	News
Horoscopes	Weather
Maps	What's On

Travel
Activities	Reservations
Destinations	Transportation
Lodging	Trip Planning

Personal
Belief	Home
Family	Kids
Health	Relationships

Today's Top Stories
- High Court Curbs Grandparents' Rights
- Earthquake Shakes Sumatra, 58 Dead
- Ray Lewis Avoids Murder Charge
- More ...

@ LookSmart
Submit a Site
Father's Day

Your Daily Clicks
Horoscopes
News
Stocks & Portfolio
Weather

LookSmart Centers
Automotive
Beauty & Fashion
Careers
Home & Garden
MP3
Real Estate
Small Business

LookSmart Services
Beseen Web Tools
Custom Styles

Can't find what you're looking for?
LookSmart Live! will help you find it, and reward you for helping others.

City Guides
Localize your search in more than 70 US cities.

5

LookSmart

Licensing Navigation Solutions

"It's very powerful when you have a vision and the opportunity to go out and make it happen."

—Tracey Ellery

CUTTING THROUGH THE CLUTTER

For Tracey Ellery, a passion for the Internet originated out of sheer necessity. In 1995 she was pregnant with twins and housebound. "It was pretty early days for the Internet, but I learned to do everything from business research to grocery shopping online," says the 38-year-old Aussie entrepreneur. However, finding what she needed in the Net's salad days before it was a mass-consumer medium took a very long time.

This frustration inspired Ellery's idea for an online directory that would offer links only to "hate-free, porn-free," high-quality Websites. While early search engines and directory sites such as Yahoo! were already online, their search results often contained too many listings, and poor-quality or irrelevant sites. Ellery envisioned a consumer-friendly directory that would organize handpicked sites into granular, easy-to-navigate categories. "It was clear to me that as more and more nontechie people started using the Web, they would need services that would organize it in an intuitive way and weed out the junk that was overwhelming the good stuff even back then," she says.

Today LookSmart, the online directory business she cofounded with her husband in Melbourne, Australia, has offices in San Francisco, Montreal, Sydney, London, and Amsterdam, and employs more than 600 people. Its headquarters, located in a converted brick-and-timber train-storage warehouse in San Francisco's Media Gulch, reflects an industrial technohip style that's the trend among San Francisco–based dotcoms. But conference room names like Dingo, Koala, and Kangaroo, as well as a huge inflated platypus sitting on an office table, give away the company's Aussie roots.

LookSmart is a leading Internet search and navigation company dedicated to helping Web users around the world quickly find what they want. It allows visitors to search the Web by browsing a directory of categorized Websites or doing a keyword search. Visitors who get stuck can post a question on the site's *LookSmart Live* message boards: If another visitor doesn't answer right away, one of the company's many search experts will. The site also offers regional content, such as weather, restaurant reviews, and movie listings, for more than 70 U.S. cities.

Ellery, who is the company's president, and her husband, Evan Thornley, who is CEO, have overseen LookSmart's rocket-fueled growth from a straightforward idea to a billion-dollar-plus market cap. Look-Smart's search and directory services are used by nearly three-fourths of all Internet users in the United States, and the company was named one of the 100 top shapers of the Internet by *The Industry Standard*. At the time this was written, LookSmart was among the 10 most highly trafficked navigation Websites and was a top-20 site overall. "When we first drafted our business plan in 1995, we set an objective of owning a top-20 site by the year 2000," says Ellery. "We knew that if we achieved this goal, we would have an incredibly valuable business, but we had no idea how valuable it would be."

AN UNLIKELY BENEFACTOR

It's no wonder that starting an Internet business held a lot of appeal for Ellery. From an early age, she has run with new ideas and headed up organizations. She grew up outside of Melbourne in a working-class family, and her parents were very supportive of her emerging leadership abilities. While an undergrad studying law and drama at Australia's Deakin University, she was founding president of the National Union of Students, a powerful lobby group focused on improving the welfare of university students. After graduating, she served a three-year stint as a lobbyist for the Consumer Advocacy and Financial Counseling Association, a Ralph Naderesque consumer watchdog group. And before starting LookSmart, she founded and headed Student Services Australia, a university publishing and computer retailing company.

She and Thornley shared a longstanding dream of starting a business together, so when Ellery hit on the idea for LookSmart, she was convinced it was their opportunity. With the Internet industry still largely virgin territory, she believed that the idea had the potential to grow into something very big. So she started doing online research to pinpoint the best business strategy. At the time, there was a huge partition on the Internet: On one side were proprietary, closed services such as AOL; on the other, the Web's inchoate free-market chaos. "The Web was clearly going to win out over proprietary services in terms of consumer access," says Ellery. "There needed to be an AOLization of the Web to make it attractive to consumers."

As the business strategy gelled, she and her husband sought feedback from a wide range of people. Most said they were completely nuts. "Many of our friends and colleagues thought we were leaving our careers to start something equivalent to a ham radio business," Ellery says, laughing. But one of the people they spoke with took their idea seriously: the chairman of *Reader's Digest*, whom Thornley knew through working as a consultant for McKinsey & Co. Intrigued by their idea, *Reader's Digest* invested $200,000 in seed funding so they could develop the business plan and produce a prototype of the Web directory.

With the prototype completed, they did market testing, which further convinced them of the need for their product. Then, with positive market-test results in hand, Ellery and Thornley negotiated an additional $1 million from *Reader's Digest* to turn the prototype into a consumer-ready Website.

They leased office space in Melbourne and began recruiting, looking for job candidates who could flourish in a startup environment without being overwhelmed or stymied by the unpredictability. Few people had Internet experience, so they recruited those they thought could quickly climb a very steep learning curve. But convincing people to leave secure jobs and place their career bets on the Net wasn't easy in 1995, when the Web was viewed with far greater uncertainty than it is today. "People self-selected," explains Ellery. "The ones who joined LookSmart early on were exactly the people with the passion and vision to make things happen."

They hired HTML coders and designers to create the site, and database engineers to set up its back-end systems. But their biggest startup expense was editorial staff: They spent 60 percent of their $1 million paying a small army of "Webrarians" to cull through, evaluate, and categorize Websites. (The remaining 40 percent was spent equally on engineering and market reseach.)

UP FROM DOWN UNDER

Ellery and Thornley were acutely aware that they needed to move fast. They knew that even a great Net product or Website that hits the market too early or late can easily fail. Their solution was to outsource whenever they needed to accomplish something and didn't have the necessary in-house resources. "We used technical consultants so we could get moving on projects fast, even if we didn't have the staff in place to do so," says Ellery. "Even now, we'll orchestrate any outside resource if that's what it takes to get the right thing done quickly."

As a result of this strategy, the LookSmart Website launched just six months after the prototype debuted. While traffic to the site was growing dramatically, *Reader's Digest's* own fortunes were souring, and it couldn't continue funding the upstart. On top of this, *Reader's Digest* refused to let Ellery and Thornley raise capital from other investors because it considered LookSmart too strategically important. So LookSmart treaded water as Ellery and Thornley watched their well-funded competitors grow and go public.

In 1997 new management stepped in at *Reader's Digest* and informed Ellery and Thornley that LookSmart was out of business and requested an estimate of shutdown costs. "In retrospect, we really should have gone to California and raised classic venture capital very early on," acknowledges Ellery. But they weren't willing to let their business die so easily, so they proposed an alternative: If *Reader's Digest* would let them buy LookSmart back on no-cash terms, they would finance it themselves and assume its debts.

An ailing *Reader's Digest* agreed, and Ellery and Thornley bought back equity in LookSmart. But with no investor, they were in a pinch. They had recently opened up an office in San Francisco and moved their top managers and their families there to center LookSmart squarely in the midst of a main Internet business hub. And they were running out of cash. "We were the proud owners of the number 903 Website in the world when we bought it back," remembers Ellery. "We were burning $650,000 a month and had only 75 days worth of cash in the bank—all of which was spoken for by creditors."

BOOMERANGING BACK

The duo courageously set out to raise Sand Hill Road venture capital. By this time, though, leading portal sites such as Yahoo!, Excite, Lycos, and Infoseek had already gone public. VCs had invested in their fill of search engines and directories, and viewed LookSmart as a Yahoo! copycat that had missed the boat.

Fortunately, they were able to use small amounts of money from Australian investors to tide them over. "It was the worst time," says Ellery. "We had no experience raising venture capital and few contacts in the States. We came within two days of missing payroll six times." Nonetheless, LookSmart's many partnerships and growing traffic volume eventually made it attractive to major content players, and after eight months of barely scraping by, Ellery and Thornley raised an $8 million round led by Cox Interactive Media. After that, raising money got much easier as the company's momentum picked up. Just three months later they raised a $60 million mezzanine round—one of the largest investments for a private Internet company at the time.

LookSmart's pre-IPO investors were captivated, among other things, by how quickly the site was climbing the Web rating charts. Their capital infusion helped fuel the company all the way to a spot among the top 20 Websites, and it enabled the founders to make key strategic acquisitions, expand their overseas offices, and launch a $20 million ad campaign to further establish the brand.

Although other major broad-based portals had gone public before LookSmart, the company's August 1999 IPO was a shining success despite the lackluster IPO market at the time. Shares were priced at $12 and jumped 44 percent to $17.50 by the end of their first day of trading, raising $92.5 million and making Ellery and Thornley paper multimillionaires overnight. (They own 15 percent of the company, which was valued at $1.8 billion at the end of the first trading day.) The company's post-IPO stock market success enabled it to continue attracting and hiring taxonomists, editors, and subject-matter experts even in an overheated labor market in which most job seekers were on the lookout for the next hot prepublic startup. "For most of our current employees, the value they're realizing from their stock options each year exceeds their salaries," says Ellery.

THE BUSINESS MODEL

Ellery and Thornley are the kind of enterprising entrepreneurs who not only sell lemonade, they sell their lemonade recipe. Besides coming up with a first-rate Web directory, they're selling their infrastructure. Heavyweight search engines such as Excite and Alta Vista, eager to outsource their Web directory needs, have become customers. The company has partnered with Inktomi, which licenses search engine technology, to offer custom directory and search solutions to both consumer and business portals. Portals and search engines aren't the only businesses using LookSmart's directory—ISPs and other Websites are seeing its value too. One reason: Building a robust directory is very labor intensive and therefore expensive. It's not something most Net companies can justify creating from scratch.

Why would other portals, in particular, look to LookSmart? Search sites typically come in two flavors: search engines and directories. Many portal sites are built around search engines, which use a program called a *spider* or *bot* (short for robot) that crawls through Web pages and automatically indexes them by keyword. When a user performs a search, the indexed pages with the highest incidences of the keyword appear at the top of the results. The problem is that poor-quality sites frequently crop up, partly because unscrupulous Web page creators spike their pages with hidden text that repeats popular keywords to improve their search-result ranking.

To ensure that users can find what they're after, major search engine sites also offer browsable directories of sites as a complement to their search engines. This is where LookSmart steps in and licenses its directory. While some portals such as Yahoo! and About.com also use hordes of human editors to create directories of sites manually, unlike LookSmart, they don't necessarily filter out hate and porn sites with the rest of the Web's garbage, and they don't license their directories.

Embracing a business model that included licensing their directory to competitors took a leap of faith and a willingness to chuck out old ideas about how traditional businesses are run. "It actually took us a long time to figure out who should pay whom," explains Ellery. "Do I pay you to use your content or do you pay me to take it and distribute it?" However, LookSmart's licensing strategy has carved out a niche that sets the company apart from other consumer portals. Unlike most search and navigation sites that zealously protect their brands and therefore wouldn't consider licensing their infrastructures, LookSmart doesn't worry about brand dilution. It creates custom directories for clients, hosting and delivering them in the look and feel of the clients' sites. The result of thinking outside the box? LookSmart has been able to syndicate its directory to more than 400 ISPs and 600,000 affiliate sites around the world.

LookSmart allows ISPs and other Websites to integrate a cobranded LookSmart directory into their sites using the company's

Portalmaker tool (www.looksmart.com/portalmaker/). Since banner ads are included in the cobranded directory, LookSmart pays sites that syndicate it a $2 CPM (cost per thousand) for the pageviews they deliver. This is a win for the ISPs and other sites: They earn a slice of advertising revenue and get to integrate LookSmart's directory with their sites. And it's a huge win for LookSmart, which sells banner ad space at a much higher CPM and pockets the difference.

Beyond licensing and syndication, LookSmart earns money through selling advertising space on its consumer portal site. Because the site is organized into very specific categories and sub-categories, advertisers pay $30 to $60 per thousand page impressions to place targeted ads. The company also sells *run-of-site* inventory (which means the advertiser's banner is placed anywhere on the site with available ad space). Because run-of-site placements are untargeted, they're less expensive. LookSmart typically charges between a $4 and $12 CPM for this type of placement, depending on supply and demand each month.

The company earns the remainder of its revenue through e-commerce. Merchants gladly pay hosting and placement fees to have a presence in LookSmart's shopping area, thereby expanding their reach to its large user base.

LOOKING SMART

Because LookSmart is both a consumer-oriented directory site and a company that licenses its infrastructure, it faces two types of competition. In the technology and directory licensing arena, Info-Space, a company that creates custom consumer-oriented portals, is the biggest competitor. Another potential competitor is GoTo, which pays Websites that add its search and other functionality to their pages. And, while at first blush sites like Yahoo!, AltaVista, and Excite might appear to be LookSmart's consumer rivals, AltaVista and

Excite@Home are actually LookSmart partners, licensing the company's directory. More recent entrants putting a new spin on traditional searching methods also offer competion. One such site is Google, which ranks Websites based on how many other sites link to them. Another is Ask Jeeves, which lets users ask a question in plain English and points them to sites with an answer. But despite these rivals, LookSmart's position is exceptionally strong. It has secured distribution through partner Websites that would be extremely difficult for competitors to replicate.

As a successful Net company with origins outside the United States, LookSmart has been focused on international markets for a longer time than its rivals, securing a broad international reach. The company has localized versions of its site for the United Kingdom, Canada, the Netherlands, Singapore, Mexico, New Zealand, and, of course, Oz. It has also built directories for Japan, Korea, and France, among many other countries. And it's continuing to aggressively roll out offerings around the world. In early 2000, LookSmart entered into a joint venture with British Telecom that added 31 million new Internet and wireless users globally to LookSmart's reach.

While the company has yet to turn a profit, its revenues are climbing fast. Ellery expects it to be in the black by 2002. The company brought in $48.9 million in 1999, more than a fourfold increase over its 1998 revenues. Ellery and company are developing new revenue streams too. They've introduced Express Listing, a service that allows businesses that pay $199 to have their sites reviewed and added to LookSmart's directory within 48 hours.

What's Ellery's biggest take-away from her Internet business experience so far? That there are no easy answers. "Every day, I think 'Wow. Look at how the Internet economy is working *today*. How can I benefit from that? How should I respond?'" she says. "I've thrown away all dogma about how I think things should work." This open-minded approach is right on. It's proving to be part and parcel of what it takes to thrive on the Net, and is helping to ensure a smart-looking future for LookSmart.

Tracey Ellery's
TOP THREE LESSONS LEARNED

1. *"There are no rules in the Internet space.* You need to make them up as you go. To thrive, Internet companies need to constantly think outside the box."

2. *"You have to be unreasonably determined to succeed.* You need to be really clear and focused on where you want to be in the long term."

3. *"People decisions are the most important ones you can make.* Hire people who are prepared to take risks and have the tenacity and loyalty to stay in the game through the ups and downs."

LookSmart: KEY STRATEGIC TAKE-AWAYS

- Outsource to get your business moving fast and keep it nimble. LookSmart relies on consultants and outside help whenever it's faced with a looming task beyond its core areas of expertise.

- When barriers to entry are low, look for ways to develop your "unfair competitive advantage." LookSmart leapfrogged up the Web rating charts when it shifted its strategy to include licensing its directory.

- Tap your existing relationships as you seek out capital. Ellery and Thornley initially had an easier time raising funds in Australia, where they knew people, than in the United States. "VCs want to have a sense of who you are, your reputation, and whether they know somebody who knows somebody who knows you," explains Ellery.

- Don't automatically assume competitors can't be partners or customers. Ellery and Thornley credit LookSmart's success to their willingness to partner with competitors.

- If your Website uses a unique technology or proprietary content, consider selling it. While Ellery and Thornley started their business solely as a consumer-oriented site, they realized they could create a lucrative new revenue stream through licensing.

- Understand that you'll need to reinvent the business as you go. Ellery and Thornley are constantly shaping their strategy and pricing models in response to changes in the marketplace and their evolving sense of what works online.

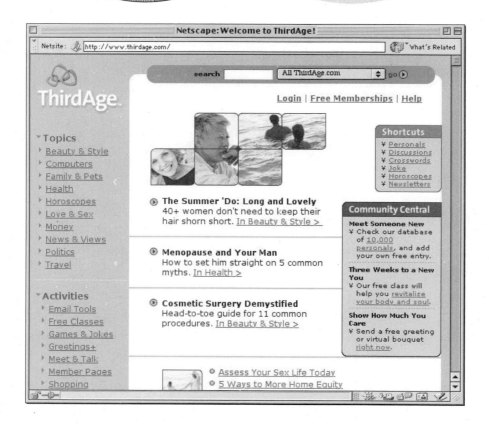

VITAL STATS

- Founder: Mary Furlong, chairwoman
- URL: www.thirdage.com
- Stock: Private
- Founded: 1996
- Headquarters: San Francisco

6

ThirdAge Media

Branding a Generation

"Don't ever believe that you can't take an idea out of the trunk of your car and make it happen."

—Mary Furlong

A TURNING POINT

In August 1995, Mary Furlong sat on the top of a Ferris wheel at the Windows 95 launch party in Redmond, Washington. Her vantage point gave her a bird's-eye view of the Microsoft campus and a sea of white party tents and enthusiastic techies swirling past below. Perhaps it was the summer air or being immersed in the launch party's buzz, but at that literal turning point Furlong had an epiphany that would soon alter the course of her life. "At the top of that Ferris wheel, I realized that the Internet market was going to be much bigger than I had ever imagined," she recalls.

At the time, Furlong was leading SeniorNet, a nonprofit computer-training organization for older adults. Today she's surfing the Internet tidal wave that she first caught sight of from the top of that Ferris wheel. As the chairwoman and first CEO of ThirdAge Media, she's the visionary entrepreneur behind one of the leading Websites for babyboomers. ThirdAge.com caters to people between the ages of 45 and 59, offering them content in eight categories: family, health, living, money, news, romance, technology, and travel. The site has all the fixings of a robust online community—active discussion forums, chat rooms, and plenty of advice from members and resident experts. It features popular online classes that span a wide range of topics from "Alternative Health for Beginners" to "Finding Romance on Vacation." ThirdAge.com is a place where people start new friendships, offer each other support through life transitions, and even fall in love. (Furlong knows of half a dozen couples who met via the site and tied the knot!)

In the heart of San Francisco's Media Gulch, ThirdAge's brick-walled, loft-style office is buzzing with energy. The company's 100-plus employees work away at their monitors and have animated discussions in conference rooms. Visitors waiting to meet with ThirdAge staffers engage in lively conversation on a sofa in the entryway lounge, resting their feet on a J. Petermanesque, leather-covered trunk.

Why all the excitement about a Website catering to midlife adults, a category that now includes the Clintons and the Rolling Stones? As a demographic segment, baby boomers are golden. They own their homes, keep more than 80 percent of their wealth in financial institutions, and represent a very powerful consumer group. With the over-50 crowd the fastest-growing and wealthiest segment of the population both online and off, Furlong has found a promising niche and was able to convince equity investors about it too—to the tune of $103 million. ThirdAge Media boasts an investment level that's simply phenomenal for an online community site: In June 1999, the company raised an enormous, oversubscribed $89 million third round of financing, one of the largest placements ever for an Internet startup.

PASSION FOR HER PEOPLE

Furlong, a vibrant, 50-year-old former professor of education turned dotcom entrepreneur, has spent the last 17 years of her life educating older adults about technology. In the 1980s, while teaching at Catholic University in Washington, D.C., she wrote a book called *Computers for Kids Over Sixty*. As part of her research, she began teaching basic computing at senior centers. "In my first series of classes, I saw that older people had a lot of talent, knowledge, and experience to bring to computers and telecommunications," says Furlong, repositioning a vase of tulips on the conference room table to better show off the blooms. "But they had been left out of the information revolution."

Furlong decided to tackle this problem, and in 1986, with funding from the Markle Foundation, she started SeniorNet. Over the next 10 years she grew it into a successful nonprofit, establishing more than 100 technology learning centers run by and for seniors throughout the United States. SeniorNet continues to flourish today, and ThirdAge has endowed it to ensure that the nonprofit would benefit if ThirdAge were to strike dotcom gold.

FROM NONPROFIT DIRECTOR TO CEO

How did Furlong transform her SeniorNet experience and vision about the looming growth of the Internet into one of the top Websites catering to the needs and tastes of midlife adults? Realizing that SeniorNet wasn't in a position to launch a risky commercial Web venture, she began networking to find a way to start the business. She was introduced through some mutual friends to angel investor Gary Hromadko, who was so excited about her idea that he provided initial seed funding. Investment bankers Robert Huret and Alan Rothenberg also made contributions. Together, Furlong and Hromadko formed ThirdAge Media in June 1996, mapping out a business plan for a community Website for midlife adults that would capitalize on the baby boomer phenomenon and generate revenue through a mix of e-commerce, corporate sponsorships, and advertising.

"A lot of my idea had to do with my passion for the audience I was serving and a desire to know what was in their hearts and on their minds," says Furlong. "I saw that SeniorNet's centers were not just technology venues, they were social venues. I knew early on that communities in cyberspace were especially important for older people dealing with grief and loss."

Furlong's career transformation required a crash course in executive management. "I read over 40 books about being a CEO between the time we started the business and the launch of ThirdAge.com," she says. She learned the ropes on the job and, together with her partners, assembled a first-rate board of directors and advisers. With a social mission to empower baby boomers and older adults, she's been able to engage investors, advisers, and employees alike. "She can sit next to the head of a major corporation for just a few minutes, and the next thing you know, they've become her best friend," attests Judy Walklet, vice president of sales at ThirdAge, when describing Furlong's talent for connecting with people.

Big names like Melinda French Gates (chairwoman of the Gates' Learning Foundation and Bill's wife), Mort Meyerson (chairman and CEO of 2m Companies, a private investment firm), and Daniel Socolow (director of the Fellows Program for the MacArthur Foundation) are all members of ThirdAge's advisory board. "Melinda Gates helped us with our branding and counsels us about industry trends," explains Furlong. "Mort Meyerson, my digital mentor, helps us see when we need to make critical business changes."

Furlong, however, is every bit as accomplished as her mentors and advisers. She holds a presidential appointment to the National Commission on Libraries and Information Sciences and has provided counsel to the U.S. House of Representatives on aging. And the list of her distinctions goes on: *Interactive Week* named her one of the "25 Unsung Heroes of the Web," *Upside* magazine chose her as one of the 100 most influential CEOs of the digital age, and *Time Digital* heralded her as one of the "50 most important people shaping technology today."

In adjusting to business life at a dotcom startup, Furlong has found it critical to give her full attention to key priorities. "I've never been more focused on my life and the things that are important," she explains. "I have very good time management around that, and I've learned to execute through other people to amplify my vision." She says learning to talk the talk has been central to establishing credibility. "You need to own words like 'enterprise valuation' and 'maximizing shareholder value,'" she advises. "This is especially important for women entrepreneurs."

RECRUITING THE BEST AND BRIGHTEST

To build a great organization, Furlong recruited nationwide, seeking every possible set of "bright eyes"—people with extraordinary drive and leadership ability—she could find. The company has attracted Gen-X Internet mavens from first-rate technology companies, as well as

ThirdAgers themselves, who can apply their many years of experience in traditional fields to the Web.

Furlong also used her connections as one of the nation's foremost experts on aging to recruit staff members from unlikely places. A delegate to the 1995 White House Conference on Aging, she recruited a young PR person from the conference as her fifth employee. "When you start to galvanize people around a social mission as well as building a great company, suddenly they want to tumble out of their current jobs and work for you," she explains.

Through the efforts of a small but dedicated team, the ThirdAge site was launched in June 1997 with a mile-long list of corporate sponsors and an army of 1000 experts and hosts ready to facilitate message-board discussions and chats. Since then the ThirdAge community has grown like gangbusters. In 1999 the number of registered users (a chief metric community sites use to gauge their success) grew a spectacular 400 percent to one million. Furlong expects the site to have six million registered users by 2002—a milestone that should be within reach given Forrester Research's prediction that by then boomers will represent more than a third of all the people online.

UNDOING STEREOTYPES

Furlong doesn't strive to simply provide midlife adults with the Net's three Cs—content, community, and commerce. Her goal? To make it hip to be 50. Through ThirdAge, she's striving to create a positive, life-affirming brand that eliminates the negative stereotypes associated with aging. "I was 46 when I decided to start ThirdAge, and I was moving into the category of 'older adults'. . . I don't look forward to being called a 'senior' or an 'older adult,' nor does anyone else who's a member of the baby boomer generation," she says.

Hence the name *ThirdAge*, a translation of the French phrase *troisième age*, which refers to the empty-nester stage of life: the time after children leave home but before "old age" begins. ThirdAge is a period when people can repossess their lives and pursue passions, projects, and activities they put on hold while raising children. "You will live 20 years longer than your parents, and the extra time is tacked on in the middle of your life, not at the end," says Walklet, Furlong's right-hand woman. "It's a rubber band that stretches in the middle, and that stretching ground is the gift that ThirdAge is all about. It's not cool to get an AARP card, but it is cool to be a ThirdAger." To this end, a $20 million national television, print, billboard, and radio ad campaign is in the works. Featuring the Who song "Talkin' 'Bout My Generation," the campaign is part of the company's effort to brand midlife adults (a demographic that currently includes the first wave of baby boomers) as "ThirdAgers."

A MULTIDIMENSIONAL ENTREPRENEUR

Furlong is a blend of contrasts. That she was able to move from a successful academic career to an equally successful one in the nonprofit world and then land squarely on her feet in the frenetic dotcom whirl is nothing short of remarkable. "As a tenured professor on leave and the founder of a $2 million-per-year nonprofit organization, I went from the most secure job to the least secure," she says.

Furlong's mix of business savvy and social skills is one reason she's so successful. She attributes her sharp business instincts to her father, and her sociability and enthusiasm for supporting good causes to her mother. "My father was an entrepreneur and he taught me a lot of what it takes to build a business—a big idea, a great team, timing, stellar partners, a great value proposition, luck, and faith," she says. "My mother is from the South, and she taught me about the value of building community and treating people well."

THE BUSINESS MODEL

Like most dotcoms focused on building their brands and grabbing mindshare at Net speed, ThirdAge Media is not yet profitable and, as a still-private company, chooses not to disclose its revenue numbers. But the company's revenue streams are diversified and, according to Furlong, on the rise. "Our growth curve is shaped like a hockey stick," she says employing the bullish cliché oft-uttered by Net entrepreneurs with big plans for their company's future.

ThirdAge consists of three distinct revenue-generating areas: ThirdAge.com, a news service, and a research division:

ThirdAge.com

ThirdAge Media has a strong knack for securing key distribution partnerships and large sponsorship deals. In March 1998 it became an anchor tenant in the Lifestyles Channel on AOL. This partnership boosted the site's traffic and gave AOL's boomer population access to ThirdAge content tailored to its preferences. ThirdAge has also partnered with other popular portal sites including Excite, Infoseek, and Yahoo!, distributing its content through them, which in turn drives traffic back to ThirdAge.com.

Sponsorships are ThirdAge.com's cash cow. Among the site's many sponsors are traditional heavyweights such as Intel and Procter & Gamble as well as dotcoms such as Amazon and Match.com. America's strongest brands are willing to pay rates beginning at $500,000 per year for a sponsorship placement on the site. At the time of this writing, the company was finalizing some long-term, multimillion-dollar sponsorships.

ThirdAge also sells advertising space both as banner and box ads. Because of the site's attractive demographic, space sells at $50 per thousand page impressions for banners and $20 for box ads. But advertisers are lucky to get a spot on ThirdAge.com at any price: "Our ad space inventory is often sold out," explains Furlong.

ThirdAge.com currently derives e-commerce revenue through its shopping channel and is focused on enhancing the ThirdAge shopping experience to make it highly contextual and personalized: "If we know a ThirdAge member is part of an online writers' club and that they also like traveling to Europe, we can offer a ThirdAge travel adventure specific to their interests," says Furlong.

News Service

ThirdAge's award-winning, 25-person editorial staff produces more than 100 weekly news and feature stories tailored to baby boomers.

This material is distributed nationwide to more than 200 newspapers through the Universal Press Syndicate, as well as online through portal sites such as Yahoo!, Netscape NetCenter, and Snap. ThirdAge also creates and distributes more than a dozen daily and weekly electronic newsletters to a subscriber base of more than a million.

Research

ThirdAge Media conducts marketing and demographic research about ThirdAgers on behalf of clients. In partnership with Excite, the company published the first psychographic study of Web users over age 50. This study and 12 subsequent ones provided detailed insight on successfully marketing to midlife adults. ThirdAge also does custom research for sponsors to assess awareness of brands among baby boomers.

BOOMING AHEAD OF THE REST

With a two-year lead on competitors such as Myprimetime.com, which launched in September 1999, ThirdAge's position as the top Website for boomers is as rooted as anything can be in the ever-shifting Internet landscape. The company currently faces little direct competition. Even Myprimetime.com is going after a slightly different niche: the full spectrum of boomers rather than the 45-to-59 set.

In late 1999, Furlong and company recruited James Barnett as ThirdAge's new CEO, bringing in an experienced corporate executive, which has enabled Furlong to focus on her responsibilities as chairwoman of the board. In this role, she continues to be the company's visionary, resident expert on ThirdAgers, spokesperson, and chief evangelist. Ever the relationship builder, she's also responsible for many of the company's key accounts with sponsors.

Looking back on her experience so far as an Internet entrepreneur, Furlong points to one thing she would do differently and advises other entrepreneurs to do: "Spend half a day a week in learning mode. Ask yourself, 'What business models are working on the Internet? Who are the industry leaders in different segments? What are they doing?'" With Internet business rules constantly morphing, keeping on top of the changes and keeping your industry knowledge current take a dedicated effort.

How does Furlong, who recently sent her eldest child off to college, plan to spend her own ThirdAge? Not on the beach in the Bahamas. Having honed her business-building talents, she's looking forward to someday starting a business incubator and applying her experience and know-how to mentoring rookie entrepreneurs. She also wants to encourage more companies to practice social responsibility through philanthropy and community involvement. In the meantime, she'll continue to build ThirdAge as a brand and business. "I know ThirdAge is working on a large scale and will continue to grow fast," she says confidently. "I suspect that we'll have our IPO soon since we're hitting the ball outside of the park on all our objectives."

Mary Furlong's
TOP THREE LESSONS LEARNED

1. *"Start with a big, important idea,* one you're passionate about and that people believe in. I set out to produce a new model for giving a generation a voice and a vehicle for change."

2. *"It's all about the team.* Your management team, investors, sponsors, strategic alliances, employees, and online community members lead you to success. Leverage the talents of others in support of your vision and highlight the efforts of people who help you along the way."

3. *"Balance work with the rest of your life.* Never lose sight of the fact that making time for family, friends, yourself, and causes that matter keeps things in perspective."

ThirdAge Media: KEY STRATEGIC TAKE-AWAYS

- Pick your audience carefully. Target your online offerings to the needs of an underserved demographic segment that's attractive to advertisers and sponsors.

- Choose a growth market. Furlong picked adults in midlife as ThirdAge's demographic segment, in part because it currently coincides with the baby boomer generation, a population bulge that will have a major impact on the economy over the next 25 years. Because of its affluence, this demographic segment will continue to be an attractive one even after the baby boomer generation.

- Leverage the strengths of your partners. ThirdAge's sponsor- ship- and partnership-heavy strategy works to create a variety of nodes for generating revenue and distributing the company's content, services, and marketing messages.

- Don't rule out job candidates who lack Internet experience. Some of ThirdAge's most valuable employees have extensive experience in traditional fields that is directly applicable to the work they do for ThirdAge.

- Become a master networker. The more allies you can create, the more advisers, mentors, business associates, potential partners, and investors you'll have.

- Learn how to tell a good story. This is one of the most impor- tant skills you can possess as an Internet leader or entrepreneur, whether you're pitching to investors, coaching team members, or promoting the company.

- Have faith that you can and will learn as you go. This is espe- cially important for first-time entrepreneurs to keep in mind. Like most entrepreneurs, Furlong learned how to start a busi- ness through trial by fire.

Part
II

WEB-BASED SERVICES VENTURES

VITAL STATS

- Cofounder: Katie Burke, CEO
- URL: www.desktop.com
- Stock: Private
- Founded: 1998
- Headquarters: San Francisco

7

Desktop.com

Shifting the Paradigm from Desktop to Webtop

"This is something I wanted to do all my life. I wanted to start a company and be a CEO. I saw this opportunity and jumped on it."
—Katie Burke

TOSSING AND TURNING

In October 1998, Katie Burke rested her head on her pillow for the night but couldn't sleep. She was trying to decide whether to give up her job at Yahoo! to venture out on her own and start a company with friend and colleague Larry Drebes. Everything in her life had seemed to lead up to this moment. Burke had the perfect partner, was already a veteran Web entrepreneur despite the industry's newness, and had six viable consumer-oriented Web business ideas. Opportunity was knocking, the time seemed ripe, but the stakes were high. Leaving Yahoo! to start her own company would mean walking away from tens of millions of dollars worth of unvested stock options.

At that time in 1998, Yahoo! was a large and growing company and that didn't make Burke's blood pump the way the unknown startup adventure did. In a series of stints at startups before working at Yahoo!, she had caught the entrepreneurial bug bad. Although the idea of leaving behind her unvested Yahoo! options made the decision difficult, Burke's entrepreneurial drive ultimately made the decision: She would leave Yahoo! to start her own company, which she and Drebes named Desktop.com.

A fast-growing, San Francisco–based Web venture, Desktop.com is revolutionizing the way people use the Web and their personal computers. Its product is a WebTop, a Web-based re-creation of a PC desktop that allows users to access Web-based applications and store up to 10 megabytes of files. At Desktop.com, you can log in to access your own virtual desktop from any personal computer with an Internet connection. The site offers PC-like applications complete with drag-and-drop functionality, windows, and pull-down menus. It's a boon to mobile Web users: no more frustrating moments being unable to access your files, addresses, email, calendar, passwords, and bookmarks away from your own PC. Every day, through the unassuming glass doors of the company's South of Market offices, Desktop.com's bevy of engineers is adding more functionality to this new breed of Website. And best of all, Desktop.com is free.

Desktop.com's effort to be everyone's online home on the Web represents a paradigm shift in computing that is forcing tectonic changes for Microsoft and other software giants. Software is transitioning from a shrink-wrapped product to a rented or free Web-based service. The concept of storing and accessing files on Web servers is shaking up the notion of the personal computer altogether and creating huge markets for Internet appliances—Internet-access devices that contain small programs and minimal hard disk space. Sites such as Desktop.com are helping foster this shift away from desktop to WebTop computing.

INCREDIBLE HINDSIGHT

Burke is playful, optimistic, and down to earth. She's at home in the casual jeans and T-shirt atmosphere that is de rigueur at Bay Area Net startups like Desktop.com. She bubbles with the energy and enthusiasm of someone who's convinced she's helping to create the Web's next big thing. At 30, she's already involved with her fourth startup. Her entrepreneurial itch is so strong that she couldn't wait to finish her MBA at Harvard before moving to Silicon Valley. In fact, she was so eager to start working for a Web startup that she headed out West and finished her last two months of coursework remotely, earning her degree in 1995.

After graduate school, Burke's Silicon Valley beginnings were humble. She spent her first six weeks sleeping on a futon in the living room of a friend from her undergrad days at Stanford. Her first job with a startup wasn't anything to write home about—at least at first blush. She had turned down two "real" job offers—one with Silicon Graphics and the other with a New York–based Internet Service Provider (ISP)—to join Spider Technologies, a four-person Web startup with a cramped, 400-square-foot office and no funding. Space was so tight that Burke found herself sharing a desk with three engineers and using the fax machine as a phone by the time they finally moved to a bigger office.

Although her parents were understandably nervous when they heard that their daughter would be working sans paycheck, Burke's decision to join Spider Technologies was the right one. At the company, which was later renamed NetDynamics and sold to Sun Microsystems in August 1998, Burke had the opportunity to work on every aspect of building a business. She raised $2 million for the startup from Hummer Winblad, an experience that would later give her solid hindsight when making critical decisions at her own company.

So where does Burke get her phenomenal entrepreneurial drive? Her father, a manufacturing entrepreneur, was a key influence on her. "My father is a turnaround specialist, and I grew up working in small manufacturing companies with him," she says. During high school and college summers, she worked in every department of her father's power supply manufacturing companies throughout the Northeast, assembling bills of materials one week and soldering boards the next. This experience got her excited about the prospect of someday starting, growing, and running a business.

ROCKETMAIL AND BEYOND

Burke met her future business partner, Larry Drebes, in 1996 on the insistence of a friend who felt she was destined to work at Drebes's fledgling 15-person startup, Four11. Burke wasn't really expecting to join Four11, one of the Web's original "white pages" directories that helped Web users find long-lost friends. She believed there was simply too much competition in the niche for comfort. But after meeting Drebes and Four11's management team, she decided to join—she liked the people, and the chemistry was good. When Four11 was ready to expand, Burke and Drebes helped develop the quintessential killer Web app: free Web-based email they named Rocketmail. This was the beginning of their working relationship, which would blossom into their Desktop.com partnership a year later.

"We saw Web-based email as a large market opportunity," says Burke. And, sure enough, it was. Even though Hotmail was the first mover in the free Web-based email space, Rocketmail had one million users by the time it was acquired by Yahoo! in October 1997 (for a cool $89 million) and reborn as Yahoo! Mail. Burke's experience as director of marketing and business development at Four11, and later at Yahoo! developing Yahoo! Calendar and Yahoo! Address Book, helped her identify what would become the basis of her future Web business: free Web-based software and services offered in a familiar PC-like environment. "We decided to take the popular concept of free Web-based email and extend it to all the things you use on the Internet," she says.

A SECRET WORTH KEEPING

Soon after leaving Yahoo!, Burke and Drebes had half a dozen business ideas on the drawing table. After scrutinizing them thoroughly, they decided to pursue the most ambitious one: creating a Web-based desktop environment. "Our thought was if we were going to pick up and leave Yahoo!, we wanted to swing for the fences and make our business the most exciting thing we possibly could," says Burke, her shoulder-length brown hair fastened back hastily with a barrette, underscoring her roll-up-your-sleeves and dive-right-in personality. Convinced that the WebTop would be the next killer app of the Web, they took the plunge and left Yahoo!, leaving their unvested stock options behind with a wince.

While some questioned their choice, most of their friends and colleagues—including Yahoo!'s founders Jerry Yang and Dave Filo—supported their entrepreneurial spirit and understood their need to follow their ambitions. Yahoo! management even explored the possibility of potentially having Burke and Drebes pursue their plans as part of Yahoo!, but Burke knew that she wanted to start her own company. "If we had decided to have a relationship with Yahoo! it would have detracted from the raw independent startup that has got to fight for its life," she says. "That's what we really wanted and that's what we really missed at Yahoo!"

So what were Burke's other business ideas? One was a plan to create a market-testing service for media assets like advertisements and movie trailers. As for the others, Burke is keeping her lips zipped since there's the potential to build some of them into the Desktop.com platform later down the road.

Using $1.5 million of the money they made from their Yahoo! stock options to cover rent, equipment, marketing, and salaries, Burke and Drebes funded Desktop.com out of their own pockets for their first eight months until their initial site launch. Burke's experience at previous startups had taught her that the more an entrepreneur can build the business before taking outside funding, the higher the potential valuation of the company at the time it first accepts an outside equity investment. Self-funding the company initially also allowed Burke and Drebes to operate in stealth mode for an extended period, keeping their business idea and product secret and protected from any would-be competitors. Burke was keeping her fingers crossed that Desktop.com would be the first product of its kind to market.

Operating in stealth mode wasn't easy. There was buzz in the Valley about Burke and Drebes's departure from Yahoo! to pursue a new business of their own. People were curious. Burke went to great lengths to keep the company's mission unknown. The startup went by the code name JumpData.com, and Burke and Drebes would reveal the company's true mission to job candidates only after extending job offers. "What's funny is that people would mishear me and say 'JunkData?' They thought it was a terrible name," says Burke.

THINKING BIG

When Burke did finally go after venture capital funding, it was clear that she wasn't the only one that believed in Desktop.com's revolutionary potential. In August 1999, a month before the initial site launch, Accel Partners, Sequoia Capital, and Kohlberg Kravis Roberts & Co. invested a total of $29 million in Series A financing. Because of Burke and Drebes's strong business idea, their success with Rocketmail, and their immense network of connections from past startups, landing venture capital funding didn't take long. "Because Larry and I had been working in the industry for some time, and because we both had been involved with very successful companies, we had the good fortune to be calling associates we knew from previous lives when it came time to fund Desktop.com," says Burke, talking over the big-city traffic noise coming in through the open conference-room window.

While the company is well-heeled financially, Burke is careful about the way it spends the money in its coffers. The offices are spartan, and furnished with used furniture purchased on the cheap from a startup that didn't make it. "We don't need flashy offices or fancy displays at trade shows, but we subsidize employee transportation and PC purchases for working at home," she says. "Mich Kapor, one of our board members and founder of Lotus 1-2-3, says we're financed like a Cadillac but not afraid of being a Beetle."

THE BUSINESS MODEL

Free Web-based applications are great for Web users, but how is Desktop.com making money? From advertising, sponsorship-supported services, and e-commerce transaction fees. Desktop.com sells advertising space both as icons on the WebTop and buttons within its Web-based applications. The categories of applications, such as sports, shopping, finance, productivity, and games, allow for very targeted advertising. For example, ESPN could advertise within an application for tracking workouts. Some of Desktop.com's initial sponsors include eBay, USAToday.com, and BarnesandNoble.com.

Advertising and targeted sponsorships represent Desktop.com's largest revenue opportunity. Research bears this out: Forrester Research estimates that spending on worldwide online advertising will jump to $33 billion by 2004, up from $3.3 billion in 1999, numbers that bode well for Desktop.com's future.

Desktop.com is actively pursuing partnerships to enhance the site's offerings. In November 1999 it partnered with Inktomi and integrated the Inktomi Shopping Engine into its services. The site's first two e-commerce applications, WebShopper and Shopping List, allow users to easily comparison-shop at hundreds of online merchants, find the best deals, and create customized shopping lists. These shopping lists can be plugged into WebShopper enabling users to quickly find and purchase the listed items at competitive prices. And with Inktomi's Shopping Engine integrated into Desktop.com, any developer can access it to build Web-based storefronts. This provides the company with an additional revenue stream: Desktop.com receives a percentage of all e-commerce transactions made through these online shopping channels.

STICKY FEATURES

Consumer-based Websites like Desktop.com must build an enormous amount of traffic to succeed. Without it, their advertising and sponsorship space is worthless. But once visitors have found Desktop.com, getting them to come back is easy. Like free Web-based email, Desktop.com has a highly addictive quality. After all, if you're tracking your workouts, storing your files, and accessing your email through the site, you have plenty of reason to visit on a regular basis.

But how is Desktop.com capturing new eyeballs? PR, word-of-mouth, and online advertising have been responsible for building the bulk of its traffic to date. According to Burke, "Word of mouth is not only effective, but also very economical." More than 8000 people registered as Desktop.com users the day the site launched, driven there by word-of-mouth alone. And within the site's first 90 days, Desktop.com had a quarter of a million registered users.

But to ensure success, Desktop.com will need to further build traffic. For its revenue model to fly, the site needs to have more than a million users, so the company is very focused on building its user base.

To this end, Burke and Drebes launched an offline ad campaign in 2000. And they're further attracting users to the site through strategic partnerships and distribution deals aimed at capturing as many of the people who regularly access the Internet from home and work as possible. "Initially, we actually traded visibility on Desktop.com for advertising on partners' sites," says Burke. "At this early stage in our business, new users are more important than revenue."

The site is counting on the fact that its community-building collaboration tools will help draw in new users. For example, the site has a recipe box application that lets users store their recipes in one place, share them with others, and receive recipes contributed by others.

Desktop.com is also thinking big and looking beyond U.S. markets. After gaining a firm foothold in the United States, it plans to aggressively market its site to Web users and developers internationally.

ENLISTING THE DEVELOPER COMMUNITY

Desktop.com was initially seeded with a slew of home-grown applications that allow users to do everything from charting stocks to reading news articles to checking the weather. The site provides many of the most frequently used tools and services on the Web all in one location. Desktop.com users can customize their WebTop, adding icons for the applications they use on a regular basis just as they would on their PC desktop.

Burke doesn't have her eyes set solely on developing a consumer audience for the site. Her company is aggressively enlisting the developer community at large to build applications for Desktop.com. This smart move will help ensure that the wide array of applications available at Desktop.com is unmatched by competing sites. As more individual developers create applications for the Desktop.com platform, the value of Desktop.com increases for everyone involved: users, developers, employees, and the company's founders and equity investors. In December 1999 the company released Desktop.com's technical ground rules, or API (for Application Programming Interface), to the developer community. With the API public knowledge, any developer or company can create Web-based applications for Desktop.com. Devtop, the developer area on Desktop.com, offers resources and guides to help developers get started programming using Desktop.com's application platform.

Desktop.com aims to entice developers to create thousands of programs and sell or rent them to the site's user base. What does Desktop.com hope to get in exchange? A small cut of these transactions. This strategy leverages the talent of the developer community writ large, recasts them into another part of Desktop.com's customer base, and provides Desktop.com with yet another revenue stream. "Our initial target is the estimated 100,000 to 250,000 hobbyist/enthusiast developers," says Burke.

STAYING AHEAD OF THE PACK

While Desktop.com has a strong first-mover advantage—it was the first service of its kind when it launched on September 20, 1999—it's not the only game in town. Burke is keeping an eye on competing sites such as MyWebOS and Visto, which are also striving to become Internet users' home on the Web. But so far she's undaunted by the competition: MyWebOS is focused on a different target market—small businesses and enterprises—and Visto is trying to capture the consumer market, but without Desktop.com's strategy of creating an open development platform.

Desktop.com is banking on the fact that its commitment to an open programming environment will result in an array of third-party Web applications on Desktop.com that far surpasses the limited suites of Web apps offered by competitors. "Desktop.com users can cherry-pick the best of the Web and access it from one place," Burke explains. "For example, if a person wants to use Hotmail for Web-based email and My Excite to track their finances, these icons can sit side by side on their personalized desktop."

HISTORY IN THE MAKING

Burke is fully aware that she's living a Silicon Valley dream. In 1998 her parents bought her a video camera so she could record Desktop.com's history. "This is time capsule stuff," she says to employees as she wanders the cubicle-lined corridors with camera in hand. Her gift to them for the company's first product launch: A video she edited and set to music that documents the company's first nine months.

So how does Burke keep her life in balance under the pressures she faces as CEO and founder of a company charging ahead at warp speed? She runs several times a week to help burn off adrenaline, and regularly goes camping with her boyfriend at nearby Stinson Beach or in the Marin Headlands. "Wednesday night is 'date night'; that's when my boyfriend and I usually head out into nature," she says.

The chief challenges Burke faces with Desktop.com are those of success: figuring out how to keep a playful startup culture complete with foosball tournaments even as the company grows, how to harness all the great ideas that are distributed among employees, and how to recruit top engineering and other talent quickly enough to keep up with the company's swift expansion. The company, which started on the second floor of its office building, also took over the third as soon as the previous tenant moved. Burke expects the company to grow from 50 to 200 employees by 2001.

But there are technical challenges ahead too. Desktop.com's current performance is slow. Applications typically take several seconds to load. Desktop.com's engineers are aggressively working on improving the speed of the site, and Burke says the site's performance will be zippier soon. With this wrinkle ironed out, Desktop.com should have no trouble maintaining its advantage over competing sites. Its large developer community, breadth of applications, and strong functionality are likely to keep Desktop.com a step ahead.

Katie Burke's
TOP THREE LESSONS LEARNED

1. *"Think fast and make decisions fast.* Learn how to cut corners and move quickly. While it would be great to have more information when making decisions, sometimes the cost in time and resources just isn't worth it. You have to know when it's time to make a decision and move on."

2. *"Have the patience to find and hire the best person for the job.* Staffing resources are incredibly tight and it's very tempting to fill positions as soon as you find someone who is 'good enough.' In the end game though, it's much better to have the right person. Hiring the wrong people can be extremely costly."

3. *"Be pragmatic.* Business plans don't make a business. Execution does. Always keep focused on what you can do to really get strong leverage in your business."

Desktop.com: KEY STRATEGIC TAKE-AWAYS

- Think big. Don't be afraid to embrace a revolutionary business idea. The bigger the idea, the bigger the potential business. With Desktop.com, Burke is thinking beyond the tradition desktop-computing paradigm.

- Be paranoid about the competition. Things move so quickly in the Web space that a lead on the competition of just a few months can mean the difference between failure and success.

- Site performance is key. If your site isn't speedy, visitors won't wait—they'll move on to another site. This is the reason Desktop.com's developers are so focused on improving performance.

- If you can hold out and build your business before accepting outside funding, your company will garner a higher valuation when you do go seek out an equity investment.

- Spend carefully. Even if your business is well-funded, be prudent about spending. If your startup has leather chairs and mahogany desks, you're wasting money—it will hurt your business and irritate your investors.

- Look for "viral marketing" opportunities. Keep your eyes open for ways to enlist your user base or a large group of people to help you evangelize your Website or business. Don't underestimate the power of word-of-mouth when getting your message out.

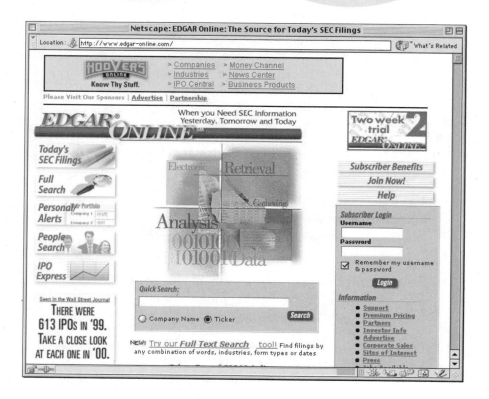

8

EDGAR Online

Democratizing Distribution of Financial Information

"I really like the beginnings of things. Turning a good idea into a business is one of the most challenging, creative, and satisfying experiences I can imagine."

—Susan Strausberg

CAPITALIZING ON A REVOLUTION

The 1990s saw an explosion in the number of people picking their own stocks. The big bull market reared its head, online trading was born, and commissions plummeted to less than $10 a trade, bringing stock picking into the everyday lives of a much wider swath of society than ever before. But these aren't the only things that explain the trading bug that has swept the nation. The Internet lets anyone with a computer and Net connection access up-to-the-minute financial information with the click of a mouse. Whether it's stock quotes, company news, or the skinny on upcoming IPOs, breaking financial information is freely available online. It's this new democratization of information that's enabling individual investors to try and beat financial pros and the market by investing in stocks.

Susan Strausberg, CEO of EDGAR Online, is doing her part to empower investors and facilitate this financial revolution. She and her husband, Marc Strausberg, were the first two entrepreneurs to provide Web surfers access to Securities & Exchange Commission (SEC) filings. These filings, which include annual reports (10-Ks), quarterly updates

(10-Qs), proxy statements, and notices of security sales, deliver the inside scoop on corporate financial activities—information that was previously available only to Wall Street analysts, money managers, and deep-pocketed parties willing to fork over $80,000 for an annual subscription to filings delivered by overnight mail.

The SEC, still operating in the Gutenberg era until the early nineties, dealt primarily with paper reports. Subscriptions were pricey, and accessing and searching filings was cumbersome and anything but real-time. The SEC licensed filings to retailers such as TRW and Mead Data, which in turn sold paper or special terminal-based subscriptions to clients. For those without a subscription, access required a trip to the SEC's reference room in Washington, D.C., or one of its satellite offices, followed by searching through (horrors!) microfiche. "Most SEC information was filed on paper," says Strausberg. "Services that delivered American corporate financial information, such as S&P's CompuStat or Market Guide, had rooms full of people who would retype selected information from SEC filings."

But today all this has changed. Now all U.S. corporations must submit filings electronically for storage in the SEC's Electronic Data Gathering Analysis and Retrieval (EDGAR) database. The SEC began allowing companies to file electronically in the early nineties, although many continued filing on paper until 1996 when the SEC made the switch mandatory.

A BIG IDEA

How did the Strausbergs hit on their winning business idea? At the time, they were involved with Internet Financial Network, which they helped start in 1994 to sell EDGAR financial information. The couple knew first-hand how time-intensive it was to dig through SEC reports to unearth critical nuggets of information. As publisher of *The Livermore Report,* a now-defunct financial newsletter focusing on short plays in the IPO market, Marc had relied on paper versions of S-1 filings (the form companies use to file for an IPO) to do much of the research.

In 1995, with the SEC's EDGAR database reaching critical mass and Internet use exploding, Strausberg and her husband shared a flash of insight. "We realized that if we could take the electronic version of SEC filings and add search and distribution services via the Web, we could start a new business to disseminate this critical financial information in a totally new and streamlined way," says the sixty-one-year-old entrepreneur and grandmother of five. "This was a *big* idea."

Energized by their "Eureka!," the couple moved from Manhattan to a rambling eighteenth-century house in Wilton, Connecticut, which according to local lore was once a tavern frequented by George Washington. They launched EDGAR Online in a room above the garage. "We set out to create a virtual company. Our programmers could be from Mars, physical proximity didn't matter, and we didn't need to be on Wall Street or Madison Avenue," she explains, her New York accent a sign of many years spent living in Manhattan before this move. "It was charming to look out at a red barn across a snow-covered lawn, but the mood and tempo weren't any different than at other Net startups."

FROM WALL STREET TO MAIN STREET IN TWO MONTHS

The Strausbergs' approach was to create a Website that would appeal to individual investors and present SEC filings in a user-friendly format. "At the time we started EDGAR Online, few people really recognized the degree to which the Internet was going to empower individuals to invest," says Strausberg, who initially shared the CEO role with her husband, but is now the sole CEO (her husband is CIO and chairman).

Using their personal savings, they hired consultants from the firm Pequot Systems (now part of iXL), whom they'd met online, to design their Website and billing system, and bought a real-time data feed (called a Level 1 subscription) to the EDGAR database. In January 1996, two months after the company was founded, the site was launched. Now, anyone with a computer and Internet access could easily retrieve previously hard-to-find financial information.

While old-line financial information firms such as Disclosure subscribed to the EDGAR data feed, they weren't providing Web access to it for fear of cannibalizing their existing business. "Disclosure focused on enterprise sales," explains Strausberg. "Their approach was to build an expensive sales force and sell five- and six-figure contracts to banks and law firms to deliver this data on paper and CD-ROM."

The Strausbergs took a different tack and brought power to the people. EDGAR Online allows registered users to search 24-hour-delayed SEC filings free, and supports this capability through advertising. It also allows visitors to search proxy filings by individual name. Wonder how much Amazon.com CEO Jeff Bezos took home in salary in 1998? A relatively modest $81,840. How about Susan Strausberg herself? She took home $150,000. Simply enter an exec's name into the site's "people search" function to find out.

For $9.95 per month the site offers a premium service that allows subscribers to view up-to-the-minute filings, create a customized portfolio of companies and industries, access insider trading information, and get automatic real-time email notifications about new IPOs and other filings that meet the criteria they specify.

If you want to know when the 25-day quiet period after an IPO announcement ends, for example, EDGAR Online will tip you off. You can also be alerted when the post-IPO lockup period ends (if company execs start dumping their shares, it usually signals bad news for the stock). The practical uses of the site are endless: "One customer recently told me he was job-hunting, so he set up his watch list to alert him every time a technology company in New York City filed an S-1," says Strausberg. "The minute he got the alert, he'd send the company an email that said 'Congratulations! Now you're going to need a business development person, and I'm that guy.'"

BUILDING TRAFFIC ON A SHOESTRING

Traffic to EDGAR Online grew quickly as word spread among investors. "After we launched, every night was like Christmas Eve. We'd get up in the middle of the night and look to see who had registered. I'd say, 'Look, there's someone from Japan and another from Alaska,'" recalls Strausberg with a smile. Soon there was no elbow room left in the room above the garage. The company was up to seven employees when the Strausbergs decided it was time to get real office space and moved to their current headquarters in Norwalk, which now houses more than 50 EDGAR Online employees.

To attract more site users, Strausberg set out to brand EDGAR Online as the premier source for SEC data. The company negotiated deal after deal with major search engines, portals, and highly trafficked financial Websites. "Our first executive hire was Jay Sears, our vice president of business development," says Strausberg. "He helped us pioneer our cobranding model and negotiated deals with CBS Marketwatch, Snap, Lycos, and AltaVista."

EDGAR Online–branded data feeds and content now flow to more than 100 sites, including Yahoo!, SmartMoney.com, TheStreet.com, and the GO Network. In exchange, EDGAR Online gets tremendous brand exposure, licensing fees, and a cut of advertising revenue, in some cases as high as 100 percent. "This is an effective and profitable way to build our brand, generate advertising and licensing revenue, and upsell subscriptions," says Strausberg. The company's content is distributed through so many channels that EDGAR Online has become the leading online brand for SEC filings. *Barron's* has twice named it a top-20 site.

"EDGAR Online has opened up a whole new set of information to the consumer," enthuses Forrester Research analyst Jaime Punishill. "I'd argue that consumers now have access to more information than most Wall Street professionals did five years ago—that's pretty cool."

THE MONEY GAME

The Strausbergs funded their business out of their own pocket for the first six months. "My husband and I invested every penny we had in our business," says Strausberg, who brings her dog, Bean, to work with her every day. When the company needed more capital, she went after strategic investors such as Bowne & Company (the world's largest financial printer and adviser to the SEC on the creation of the EDGAR system), who would see the purpose and potential of her vision. "What we were doing was such a departure," she explains. "Hardly anyone knew what

EDGAR was or even what the Web was, so we decided to find investors who at least understood one component of what we were trying to do."

As the company grew, Strausberg steered clear of venture capital and stuck to a strategy of carefully selecting investors who understood the niche, raising a total of $4 million from strategic corporate investors. "My husband and I have much longer life experience than most people who start Internet businesses, so we didn't need the kind of oversight that a VC firm might have given us," she says. "Besides, we're older and married. We're not the type of entrepreneurs VCs usually fund."

The Strausbergs took the company public in May 1999. The outcome? The stock was priced at $9.50 but traded flat. "Our stock didn't have the pop that other Net stocks before us had, but we took in even more money than we expected," she says. "Our goal was to get capital into the company and we did." With the IPO, the Strausbergs' paper net worth instantly increased more than $66 million. (The couple personally owned 43 percent of the company at the time of its IPO.)

CAPTURING FreeEDGAR

Because the SEC's EDGAR database is in the public domain, anyone with the gumption can go out and mine it. Even though barriers to entry are nil, competitors to EDGAR Online were slow to emerge—an indication of just how prescient the Strausbergs' idea really was. But in 1997 one serious rival sprung up: Washington State–based FreeEDGAR.com, another EDGAR data-mining site created by a former banker.

While EDGAR Online's IPO wasn't a screamer, it did create the stock currency the company needed for strategic acquisitions. So in July 1999 it acquired FreeEDGAR in a stock deal valued at about $10 million, instantly eliminating its chief competitor and increasing EDGAR Online's traffic and user base 50 percent. With the acquisition, the company got its competitor's watch list functionality and assumed its partnership with Reuters, getting yet another distribution outlet at a leading financial Website.

Although EDGAR Online still has a few competitors, the site's brand ubiquity and strong first-mover advantage have deterred rivals from flocking to the scene. Most notable among them is 10K Wizard (www.10kwizard.com), a similar site that launched in April 1999. Other potential players include LIVEDGAR and, to a lesser degree, the SEC itself, which offers clunky access to the EDGAR database at www.sec.gov. But EDGAR Online is far and away the best-known site providing access to SEC documents. "This is EDGAR Online's game to lose," says Forrester's Punishill. "There aren't going to be a whole lot of new entrants that can find better ways of displaying 10-K data."

EMBRACING NEW B2B MARKETS

As word about EDGAR Online spreads and the ranks of online investors swell, more and more people are frequenting the site. "In 1999 alone pageviews rocketed from 5.7 million to 21 million, the number of monthly unique visitors grew from one to two million, and our registered users grew from 90,000 to 250,000," notes Strausberg. What's more, the buzz is spreading to the corporate sector.

SEC filings, crucial to investors, contain information prized by a variety of businesses and professions. Headhunters, for example, are using the data to keep tabs on executive compensation packages. Business and financial journalists use SEC filings to find juicy details (such as pending lawsuits and investigations by government agencies) that companies are obligated to report but choose not to release to the press. Moreover, entrepreneurs review S-1 filings to glean competitive intelligence about rivals' business models, and venture capitalists refer to these records to research the competitive landscape when considering potential investments.

With these new business and professional uses identified, Strausberg is shifting the company's focus to include business-to-business applications. With proceeds from its IPO, EDGAR Online has built a sales staff targeting corporate and professional users of financial data and expects B2B sales to generate at least 60 percent of the company's revenue by 2002.

With its B2B strategy in place, the company has launched several new initiatives. EDGAR Online now develops customized intranet sites for corporate investor-relations departments and has also created a Web-based application, Wealth ID, which alerts clients of insider trades. The company is marketing this latter feature to salespeople, financial institutions, nonprofits in fund-raising mode, and other professionals who cater to the wealthy. After all, knowing who has recently sold a chunk of stock and is on the verge of a big cash influx is critical information if you're trying to sell a yacht, attract new investors, or raise money for AIDS research.

THE BUSINESS MODEL

The growth in popularity of sites like the TheStreet.com, Motley Fool, Quicken.com, and IndividualInvestor.com attests to the fact that the online population has a huge appetite for financial information. Here's the breakdown of how EDGAR Online is earning money from its Net endeavors:

Corporate Sales

Corporate sales are the fastest-growing area of EDGAR Online's business and represented one-fourth of the company's $5.2 million in revenue at the end of 1999. Since the areas the company builds for corporate intranets and extranets are all custom, pricing varies. Business clients typically pay $4000 to $5000 per month under a one-to-two year contract for the creation and maintenance of a custom Website area. More complex implementations can run $50,000 per month or more. At the time of this writing, the company had more than 50 corporate clients, and this number was growing fast.

Subscriptions

EDGAR Online sells subscriptions to its premium service, and this accounts for approximately 20 percent of overall revenue. Subscriptions cost $9.95 per month, and as of spring 2000, the site had more than 13,000 subscribers.

Advertising and Sponsorships

Ad and sponsorship sales account for close to 40 percent of revenue. The company sells banner advertising space on its three Web properties—EDGAR Online, FreeEDGAR, and IPO Express—at a $55 CPM (cost per thousand pageviews) through DoubleClick, a company that manages online advertising for Websites. The site is able to garner this relatively high rate because its affluent user base is extremely attractive to advertisers: According to a 1998 Gallup survey, 10 percent of the site's visitors have portfolios worth more than $1 million (compared with two percent for the average Website), and 54 percent have portfolios over $100,000 (compared with 23 percent for the average Website). The company also earns ad revenue and licensing fees based on usage from many of the portal and financial sites it provides data to.

EDGAR Online sells sponsorships at rates from $10,000 to $50,000 per month. With EDGAR Online's traffic expanding at a rapid clip, advertising and sponsorships are expected to provide a growing revenue stream.

GOING WIRELESS, GOING GLOBAL

The company's strategy to land key distribution partnerships and acquire its chief rival is showing results. In 1999, EDGAR Online raked in $5.2 million, a 160 percent increase from its $2 million in revenue the previous year. Analysts are projecting that the company is on track to increase revenues quickly as its startup costs wind down and it turns its attention to its emerging B2B market. This is no news to Strausberg: "We're forecasting profitability for the third quarter of 2001," she says.

Strausberg isn't limiting EDGAR Online's content distribution to the wired world. In March 2000 the company launched IPO Express2go, a wireless version of its popular IPO Express Web and email service. The new service allows users to receive IPO-related alerts via personal digital assistants, including Palm Pilots and Windows CE devices.

She's also turning her sights to markets outside the United States and extending services to the United Kingdom, other European countries, Japan, and Latin America. "We'll be offering international filings as well as U.S. filings abroad," she says. "No companies overseas directly compete with us." In spring 2000, EDGAR Online partnered with Perfect

Information, a U.K.-based financial information company, to provide access to SEC filings to its corporate clients in Europe.

Have the fast pace and daily stress of running an Internet business together strained the Strausbergs' relationship? Not a bit. The two have worked together on several different businesses over many years, and they're used to close collaboration. "We have very different complementary abilities—he's more of a theoretician and I like to take ideas and turn them into reality," she says. "And we communicate with a high degree of shorthand, which is pretty efficient."

Strausberg's business accomplishments haven't gone unnoticed. In January 2000, *The Silicon Alley Reporter* named her one of Silicon Alley's top 100 Net executives. A forthright, no-nonsense entrepreneur, she credits her trailblazing streak partly to her education—she earned a BA from New York's Sarah Lawrence College, noted for inspiring originality and creative vision. She's proud to have created a Web service that empowers so many people financially and professionally, and is especially proud to have done it later in life. What's her biggest rush? "Bumping into someone on a plane or at the grocery store and, after I give them my contact information, hearing them say, 'EDGAR Online! Oh my God! You've changed my life.' That's incredibly exciting for me," she says.

Susan Strausberg's
TOP THREE LESSONS LEARNED

1. *"Take the risk.* It's never too late to try something new. My husband and I are living proof of this."

2. *"Hire smart people.* The success of your company rests on the quality of your team."

3. *"Execute, execute, execute.* Execution is 99 percent of the game. Stay focused and stick to your idea. Don't let other people throw you off course."

EDGAR Online: KEY STRATEGIC TAKE-AWAYS

- If you provide very valuable, hard-to-find content, don't rule out a subscription model. Although they haven't generally taken off on the Web (people would rather look at an ad and get content for free), they can work well given the right circumstances. For EDGAR Online, going with a subscription model provided revenue from day one.

- When barriers to entry are low, a strong brand and wide distribution are critical. EDGAR Online focused on building its brand early and locking up numerous distribution deals with portal sites, which gave it a leg up on later entrants.

- Evaluate competitors carefully. Undifferentiated competitors can dilute awareness of your business and brand. EDGAR Online decided to solve the problem of a similar competitor by acquiring it.

- Outsource areas that aren't your core competency. EDGAR Online outsources its Website maintenance, public relations, customer support, and advertising sales, which allows it to focus on what it does best: business development and strategy.

- Venture capital isn't for everyone. Partnering with corporate investors worked best for EDGAR Online and allowed the Strausbergs to retain ownership of a large portion of their business.

- Pick your content distribution partners with care. If you're trying to build a strong brand, associate yours only with other premium brands. EDGAR Online limits content distribution to well-known portals and brand-name financial sites.

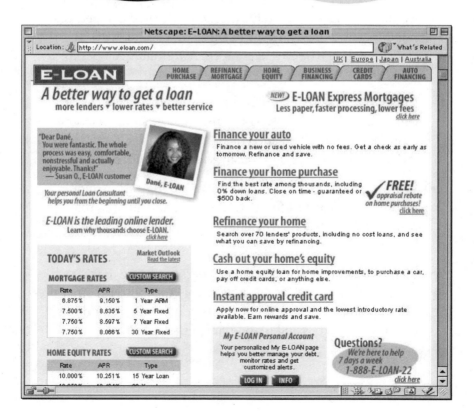

VITAL STATS

- Cofounder: Janina Pawlowski, chairwoman
- URL: www.eloan.com
- Stock: EELN
- Founded: 1996
- Headquarters: Dublin, CA

9

E-Loan

Streamlining an Industry Riddled with Inefficiencies

"Start a business because you want to make a difference, not because you want to make a lot of money. We had opportunities to sell E-Loan, but we didn't because we wanted to build something sustainable that would change an industry that wasn't working very well."

—Janina Pawlowski

SEE YOU AT THE IPO

On June 29, 1999, Janina Pawlowski woke up early in her New York City hotel room with a knot in her stomach. Today was the day that E-Loan, the company she cofounded three years earlier, was going public on the Nasdaq. She rushed downtown to Goldman Sachs, the investment bank that was taking the company to market. Already there was her partner, Chris Larsen, who was as bleary-eyed as she was from two grueling weeks of crisscrossing the country pitching to institutional investors.

Together, Pawlowski and Larsen stood watching the huge trading floor, feeling powerless. All they could do was wait for their ticker symbol, EELN, to appear on the large green screen and hope for the best. Finally, the stock opened . . . at $21, which was 50 percent higher than the offering price. In exchange for selling 10 percent of the company to the public, they'd raised more than $50 million to grow it even more. The closing price that day was $37, which gave E-Loan a $1.4 billion market cap and made the personal stakes of the founders each worth more than $200 million.

Launched in June 1997, E-Loan was the earliest entrant to the field of online mortgages, and the first to go public. Using the E-Loan Website, potential borrowers can search and compare loans offered by multiple lenders, and apply for and obtain the best loan entirely online. The site provides borrowers with the most suitable and affordable home mortgages, auto and small business loans, and credit cards. E-Loan also provides credit approval for all types of loans, and enables borrowers to track the status of their mortgage applications from submission to closing, as well as monitor their debt. The company's customer service staff is available seven days a week via email or a toll-free number, which is printed on every page of the site.

But one group of professionals is missing among E-Loan's staff of 170 loan processors and underwriters: loan brokers. The company is turning the traditional lending industry on its head by slashing transaction costs, replacing commissioned loan agents with easy-to-use comparison shopping tools, and passing the savings on to borrowers. Whereas typical mortgage brokers charge up to two points in fees for originating a loan, E-Loan charges only three-eighths of a point. For a 30-year mortgage on a $220,000 home, that's a savings of roughly $1500.

E-Loan offers loans from more than 70 lenders and more than 50,000 loan products, a far greater number than brick-and-mortar brokerages can provide. This vast selection means consumers can land better rates than those typically offered by loan agents. The company also approves and funds more than 50 percent of its own loans, which gives it the ability to eliminate the inefficiencies caused by scads of intermediaries in the traditional cumbersome lending process. "Savings are possible because we use the Internet to make the paper-laden, middleman process much more consumer-friendly and efficient," Pawlowski explains.

A WONDERFUL LIFE

How did Pawlowski make the journey to become the cofounder of a successful dotcom dedicated to taking the pain out of borrowing money?

The daughter of postwar Polish immigrants, she grew up in Rochester, New York, and as a teen worked in her father's credit union, which helped other Poles buy their first homes in the United States. Little did she know that she was learning the facets of a business that would help shape E-Loan more than a decade later. "Working in this version of the building and loan in *It's a Wonderful Life* formed my personality of fighting for the consumer," says the 40-year-old entrepreneur.

Pawlowski graduated with a degree in agricultural economics from Cornell University, but then stepped on the road to finance, earning an MBA from the University of Rochester, where she met her first husband. Shortly after the wedding, he got a position at aerospace contractor Lockheed-Martin, so they moved to Palo Alto, California. Pawlowski's wanderlust was apparently as strong as George Bailey's, the lead character in *It's a Wonderful Life,* who wants nothing more than to see the world. Far from being sad about leaving her hometown behind, she was excited. "Rochester was getting too small, and California was always this dream place I wanted to live in," she says. Even the fact that she moved there two days before the massive 1989 Loma Prieta earthquake didn't squelch her enthusiasm.

In 1990 she got a real-estate broker's license, gave birth to a baby boy, and began working for a San Jose–based mortgage brokerage. After two years she joined a Palo Alto brokerage, where she met and developed a close friendship and soon-to-be business partnership with coworker Chris Larsen. "We hit it off right on the spot," she says. "We thought alike, both had MBAs in finance, and both felt we were overeducated for our positions."

But Pawlowski's relationship with her employer turned sour when her boss tried to make her push higher margin loans. Swimming with "loan sharks" held no appeal for her or Larsen, so they jumped ship to start a more ethical brick-and-mortar mortgage brokerage called the Palo Alto Funding Group (PAFG). The adaptation to selling over the Net was soon to follow.

In 1995, Pawlowski received a call from CommerceNet, a nonprofit consortium of technology companies that saw potential—and profit—in the Internet, which was more buzzword than business application at the time. CommerceNet was helping small businesses get hooked up to the Net at no cost and wanted to know if PAFG was interested in a free router and ISDN line. Pawlowski wasn't sure what this all meant, but since there was no catch, she approved the installation. CommerceNet reps came in, networked PAFG's Macs, and installed Netscape Navigator on them.

Soon Pawlowski and Larsen were surfing the Web. One of the first things they noticed was the absence of any Websites offering mortgages. And their big idea struck: They would become an online originator of cheaper, better, faster loans, cutting out brokers and their fat commissions.

BUMPS IN THE ROAD

A great idea doesn't necessarily translate into a stress-free business-building experience, however. The demands of starting E-Loan left Pawlowski with scant time for her husband and contributed to the breakup of their marriage, which ended in 1995. She invested everything she had in the business and then some—maxing out her credit cards and damaging her credit rating so badly that when she tested out a rival loan site by applying for a loan, she was denied. It also wasn't easy for her to juggle starting a new business with being a single mom.

Raising capital proved tough too. Even though Pawlowski knew from her experience as a mortgage broker that borrowers hated reviewing their credit reports and sharing information about their income and assets with a broker, convincing VCs that people would be willing to secure mortgages without this face-to-face interaction was a hard sell. And the fact that Pawlowski was female didn't pass unnoticed. "One group of VCs that I'll never forget took me to lunch and told me that they didn't have a problem with the fact that I was a woman—not just once but all throughout the meal," she remembers. "I wondered why they were so focused on this instead of the business. Needless to say, we didn't work with them."

It got worse. By January 1997 Pawlowski and Larsen had created a glitzy, Shockwave-based, animated prototype of their site for their presentation to investors. But when they showed it to Scott Russell, a partner and managing director at Softbank Technology Ventures, the room fell silent. Finally, he spoke. "I'm going to be brutal," he said. "What is this animation crap?"

After the disastrous meeting, the pair picked up books on Perl and HTML and, six months later, officially launched the mortgage site they dubbed E-Loan. Despite little fanfare, the online service took off. When a mention in a *San Francisco Chronicle* article got them 240 mortgage applications in a single day, Pawlowski knew they had the workings of a Website that could appeal to loan applicants nationwide.

They made more pitches to investors showing off their now-live Website that emphasized ease of use over eye candy. By December 1997, they secured a first round of $5.5 million from Benchmark Capital. Managing director Bob Kagle was the dream investor, says Pawlowski. "He's one of the most intuitive men I've met and goes with his gut."

Despite E-Loan's growing popularity and revenues, by fall 1998 the company was running out of cash. It was burning $250,000 a month paying its 150 employees and financing an ad campaign that poked fun at the traditional loan industry. With cash in the kitty low, Pawlowski and Larsen faced a tough decision: seek a second round of funding and continue building the business, or sell it for a price that would make them both multimillionaires. The latter option was offered to them by Intuit, which already had a loan site, QuickenMortgage, but wanted to buy E-Loan's proprietary technology and market share for $130 million. This would have let the two founders, who together held 40 percent of E-Loan, each walk away with $10 million in cash and $16 million in Intuit stock, but E-Loan would have been absorbed by Intuit and ceased to exist as its own entity.

HOLD OR SELL?

Pawlowski was at odds with her business partner. She wanted to keep the company independent (she didn't like the idea of selling a business they'd been building to last), but Larsen, anxious because E-Loan was on the brink of running out of cash, wanted to take the money. To get beyond the impasse, Larsen set an ultimatum: He'd walk away from Intuit's offer if Pawlowski drummed up an equity investment that paid them each at least $5 million in cash and carried a similar valuation for the company. With only a few days to go before their deal-closing meeting with Intuit, Pawlowski had to think fast. She boldly called Tim Koogle, Yahoo!'s CEO, and explained the situation.

To her surprise, he wanted to help. As timing would have it, the next evening he had dinner with Japanese billionaire Masayoshi Son, head of Softbank, and they worked out an offer that met Larsen's terms. The next morning, just hours before the Intuit meeting, Pawlowski's phone rang and Koogle gave her a verbal offer: a $25 million investment in exchange for a 23 percent stake in the company and $5 million in cash for each of the founders, who would retain about 30 percent ownership. Even though Yahoo! set the valuation for E-Loan slightly lower than Intuit had, an equity investment, unlike an outright buyout, would let E-Loan live on as an independent company run by Pawlowski and Larsen, so they quickly accepted.

With this investment, Koogle joined E-Loan's all-star board of directors and started doing his part to help build E-Loan into an online-lending powerhouse. When the company faced the growing pain of figuring out how to scale operations fast enough to handle hundreds of loan applications each day, Koogle helped hammer out a solution. He reviewed the company's entire back-end processes, making suggestions about ways to streamline operations at every step. "He had little knowledge of mortgages, but has a strong background in manufacturing and building Websites that he's able to apply to all kinds of different processes," says Pawlowski. "The guy's a genius."

THE BUSINESS MODEL

The size of E-Loan's potential market is mind-boggling. Forrester Research estimates that the U.S. consumer lending industry was worth $1.9 trillion in 1999. At $1.2 trillion, mortgages make up the largest portion of this market. (Home equity loans, auto loans, and credit cards make up the rest.) Online mortgages reached 1.4 percent of all mortgages in 1999—roughly $18 billion. And according to Forrester, they'll climb to $91.2 billion by 2003, becoming almost 10 percent of the entire mortgage market.

Loans are ideally suited to being sold on the Internet. They're complex and paper-intensive, require extensive research to pinpoint the right product and provider, and don't require physical proximity between the borrower and lender. What's more, the industry is incredibly fragmented: The five largest lenders have only a quarter of the total market. And because complicated processes, unnecessary fees, and the difficulty of comparison shopping make so many people dread applying for a loan, consumers are readily adopting the Net as a preferable source of loans.

E-Loan's principal revenue comes from mortgage origination fees and gains from reselling these loans on the secondary market. These sources represent more than 40 percent of the company's revenue, which was $22.1 million in 1999. E-Loan sells the servicing value of both its self-funded and brokered loans to the highest bidder in the capital markets.

The company earns another 40 percent of its revenue through originating and reselling auto loans. The remaining 20 percent comes from the interest the company earns on mortgage and auto loans during the period it holds them before reselling, as well as money made from offering small business loans and credit cards.

LEADING THE WAY TO CHEAPER LOANS

Since it was launched, E-Loan's volume of closed loans has grown dramatically. In 1999 the company closed $1.5 billion worth of mortgages and more than $130 million in auto loans, making it the top-ranked site in the online mortgage and auto financing markets. That put 1999 revenues at more than $22 million, up 223 percent from the previous year. If E-Loan continues executing against its plan, it will be turning a profit by 2003.

E-Loan has been fortunate to be able to ride the wave of a strong U.S. economy. In 1998 falling interest rates drove up the number of mortgage originations by 70 percent, and E-Loan processed 5000 loans that year—one-fourth of all online mortgages. Because the volume of refinanced mortgages drops in times of rising interest rates, the company is structuring its business so that it's less reliant on refinance loans and therefore less affected by rising interest rates.

To further reduce its dependency on the whims of any one country's interest rates, E-Loan has expanded itself overseas. In 1999 it established joint ventures in the United Kingdom, Australia, and New Zealand through Softbank affiliate eVentures. It also started E-Loan Europe in partnership with Groupe Arnault in Paris, and began marketing online mortgages in Japan and Korea.

Going beyond the home mortgage market, E-Loan has formed alliances to offer home equity lines of credit and small business loans, and to process subprime mortgage loans. "When anyone wants any type of loan, we want them to come to us," says Pawlowski. To this end, the company has forged exclusive deals with strategic Internet partners to direct prospective customers to its Website. A third of its loan applicants are referred from Websites with huge audiences such as Yahoo!, E*Trade, and Charles Schwab, as well as online banks and auto sites. "These alliances aren't done for the sake of branding," says Pawlowski. "We're always asking, 'Are we getting the revenue per loan to pay for this?' It's an ongoing analysis."

As for competition, it's fierce, both online and off. But as the first mover and first company to go public in this niche, E-Loan has an advantage. "Entering the market first definitely gave us an upper hand when it came to making deals and acquisitions afterward, and helped propel us forward quickly," Pawlowski says, noting that the IPO enabled them to buy CarFinance.com from Bank of America and extend their offerings to include auto loans. Sites such as Intuit's QuickenLoans, iOwn, and Mortgage.com represent E-Loan's online competitors. Offline mortgage brokers such as Countrywide Home Loans represent E-Loan's brick-and-mortar rivals, but the company has a cost-savings advantage over them since it doesn't have to maintain branch offices. Banks such as Wells Fargo and Bank of America have created Websites that sell loans directly, but because they are single institutional sellers, they can neither offer a multilender selection nor reduce their fees, for fear of cannibalizing their offline distribution channels.

RADICALLY PRO-CONSUMER

For Pawlowski, fighting for consumers' rights is key to ensuring E-Loan's continuing success. In a bold move, the company made consumer credit scores available over the site. Mortgage shoppers nationwide could see what they looked like to lenders in terms of credit risk. Fair, Isaac Co., the developer of these scores (known as FICO credit scores), which are used by nearly all mortgage companies to determine a person's mortgage destiny, considers the scores proprietary and safeguards them from consumers, as do most lenders. When Fair, Isaac found out that E-Loan was publishing the scores online, it made Equifax cut off data flow to the company, so E-Loan turned to another credit bureau to continue this service. Although Fair, Isaac wasn't happy to see credit scores made public, savvy borrowers were. E-Loan was swamped with new visitors who wanted to register to see their never-before-publicly-available scores and get advice to help increase them. "Why should these scores be kept secret when they're so important?" asks Pawlowski. "The policy goes against the whole idea of the Internet, where you have free access to the information that's important to you and you use that information to accomplish what you want." She is encouraging E-Loan users to lobby their legislators and to put pressure on Fair, Isaac to make the scores public.

Since starting E-Loan, Pawlowski has alternated being CEO with Larsen every two years, but when it came time for her to take the CEO role once again in 1999, she opted to become chairwoman instead. "Chris is more patient with analysts and better able to focus on Wall Street and investors," she explains. "I'm more focused on the company internals and the product itself." She's enjoying her busy life as a high-powered dotcom exec and the rest of her life. She's happily remarried, and E-Loan's success has certainly helped mend her credit rating by now. She's focused on making the company the best it can be and is fanatically dedicated to serving the needs of the site's customers. "I think I'll do this forever," she says. "There's so much left to do to make borrowing better for consumers."

Janina Pawlowski's
TOP THREE LESSONS LEARNED

1. *"Don't blindly believe the experts.* They're usually following some other expert, who heard from some other expert, and so on. Trust your instincts and use your own judgment."

2. *"Build a strong management team quickly,* and pay for the best talent you can find."

3. *"Aim for the impossible.* Too few people challenge what already exists, and it's the only way to make progress."

E-Loan: KEY STRATEGIC TAKE-AWAYS

• When searching for a business idea, look for one that streamlines a process or cuts out intermediaries using the Internet. A main reason for E-Loan's success is its ability to offer lower-priced loans by cutting traditional mortgage brokers (and their commissions) out of the loop.

• Before you present to investors, get feedback. Pitch coaches, investors who are friends or colleagues, and executives can be great sources of honest, direct feedback.

• Use partnerships as marketing tools. E-Loan has partnered with highly trafficked sites that refer visitors.

• Expand your revenue base from one to multiple sources. E-Loan was satisfied with its stream of refinance mortgage loans but, in an interest-rate-sensitive economy, found it best to offer a wide variety of loan types, both domestically and abroad, to be better protected during times of rising interest rates.

- If another company wants to buy yours, consider whether the money, or having control and running the business the way you want to, is more important.

- Understand that the IPO process isn't objective or efficient. Pawlowski was surprised to learn that taking a company public is, as she puts it, "a big game with flaky rules." For example, institutional investors generally don't show interest or enthusiasm during road show pitches since doing so could raise the stock's offering price. "You'd think the process would be more related to real demand, but it's not," she says.

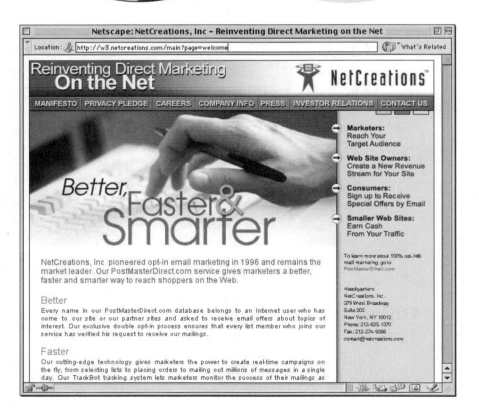

Netscape: NetCreations, Inc - Reinventing Direct Marketing on the Net

Location: http://w3.netcreations.com/main?page=welcome   What's Related

Reinventing Direct Marketing On the Net   **NetCreations**

MANIFESTO | PRIVACY PLEDGE | CAREERS | COMPANY INFO | PRESS | INVESTOR RELATIONS | CONTACT US

Better, Faster & Smarter

Marketers:
Reach Your
Target Audience

Web Site Owners:
Create a New Revenue
Stream for Your Site

Consumers:
Sign up to Receive
Special Offers by Email

Smaller Web Sites:
Earn Cash
From Your Traffic

To learn more about 100% opt-in
mail marketing, go to
PostMasterDirect.com

Headquarters
NetCreations, Inc.
379 West Broadway
Suite 202
New York, NY 10012
Phone: 212-625-1370
Fax: 212-274-9268
contact@netcreations.com

NetCreations, Inc. pioneered opt-in email marketing in 1996 and remains the market leader. Our PostMasterDirect.com service gives marketers a better, faster and smarter way to reach shoppers on the Web.

Better

Every name in our PostMasterDirect.com database belongs to an Internet user who has come to our site or our partner sites and asked to receive email offers about topics of interest. Our exclusive double opt-in process ensures that every list member who joins our service has verified his request to receive our mailings.

Faster

Our cutting-edge technology gives marketers the power to create real-time campaigns on the fly, from selecting lists to placing orders to mailing out millions of messages in a single day. Our TrackBot tracking system lets marketers monitor the success of their mailings as

10

NetCreations

Pioneering One-to-One Web Marketing

"The only way to find out what business models are going to work on the Net is to dive in and start swimming."

—Rosalind Resnick

HOLD THE SPAM, PLEASE

As a business reporter for the *Miami Herald* in the eighties, Rosalind Resnick never would have guessed that a decade later she would found and lead a hugely successful Internet company. And in a Silicon world where the word *dotcom* has become a synonym for bleeding cash, Resnick has pulled off something out of the ordinary: She has created a Web company that has been profitable from day one, and she has done it without ever taking outside funding.

SoHo-based NetCreations, a $400-million-plus company that Resnick bootstrapped all the way to an IPO with just $1000 in personal savings, is dedicated to keeping spam out of the email boxes of America. The company collects and sells topical "opt-in" lists of email addresses to direct marketers. What differentiates mailing to an opt-in list from unsolicited email broadcasts is that everyone on an opt-in list has given permission to receive messages on a specific topic.

This makes the tightly focused messages sent to NetCreations' lists a welcome antidote to mailboxes filled with annoying spam. As a result, Resnick is able to send 1.5 million emails per day without being flamed by angry recipients. In fact, recipients *like* to receive the messages. At the

NetCreations site, consumers can sign up to receive special offers tailored to their interests. Want to be kept apprised of killer deals on ski equipment and ski trips? Or perhaps the latest and greatest aromatherapy scents? Just join NetCreations' lists on these topics.

MARKETING'S NEW KILLER APP

Resnick has cornered the right corner of the market at just the right time. Email marketing has been rediscovered as one of the hottest tools in the direct-marketing toolshed. In earlier Web times, respectable marketers would run for the hills at mention of the words "direct email marketing"—after all, it is the preferred Web marketing method of pornographers and pyramid schemers alike, as well as the easiest and quickest way to anger and alienate customers forever. Recipients' ire over spam is the reason so many email providers have created "spam filters" to reroute bulk mail to a separate folder where it can be ignored.

But with click-through rates for banner advertising on the decline (they've dropped to less than one percent), respectable online advertisers are turning to email. And they're discovering that, when done right, permission-based email marketing is cheap and extremely effective, generating customer response rates that make even the most staid advertisers giddy: According to a spring 2000 Forrester Research report, average rates are 3.5 percent for a rented list and 10 percent for a company's in-house list.

"Banner advertising is dead," decries the self-styled manifesto at Net-Creations' Website. Indeed, sending a marketing message to someone's email box is far more effective than waiting for that person to stumble across and click on a banner ad or button. In fact, after affiliate marketing, email is the second most effective technique for driving traffic to a Website.

What's more, marketers are reporting especially high click-through for email sent to their in-house lists of customers, and are discovering that email is a hugely effective way to generate repeat purchases from existing customer bases. If L.L. Bean knows you've bought their size 8 all-cotton double-pleated pants in black and khaki, they can use email to suggest individual items to you that you're very likely to buy. Because email marketing can be so personalized and effective, smart companies are increasingly creating their own in-house lists by gathering customer email addresses over the phone, on the Web, and in brick-and-mortar stores.

FROM MILD-MANNERED REPORTER TO NETGIRL

Resnick might never have made the leap into the wild and woolly world of entrepreneurship if it hadn't been for the archaic employment practices of the *Maimi Herald*. After the birth of her first child in 1989, Resnick needed to work part-time or telecommute to make time for being a mom, but the *Herald* said she'd have to return to work full-time at the office if she wanted to keep her job. Unwilling to compromise, she quit, and set up shop as a freelance business writer working at home. The move was not only lucrative (within three months Resnick was making $4000 a month, more than she ever had before), it led her into a whole new realm of possibilities.

To research business stories, Resnick relied on early Internet services like CompuServe, Prodigy, and AOL. However, she soon became more interested in the online world itself than writing business articles. When she got wind that AOL was hiring journalists to create content, she jumped at the opportunity. That's how she landed her first online gig and became NetGirl, AOL's cyberrelationship sexpert and romance advice columnist, whose forum was the most highly trafficked one of its time. While she was certainly most qualified to host an Internet business forum, she chose relationships instead. "From my experience on AOL, it was crystal clear to me that users would want a 'Dear Abby' forum where they could pour out their love troubles," she explains.

Through her NetGirl experience, Resnick became increasingly interested in the best ways to publish and market online. In 1994, figuring that if she was hungry for this type of information others probably were too, she began publishing "Interactive Publishing Alert," a semimonthly email newsletter giving publishers tips and insight about making money online (Resnick sold subscriptions for a tidy $295 per year). She also disseminated her rapidly expanding Net marketing know-how through books she coauthored about doing business online, including *The Internet Business Guide*, published in 1994—well before the commercial world had embraced the Net on a large scale.

THE BIRTH AND TRANSFORMATION OF NETCREATIONS

With the Web taking off, Resnick's business instincts told her there was a huge, growing demand for Website design services. Although her business and editorial talents were tops, she lacked the technical skill to go it alone, so she teamed up with technical whiz Ryan Druckenmiller, whom she met through her local ISP. Together they started NetCreations in March 1995 and began designing Websites, with Resnick as CEO and Druckenmiller as CTO.

The duo soon discovered that getting customers to visit a client's site was tougher than creating the site itself. "At first we thought the world would beat a path to our clients' doors if we put up a cool Website for them," explains Resnick. "But as more commercial sites came online, we realized this wasn't happening." Seeing yet another market need, Resnick and Druckenmiller in August 1995 developed PostMaster, a Web-based application that automatically registered Websites with search engines. The app was a hit—more than 15,000 Webmasters soon started using it to register their sites. But as the number of commercial sites continued to multiply, NetCreations' clients began complaining that PostMaster was losing its effectiveness. "We could get them listed on Yahoo! under 'Books,' but if they were number 672, nobody was going to find the link and click on it," says Resnick. "Our clients were demanding a more direct way to get people from point A to their site."

As good timing would have it, a circulation manager at technology publisher Ziff-Davis asked Resnick if he could rent NetCreations' 15,000-person email list of Webmasters who had used the company's PostMaster service. As soon as Resnick heard the request, an entrepreneurial lightbulb flashed on: She realized that she could give all kinds of marketers and her existing traffic-hungry client base the same narrow-cast reach by creating a slew of tightly defined email lists. But Resnick knew how annoying it was to receive unsolicited email. So in early 1996 she came up with a solution that worked: what's now referred to as opt-in email marketing. And that's how she transformed NetCreations into an email list managing and brokering business.

FROM NETGIRL TO NET WORTH $120 MILLION

NetCreations was a money maker from the start, and Resnick was able to fund the company's growth through operating profits. "I've never run NetCreations as an Internet business," she explains. "I'm not a 22-year-old software whiz kid, but a 41-year-old mom with her head screwed on straight. My heroes are brick-and-mortar entrepreneurs who found a need, developed a product, shipped that product, and executed their business in a big, big way."

Although Resnick had many opportunities to sell NetCreations and many venture capitalists wanted to invest, she preferred to keep the company independent and never took outside funding. "We didn't start the company to get rich but to call our own shots and pursue our vision," she explains. "To me, there's just no amount of money in the world that can compensate you for that. A lot of deals have been thrown at us that would have looked great in a press release, but the numbers just didn't add up."

When Resnick was ready to take NetCreations public, finding an investment bank to underwrite the IPO proved to be a challenge. "The big investment banks didn't know what to make of the fact that the company was profitable but hadn't taken VC money, didn't have sponsorship deals, and was still run by me and my partner," says Resnick, who ended up taking NetCreations public in November 1999 through a small Virginia-based investment bank.

What was the IPO experience like for Resnick personally? "A 10-mile hike straight uphill," she says. "After managing to find an investment banker willing to take us public, we suffered delay after delay until we finally went out on the road show. I flew to 13 cities and gave 71 investor presentations (often six or seven a day) in three weeks. I was really glad when it was over!"

But Resnick's memory of an exhausting road show was sweetened by the IPO's success. It raised more than $43 million for the company, and Resnick's paper net worth instantly skyrocketed to $120 million (she personally owns about 38 percent of the company, while Druckenmiller holds 36 percent—the rest is owned by the public). But her life remains largely unchanged. "All the stock, all the money, it really doesn't seem real," she says. "I still come into the office at nine, work until 7:30 or eight, and go home to my kids."

THE BUSINESS MODEL

Using NetCreations' PostMasterDirect.com service is easy. "A marketer can come to our site, query our database, and mail out a campaign the same day," says Resnick. "They don't need to spend weeks and deal with a letter shop to get it done." And marketers love the results: Response rates from NetCreations' opt-in email lists typically run as high as 5 to 15 percent, much higher than the two to three percent response that's considered a success for direct snail-mail campaigns. Because customers voluntarily segment themselves by interests and preferences, NetCreations lists are of extremely high quality; and list quality, more than any other factor, determines how successful an email campaign will be. What's more, when NetCreations' list members sign up, they indicate whether they prefer to receive HTML or text-based email messages, so marketers using PostMasterDirect.com can easily send HTML email only to recipients who are able to view it. (Marketers prefer to use HTML-based email messages when possible because they usually have twice the response rate of text-based ones.)

NetCreations' list renters pay for quality. One-time use of a list costs anywhere from 10 to 30 cents per name per mailing. Clients can choose from the company's more than 3000 topical lists, which cover interests ranging from accounting to woodworking. Because email doesn't require stamps, paper, or printing, the typical $200 cost to reach 1000 consumers is much less than the $500 to $900 that's usually spent on equivalent paper mail campaigns. But the cost varies depending on how targeted the email list is. Sending a one-time email to 1000 headache sufferers costs as much as $300.

Through PostMasterDirect.com, visitors may sign up to be on topical email lists of interest. After registering, they receive a confirmation email, and only those recipients who confirm they really want to sign up are put on the list. This "double opt-in" process ensures that people understand what they are signing up for and prevents pranksters from, say, signing someone up on a hair loss mailing list they don't want to be on. It also sets NetCreations' lists clearly apart from those of unscrupulous direct marketers who harvest millions of email addresses from newsgroups, chat rooms, and Websites without consent.

To keep email list subscribers happy, NetCreations adheres to the highest possible privacy standards. Subscribers' personal information isn't ever revealed to the businesses that rent NetCreations' lists. List renters simply submit their marketing material via PostMasterDirect.com, indicate the list they want to use, and NetCreations handles the emailing so they never access the email list directly.

Wondering how NetCreations gets out word about its service? Need you ask? Resnick walks her talk and does email promotions through her in-house customer email list. But with the demand for outsourcing email marketing burgeoning, the trick for Resnick hasn't been acquiring customers. Since email marketing is more effective and less expensive than traditional direct mail or banner ads, clients are eager to sign up for her services. NetCreations boasts a long list of high-profile clients, including Dell, Compaq, IBM, J. Crew, The Gap, AT&T, and Sprint.

Instead, the hurdle for Resnick is signing up new subscribers for NetCreations' email lists fast enough to keep up with swelling demand. Opt-in email lists take a long time to build since they can only be created one voluntarily added name at a time. To continue building her email lists quickly, Resnick is partnering with portals and highly trafficked sites at a rapid clip. The company runs opt-in email lists on more than 200 large partner sites, including AltaVista, About.com, CNET, AllAdvantage.com, and CBS Sportsline. These heavy hitters keep 50 percent of the money earned per mailing when their lists are used.

Resnick is also using an affiliate program that enables small Websites to earn extra money by building opt-in email lists for Post-MasterDirect.com's network. Unlike Web merchant affiliate programs that pay commissions to sites that bring in sales, NetCreations' program pays affiliates a royalty of 25 percent every time their email list is used. "Based on our track record, this means that our affiliates could easily earn as much as a dollar a year for every email address they send us," says Michael Szerencsy, a Post-MasterDirect.com list manager. "To make that much through Amazon's affiliate program, you'd have to sell thousands of dollars worth of books."

BUILDING A BUSINESS TO LAST

While the market for outsourcing email campaigns was $164 million in 1999, Jupiter Communications sees it exploding to a mind-boggling $7.3 billion by 2005, cannibalizing 13 percent of traditional direct mail revenues. Jupiter foresees enormous growth in the volume of marketing messages sent via email: They predict that an average of 1600 will be received by each person online in the United States in 2005, which is 400 times more than the 40 commercial email messages received by the average Internet user in 1999. And email list clearinghouses such as NetCreations are poised to reap the rewards. In fact, the throng of companies seeking to outsource their email marketing efforts is so great that many email service companies have to turn away potential clients. All this has put profits for Resnick's company on a hypergrowth track.

Since the IPO, NetCreations has been flourishing. The company made $4.5 million in profit on $20 million in sales in 1999. Although Resnick wants to grow the business as much as she can, she aims to keep the vibe at the office cozy and friendly. "I want to run NetCreations as a small business where I know every employee, even though we'll soon grow to 100 people," she says. One of the best things about Resnick's business model is that NetCreations can scale without substantially increasing its operating costs. Whether a mailing list for new media professionals grows to 1000 email addresses or 100,000, little additional people power is needed.

In a Net economy where businesses are built and sold in a matter of months, Resnick has a fresh perspective. "We're not in this for the quick buck," she says. "We're in this to create one of the few Internet companies that's really going to last." To help her build the business for the long run, she has recruited first-rate senior executives with solid track records. She sought out people from larger companies who knew how to scale a business and structure an organization. "I didn't look for sprinters. I looked for people who could run a marathon," she says.

Although NetCreations was the first mover in its niche, competition is emerging as email marketing hits corporate America. Yesmail.com (acquired by CMGI) and Excite@Home's direct-mail subsidiary, Match-Logic, are among the rivals. Yoyodyne, an online direct-marketing firm acquired by Yahoo!, is another. And there's another form of competition: companies such as MyPoints.com, which offer consumers incentives to register and surf the Web, and then sell email lists. But Resnick's biggest rivals are online advertising firms such as DoubleClick, which are moving into email marketing as click-through rates on banner ads sag. Still, NetCreations' market niche is getting big fast, so Resnick isn't sweating it over the competition.

To further grow NetCreations' email lists and business, Resnick is extending the company's reach internationally by partnering with high-traffic sites in Europe, Asia, and Latin America. Resnick's partnership strategy is very effective: the company is currently signing up 35,000 new names for its mailing lists *each day*. Resnick will also deliver marketing messages via mobile phones, Palm Pilots, and other wireless platforms—a huge new opportunity for email direct marketing that will dramatically increase demand for the company's services.

Resnick is confident that NetCreations' ability to grow in its rapidly expanding market is a slam dunk. "I really think that if we keep on executing, NetCreations is going to be one of the world's biggest, best, most profitable companies," she predicts. "That's not going to happen next year, but it may happen 10, 20, or 30 years from now, and we're going to keep on going. To paraphrase Woody Allen, 80 percent of success is just showing up."

Rosalind Resnick's
TOP THREE LESSONS LEARNED

1. *"Trust yourself.* I used to be risk-averse, but now I know I can follow my instincts and take risks, regardless of what happens with my business."

2. *"Listen to your customers.* They won't steer you wrong. The way to grow is to let your customers tell you where they want to go."

3. *"Never give up no matter how bad it gets.* Every day there will be problems, customer-service issues, or competitors that will eat your lunch, but you just have to refuse to give up."

NetCreations: KEY STRATEGIC TAKE-AWAYS

- Look for business ideas that are scalable but have low overhead. This is NetCreations' biggest success factor. The company can grow its email lists and number of clients without hiring an army of employees.

- Pay attention to market trends. Resnick was able to build Net-Creations into the success it is today because she kept her eyes and ears open and responded to changes in the market. "When I was a journalist, I'd spot business trends and turn them into articles. As a businessperson, I've been able to spot trends and turn them into money," she says.

- Consider the type of funding that makes best sense for you. Many Net entrepreneurs seek venture capital so they can grow their businesses as quickly as possible, but this isn't the only way to go. Resnick preferred to bootstrap her company and grow it with operating profits to maintain independence and control. "Without investors, we could wander without outside pressure," she says. "The company had a chance to find its way organically."

- Solicit customer feedback and respond to it. By listening to her customers' needs and suggestions, Resnick got the information she needed to take her business to greater successes. That's why "It's the customer, stupid" is a motto in her corporate manifesto.

- You don't need an MBA to make it as an entrepreneur. Resnick holds a BA and MA in Italian Renaissance history from Johns Hopkins University. She believes the abilities she honed as a journalist—writing, communicating, and synthesizing large bodies of information—have helped her in business more than an MBA ever could have.

Part III

E-Commerce
Ventures

VITAL STATS

- Cofounders: Jessica DiLullo Herrin, VP of product marketing, and Jenny Lefcourt, VP of marketing and business development
- URL: www.weddingchannel.com
- Stock: Private (now part of WeddingChannel.com)
- Founded: 1998
- Headquarters: San Francisco and Los Angeles

11

Della.com

Marrying a Traditional Service and the Net

"When a great opportunity arises, go with it. We had no fear of quitting business school. We were more afraid of letting this idea get away from us."

—Jessica DiLullo Herrin

"Personal experience is a great way to land a business idea. My own wedding made me realize that the Internet could make wedding planning much easier."

—Jenny Lefcourt

SKIPPING CLASS FOR A NEW IDEA

Jenny Lefcourt, 31, and Jessica DiLullo Herrin, 27, didn't know each other when they entered Stanford Business School in 1997, but they both had the same goal. In their admissions essays, each wrote that she intended to start a business that would simplify a complicated process using the Internet.

The two repeatedly crossed paths at venture capital and entrepreneurship workshops on campus and soon became good friends. But their friendship took a turn toward business partnership when Lefcourt asked Herrin to enter Stanford's annual "entrepreneurial challenge" contest, in which each contestant presents a business plan to a group of high-profile CEOs and venture capitalists in hopes of winning a $25,000 grand prize. "Do you have any business plans in mind?" asked Herrin. "Well," said Lefcourt, "I was thinking about developing a concept for registering and buying wedding gifts online." Herrin's mouth dropped open and she gasped. "I wrote a business plan for that same idea two years ago!" The two immediately became engaged as partners for the contest, and soon after dropped out of Stanford to give birth to a business named Della and James that would grow up to be Della.com and would eventually tie the knot with WeddingChannel.com.

How did they choose such an unusual name? Della and James are the two main characters in O. Henry's classic 1906 short story, "Gift of the Magi." They're young, poor newlyweds who want to buy gifts for each other. James sells his watch to buy Della combs for her beautiful long hair, only to find out that she has sold her hair to buy him a fob chain for his watch. For Herrin and Lefcourt, the characters' selflessness reflected the spirit of gift-giving they wanted to propagate with their business. While they initially named their company Della and James, they later shortened it to Della.com for convenience.

The company, which they cofounded in May 1998, grew to be a leading online gift registry for brides and grooms-to-be. Taking a commission from each gift purchased, it brought together well-known brick-and-mortar and virtual retailers, such as Amazon.com, Neiman Marcus, Williams-Sonoma, Crate & Barrel, and Dillard's, all in one place. At the site, which can now be found at WeddingChannel.com (Della.com merged with WeddingChannel.com in spring 2000), engaged couples can access their in-store registries, make changes to them, and create new ones. They can also add items to their list from stores they haven't registered with. When couples register with one of the company's retail partners, their registries immediately become available through the site. Conversely, those who register from the site can access and edit their list from in-store computers. The company also has an online wedding shop that offers accessories from bridesmaids' gifts and invitations to ring pillows and ceremonial music.

TAKING THE PLUNGE

Entrepreneurs at heart, Herrin and Lefcourt both knew that they wanted to be part of a startup, and preferably run one. After graduating from Stanford with a degree in economics, Herrin joined an enterprise software company named Trilogy Development as employee number 40 and director of marketing. "This was before the time when immediately joining a pre-IPO startup after college was a popular thing to do," she says. She first saw the sea change the Internet was causing in business when she took a leadership role in sales and marketing for pcOrder.com, a Trilogy division that provided e-commerce solutions to computer suppliers and was eventually spun out as its own company. (Coincidentally, pcOrder.com was founded by another successful young woman entrepreneur, Christy Jones.) Eager to gain more Web experience and learn about consumer behavior online, Herrin next took a product management position with NetRatings, a company measuring online audience usage. Then, in order to gain entrepreneurial skills, she returned to Stanford, this time as an MBA student.

Like Herrin, Lefcourt also earned an economics degree (hers from the University of Pennsylvania), but unlike her partner, she learned that big business wasn't for her by first dipping in her toe. During a two-year stint as a certified public accountant for Arthur Andersen in New York City, she felt buried in bureaucracy and stifled. "What made me most unhappy was that no matter what I did, the outcome seemed almost predetermined because there were so many ingrained rules and processes," Lefcourt recalls. So she traded in that job, and after a year off backpacking through Europe and Asia, landed at MySoftware, a startup creating productivity software for small businesses. There, she launched the company's Internet division and oversaw product marketing efforts. This experience activated her entrepreneurial impulse, which she then opted to further feed in business school.

Lefcourt's idea for a gift-registry business was inspired by her own wedding, which took place just a week before she started Stanford's MBA program. While registering for gifts, she and her husband-to-be looked online for a way to simplify the process, but found nothing. "I knew setting up a wedding registry was a problem the Internet could solve," she says.

By January 1998, Herrin and Lefcourt were working on their business plan in earnest as an adjunct to their MBA coursework, and soon Della.com was taking up most of their waking hours. As far as the business plan contest, well, they never actually completed it. In the first round of the competition, Dave Whorton, an associate partner at venture capital firm Kleiner Perkins Caufield & Byers and one of the contest judges, asked them to pull their entry out of the contest and keep it quiet. Engaged to be married at the time, Whorton knew Herrin and Lefcourt were on to something big.

Having captured the serious interest of an elite VC firm, Herrin and Lefcourt faced a major decision: stay in school another year to finish their MBAs or drop out to turn Della.com into a real business. It didn't take the two long to decide. "When Dave approached us about starting the business, our answer was, 'Of course we will!'" remembers Herrin. And Lefcourt adds, "That was the reason we both went to Stanford in the first place."

WOOING SUITORS

Although the two admittedly had an easier time getting funded than most first-time entrepreneurs because of Whorton's enthusiasm, they weren't able to forego formally pitching the idea in VC firms' conference rooms. But even when presenting their business model to a room full of all-male Kleiner Perkins partners, Lefcourt says all they felt was adrenaline: "We were so revved up about the company we wanted to start, and so excited to have the chance to talk about it, that we weren't intimidated."

Their excitement rubbed off: Kleiner Perkins invested a seed round of $1 million in May 1998 followed by a second round of $4 million along with Trinity Ventures seven months later. From the beginning, Herrin and Lefcourt intended on hiring a seasoned executive manager as CEO. "Since we were both new to managing a business, we didn't see ourselves as the best candidates for CEO," says Lefcourt. "We looked at the situation from the point of view of stockholders, and we didn't want to be learning how to run a business on company time. We wanted this business to be a success, so we wanted a CEO who had the experience to make it big fast."

Just as the pair started to search for a CEO, Rebecca Patton, a senior vice president at E*Trade, visited Kleiner Perkins to discuss potential CEO opportunities. Patton, who *did* graduate with a Stanford MBA, had helped shape the online trader's brand, develop its marketing strategy, and build it into one of the Net's top brokerage sites, but she was ready for her next challenge. So Kleiner Perkins introduced her to Herrin and Lefcourt, and it proved to be a perfect match. "We had liked the other candidates we'd interviewed, but when we met Rebecca, we immediately loved her," says Lefcourt. "There was an instant connection." Although she and Herrin knew Patton had the experience to scale their business, they had to persuade her long and hard to join the fledgling startup. The three talked over the vision for Della.com and, finally, convinced that they would make a great team, Patton joined as CEO. Herrin and Lefcourt instead became VP of product marketing and VP of marketing and business development, respectively. "Our backgrounds were in these areas, so we knew we could add a lot of value to the company in the positions we took," says Herrin.

NO HONEYMOON

Even before top executive management was in place, Herrin and Lefcourt were already signing up retail partners. Advisers had recommended that they cut out retailers and sell directly to customers. (At the time, brick-and-mortar retailers were regarded as potential dinosaurs soon to be made extinct by the Internet.) But Herrin and Lefcourt disagreed with this strategy. "Brides want to touch and feel the items they're going to live with for the rest of their lives, and an Internet-only site would never be able to provide that experience," says Lefcourt. "We didn't want to be an e-tailer with inventory or fulfillment to worry about, " adds Herrin. "Instead we wanted to be an e-service aggregator, something that's much more profitable." Their strategy was to market Della.com to deep-pocketed customers, and that meant convincing high-end stores to offer their wares over the site. "We didn't want to have 50 houseware stores, we wanted to have only the best," explains Herrin.

But getting the best brick-and-mortar retailers to join forces with a brand-new dotcom wasn't easy. For Herrin and Lefcourt, wooing retailers was much harder than pitching to VCs. "At the time, the Internet was a little scary and new to them," Lefcourt recalls. "It was uncharted territory. We had to show them how it could improve their business and consumer relationships."

Della.com's board of directors loaned a hand. A recent addition was Phil Schlein, a partner with U.S. Venture Partners and former CEO of Macy's department stores. His knowledge of the industry and personal contacts opened the door and paved the way for the founders to meet with CEOs at top retailers. "The retailers had heard about the Internet and young entre-preneurs, but it can be a shock to the system to have two young women come in and pitch you on an idea when you've worked your way up and are a 50-year-old-man heading up a major national retailer," says Lefcourt. "Phil would come with us and sort of play the 'gray hair' role. His pres-ence was very helpful to us in these meetings." To underscore the site's technological strengths, Kleiner Perkins added Jerry Held, its entrepre-neur-in-residence and former Oracle veteran, to Della.com's board. He also participated in meetings with retailers to promote the state-of-the-art technology the site would use to link retailers with online registry users.

All the courting paid off as name-brand retailers including Crate & Bar-rel, Neiman Marcus, Williams-Sonoma, and REI signed up. "They eventu-ally said yes, but working out the details about what items would be sold and what commission they would pay was a long process," says Lefcourt. "It didn't happen at Internet speed." It took a year from initial funding to site launch to hammer out these exclusive agreements and integrate retail-ers' systems with the Della.com site.

NEW OPTIONS FOR NEWLYWEDS

Della.com unveiled its virtual wedding registry in June 1999. At launch, the site was rigged to a beeper that would go off every time a visitor made a purchase. Soon after the site went live, the beeper started going off so often that it became annoying and employees turned it off. "Right after we launched, we would actually do a little dance to the sound of the beeper," says Herrin. "Hearing all those beeps was very exciting."

As Herrin and Lefcourt see it, engaged couples, who traditionally reg-ister at no more than three stores, want to manage their gift registries all in one location, add unique items to their list from stores they haven't reg-istered with, and provide greater selection to their guests, who can easily purchase a gift over the site even if they live thousands of miles from the nearest store selling the item. Wedding gifts make an ideal e-commerce category since buyers don't need to touch the items they purchase—they already know they've been deemed gift-worthy by the to-be-weds.

Herrin was happy that the site launched in time for her own August 1999 nuptials, so she and her Stanford sweetheart could take Della.com for a real-life spin. "My wedding guests lived all over the country and many of them didn't have a Restoration Hardware or an REI store nearby," she says. "Della.com made it easier for us and them to choose gifts."

Customers played a big role in defining the site's offerings. And now, as part of WeddingChannel.com, the company continues to rely on both market research and customer surveys to find out what site tools and gifts are most desired. "We discovered that many couples wanted to add a tent and two sleeping bags to their list but didn't want to register at a camping store, so we added REI as one of our retailers," says Lefcourt. "Customers also said they wanted more unique decorative items for the home, so we added Restoration Hardware."

The site's value to wedding guests is that it lets them easily locate a couple's gift registry, view and choose a gift, and conveniently purchase it from the comfort of their own home. The site offers traditional gifts such as fluted champagne glasses and kitchen appliances, as well as unique gifts like cooking lessons and spa treatments. For personalized help, the company offers a customer service staff via phone or email who can ask a few questions about the couple-to-be and make custom-tailored gift suggestions.

THE BUSINESS MODEL

Typically the most acquisitive event in a person's life, weddings are big business. Every year, wedding guests spend approximately $17 billion on toasters, silver candlestick holders, cappuccino machines, and other gifts. When you tally the cake, band, food, and other expenses, the numbers are even more astounding: the 2.5 million couples who get married in the United States each year generate a total of $50 billion in wedding-related spending.

How did Della.com earn its biggest slice of the wedding pie? From commissions. At the time of the merger with WeddingChannel.com, Della.com was getting a cut of each sale through the site. Revenues from direct sales of wedding accessories and sponsorship fees were also tallied, although Lefcourt and Herrin demur when it comes to sharing specific figures.

Although Della.com was primarily a consumer-oriented e-commerce business, its revenue model also had a business-to-business aspect. As part of WeddingChannel.com, it continues to license its online registry technology to brick-and-mortar stores. Gump's, a 150-year-old specialty store in San Francisco, scrapped its registry database to license Della.com's technology instead. And Restoration Hardware and other retail partners use the company's bridal registry computer kiosks in all their stores. "Licensing our technology to our retailers is one more way to build strong relationships with them," says Herrin. The company also charges fees when integrating its registry technology with a retailer's existing systems. "We don't just put them online," explains Lefcourt. "Our value is bringing them into an aggregation of other, complementary retailers and services that benefit them."

Luckily, weddings are a market where it's possible to do very targeted advertising. For the most part, Della.com relied on reaching brides-to-be through advertising in magazines such as *Brides* and *Modern Bride*, the wedding-planning bibles. The company also built its customer base by offering special incentives on its site (for example, "purchase something from our Wedding Shop and receive $50 toward a spa treatment") and other promotions to encourage brides and grooms to spread the word to their wedding guests. A huge benefit of the business model is that it enabled Della.com and now WeddingChannel.com to join marketing efforts with their retailers. "When brides and grooms go into their stores, retailers hand them a registry packet that has our branding inscribed on it," says Lefcourt.

Popular thinking is that the equivalent of the Christmas rush for the wedding industry are the summer months of May through August. Not so, according to Herrin. Because of the near impossibility of booking a church or band during that time, and the fact that summer can be too hot for weddings in the South and Southwest, ceremonies are now spread throughout the year, although the concentration increases between May and October. That means the wedding business isn't subject to wild seasonal variations, and, unlike many e-tailers, Della.com was able to forego traditional seasonal advertising campaigns.

TYING THE KNOT

In order to build Della.com's customer base fast, Kleiner Perkins thought Amazon.com would make a good partner and arranged a meeting between Jeff Bezos and Della.com's CEO Patton. Although Amazon.com could have set up its own registry, Bezos liked the fact that Della.com had built exclusive relationships with high-end retailers, so Amazon.com (as well as some of Della.com's other retail partners) decided to invest. In September 1999, Della.com received $45 million in a third round of funding led by Amazon.com, which took a 20 percent stake.

The $45 million helped finance the creation of an ambitious all-occasion gift registry just in time for the 1999 holiday season. The new registry was a first step toward expanding Della.com to include baby-gift registries, as well as birthday, anniversary, and holiday wish lists. But in spring 2000, after a few months of struggling to tie all those elements together, Della.com decided to go back to its roots and focus on its wedding registry. "We realized we couldn't do it all at once, which was humbling," admits Lefcourt. "The reality for a startup is that if you don't have a complete organization in place, it's easy to take your eye off the ball. That's a lesson no business school can really teach."

The upside of Della.com's decision to refocus on its strength in wedding registries is that rivals came calling. With heated competition in the online registry market, Della.com realized the best way to secure a clear lead was to join forces with another major player in the online wedding space. So in April 2000, Della.com and the WeddingChannel.com tied the knot. Rebecca Patton, Della.com's CEO, became the CEO of the merged company, which operates under the WeddingChannel.com name, and Lefcourt and Herrin kept their same roles. Prior to the merger, the top three wedding registry sites—WeddingChannel.com, Della.com, and The Knot—were running neck and neck in terms of pageviews and unique users. Della.com and the WeddingChannel.com's strong marriage instantly vaulted the new company into the lead.

With their baby grown up and married, what are Lefcourt and Herrin's plans for the future? "For now, we want to make sure WeddingChannel.com is the category killer in the wedding space," says Lefcourt. Herrin shares this focus, though she also envisions someday starting a company with her husband. But, she quips: "I can't imagine Jenny not being in the picture, though, since I feel like I'm married to her too!"

Jenny Lefcourt's TOP THREE LESSONS LEARNED

1. *"Think positively.* You can always find a reason why your business won't work, but, to be successful, you need to focus on the reasons why it will."

2. *"Amass talent quickly.* Surround yourself with the people and skills you need as soon as possible. An idea is just an idea until it's executed."

3. *"Take it seriously, but not too seriously.* There's a fine line between pouring your heart into something and going overboard. Be 100 percent passionate, but remember that it's not a life-and-death situation."

Jessica DiLullo Herrin's TOP THREE LESSONS LEARNED

1. *"See the opportunity, not the obstacles.* You shouldn't be naive, but focusing on the hurdles will only exhaust you, not compel you to do what seems impossible. Oftentimes, when you cast away disbelief, you can succeed because you didn't focus on why you should fail."

2. *"Surround yourself with an incredible team* of equal parts experience and passion. But don't compromise on the quality of people you hire for quick growth. If you make a hiring mistake, correct it very quickly. Hire people who are driven by a genuine passion for your market."

3. *"Don't go it alone.* Whether it's the support of a business partner or a spouse, you need someone to pick you back up after the many, many bumps you will face on the long but wonderful road of entrepreneurship."

Della.com: KEY STRATEGIC TAKE-AWAYS

- When hunting for a winning business idea, look for a process that the Internet can drastically simplify. Based on her own bridal registry woes, Lefcourt knew online registries could make the process much more convenient.

- If an opportunity comes along that looks too good to pass up, don't let it get away. Herrin and Lefcourt decided to forego graduating from business school rather than delay starting their company.

- Be realistic about your leadership skills. If you don't think you have enough experience to be a CEO, hire the best person you can.

- For tough negotiations, enlist help. Herrin and Lefcourt relied on two board members for advice and assistance in approaching potential retail partners.

- Use incentives to build traffic. Herrin and Lefcourt overcame the challenge of reaching gift givers by giving brides and grooms incentives to tell their wedding guests about Della.com.

- When necessary, scale back and refocus on your core business. When Della.com bit off more than it could chew by expanding into all-occasion gift registries too early, it refocused to first make its wedding registry the best it could be.

- In overcrowded e-commerce sectors, consolidation is inevitable. Joining forces with a leader in the same niche can be a good way to ensure the long-term viability of your venture.

VITAL STATS

- Founders: Mariam Naficy and Varsha Rao, copresidents
- URL: www.eve.com
- Stock: Private
- Founded: 1998
- Headquarters: San Francisco

12

Eve.com

Bringing E-Tail to an Unlikely Class of Products

> *"Brick-and-mortar companies are our best advisers. By involving our partners in the site's development, we've been able to give our customers a great online shopping experience."*
>
> —Mariam Naficy

> *"It's so important to choose a business area you're passionate about. If you don't love what you're doing, there's no way you'll be able to give all of yourself to it."*
>
> —Varsha Rao

IT'S CHRISTMAS EVE.COM

From the time they entered business school, Mariam Naficy and Varsha Rao knew they wanted to build a successful business. But they didn't realize how far they'd come until Eve.com, the company they cofounded, had survived (and thrived during) its first holiday shopping season. This online seller of high-end cosmetics and fragrances launched its Website in June 1999 and immediately began preparing for the Christmas rush. For starters, it orchestrated a $20 million ad campaign to create brand awareness and attract traffic. In November it debuted a boutique where shoppers could buy gift baskets, get gift recommendations, and choose from 8000 available products. Purchases were shipped from the company's Tennessee-based warehouse, with guaranteed before-Christmas delivery for all orders placed before December 22. The company holiday party was postponed until January since all employees had to help out during the height of the shopping onslaught by answering 24-hour-a-day customer-service phones or wrapping gifts at the warehouse.

For all their hard work, Naficy, Rao, and Eve.com staffers received the best gift they could have imagined—publicity and revenues. Orders tripled from November to December 1999, Eve.com was named a top-50 site for customer service by FeedbackDirect.com, while *Fortune* ranked it number six in customer service—ahead of brick-and-mortar retailers such as The Gap, Banana Republic, and Nordstrom. "The season was a total validation for us," says Rao.

Despite this first flush of success, Eve.com still resembles a startup. The company has grown to more than 100 employees so fast that its Financial District offices are overcrowded and chairs are scarce—staff members lean against walls or sit on the floor during meetings. But unlike other Net startups, the majority of the employees are women— well-dressed, stylish-looking women with glowing skin and perfectly made-up faces. (Makeovers and beauty advice from Eve.com's in-house beauty advisers are among the employee benefits.)

Eve.com is the first e-tailer to offer an array of prestige beauty products, from exclusive high-end brands such as Givenchy and Elizabeth Arden to smaller, trendier lines including Benefit and Urban Decay (which was founded, oddly enough, by Cisco Systems cofounder Sandy Lerner). For women and teens who don't live near a Neiman Marcus or hip boutique, Eve.com offers the chance to purchase that metallic-blue nail polish or golden skin glitter they've seen on the pages of fashion magazines like *In Style* and *Allure*.

Naficy, 29, and Rao, 30, preside over staff meetings looking equally put together in sleek suits, color-coordinated cosmetics, and chic haircuts. Looking at them, it's hard to believe they break a sweat running their company. But their slick appearances belie the grunt work they've done to successfully sell products on the Web that women generally like to try before buying.

A BEAUTIFUL FRIENDSHIP

The two founders first met in New York in 1992. Naficy had just started a job as an analyst at investment bank Goldman Sachs and was looking for an apartment to share. A coworker introduced her to Rao, who had a room to rent and, coincidentally, was also an investment banking analyst. The two hit it off and began a friendship that would last long-distance for more than five years before they teamed up to start their business.

What made Rao and Naficy instant friends? They have a lot in common. Both have cultural roots outside of the United States—Rao is Indian and Naficy is Iranian and Chinese— and both went to East Coast colleges—Rao received a degree in economics and math at the University of Pennsylvania, while Naficy earned a bachelor's in political economy at Williams College. And they both felt that the time they'd spent in investment banking was the perfect precursor to learning how to run a business. "It taught me how to talk the lingo when it came to raising funding and how to prepare a business plan," says Naficy. It boosted Rao's confidence in successfully undertaking difficult ventures. "I felt that if I could make it in investment banking, I could make it anywhere," she says.

Even after they went their separate ways—Rao moved to Massachusettes to attend Harvard Business School, and Naficy headed West to take a position as director of marketing at a small Palo Alto–based restaurant chain called Left at Albuquerque—the two lived parallel lives. They both worked at startups, attended business school, and did consulting. After Rao finished her MBA, she ran her mother's small-town printing business for a few months, before joining the New York office of McKinsey & Co. as a consultant analyzing the digital marketplace. And Naficy helped expand Left at Albuquerque into a $20 million business before going to Stanford Business School.

After earning an MBA in 1998, Naficy decided to share her career advice with others via *The Fast Track: The Insider's Guide to Winning Jobs in Management Consulting, Investment Banking, and Securities Trading,* which became one of the top five best-selling career guides at

Amazon.com and is still a big seller on college campuses. After finishing this project, she was brimming with business ideas and ready to partner with someone to turn one of them into a business plan.

She instantly thought of her pal Rao and called her to see if she wanted to partner up. Rao didn't hesitate about joining forces. As the two started talking about potential businesses, they realized that they'd both considered cosmetics as a possible e-tail category. With busy careers, they rarely found time to shop. They figured that if they both lacked the time to buy cosmetics, they probably weren't alone. So they set out to solve the problem by creating an Internet site selling makeup and hair- and skin-care products. That summer, they did the market research, drew up a business plan, and never looked back.

INCUBATION AT IDEALAB!

Rao moved to San Francisco, and she and Naficy became roomies once again. They polished their investor pitch and began networking to find people with one degree of separation from VCs—they knew getting their business plan to the top of the stacks on VCs' desks would be next to impossible unless they were referred. Naficy worked the contacts she'd made during her days at Left at Albuquerque and Stanford. Before they knew it, someone connected them with Silicon Valley law firm Wilson Sonsini, which got them an appointment with Bill Gross, chairman of idealab!, a Los Angeles-based incubator that has spawned Internet startups such as eToys, CitySearch, and GoTo.com.

After listening to the young women's pitch for only 90 minutes, Gross decided to invest: He called the very next day and offered them $200,000 in seed funding as well as office space at idealab!. What made him instinctually decide to take a chance on Eve.com? "Cosmetics is a business particularly suited to the Internet because working women care about convenience," says Gross. "They don't have time to go to department stores and deal with pushy salespeople."

At first Naficy and Rao weren't sure whether a business incubator was for them—they had doubts about whether they'd be able to concentrate fully on developing their business while sharing space with so many other startups. But they quickly warmed up to the idea as they walked around idealab!'s office and saw firsthand the benefits that camaraderie with other startups would provide. "Some of our best advice has come from our officemates," says Rao. "We all bounced ideas off of each other." After two months of jump-starting Eve.com at idealab!, Naficy and Rao moved their fledgling company back to San Francisco.

ALL ABOUT EVE.COM

One of the first big decisions the cofounders faced was choosing a name. "We wanted one that evoked beauty, not something utilitarian like Fragrancenet or Fragrancecounter, which would be hard to build a brand around," explains Rao. They thought a woman's name would make a good brand, and picked Eve after both of their mothers independently suggested it.

But there was a small problem: The Eve.com domain was already taken, owned by a seven-year-old Virginia girl named Eve, whose mother was reluctant to sell it. But Eve named her price, and Naficy and Rao agreed to the terms: She'd trade the moniker for a computer, a $500 gift certificate for eToys, money for college, and a trip to Disney World. "It was one of the toughest deals we ever negotiated!" Rao jokes.

But their negotiating and persuasion skills were really put to the test when they were ready to raise more funding. "Early on, we had to do a lot of convincing," says Rao. "It was a challenge to communicate to male VCs that women would be a powerful force on the Web, because at that point their usage was low." VCs who heard their pitch said they were concerned that beauty products wouldn't flourish online since customers usually want to try them out before making a purchase. Moreover, they weren't convinced that high-end cosmetics—the products Eve.com would supply—would sell without the all-important personal advice offered at department-store cosmetics counters.

But Rao and Naficy's market research and conviction proved persuasive, and in February 1999, idealab!, Charter Venture Capital, and Menlo Ventures invested $3.2 million in Series B funding. After that, securing additional rounds of funding became easier as competition in the cosmetics category heated up. When it did, the VC lemming phenomenon kicked in—as more VC-backed cosmetics companies entered the fray, investors lost their doubts about the online selling power of beauty products and invested more in Eve.com, bringing the company's total funding tally to $28.7 million.

Although Naficy and Rao's business backgrounds are tops, they lacked an insider's view of the cosmetics industry, so they needed to recruit industry experts fast. As luck would have it, Naficy's next-door neighbor was a cosmetics buyer at Macy's. She led the founders to their first hire, Margo Scavarda, Eve.com's vendor relations director. Scavarda was the head of cosmetics at Macy's West and The Broadway department stores when they met her. She saw the Internet as the future of retailing and, captivated by their business idea, joined Eve.com. "Margo gave us instant credibility and opened many doors," says Rao.

Another critical hire was Charla Krupp, a 20-year veteran of beauty journalism, *Glamour's* beauty director, and a monthly commentator on NBC's *Today Show*. Like most of the other people Naficy and Rao hired, she was looking to do something new and entrepreneurial on the Internet, and responded with enthusiasm when Naficy gave her a call. Joining as vice president and editor-in-chief, she oversees editorial and product reviews on the site.

A MAKEOVER FOR MANUFACTURERS

With Scavarda and Krupp on board, many cosmetic makers overcame their skepticism about selling their wares on Eve.com. Maintaining brand integrity and consistent prices are the main concerns of high-end cosmetics suppliers, which pour millions of dollars into building their product-line images. They're adamant about selling only in upscale settings and don't allow retailers to compete on price. Their worst nightmare would be a dotcom site hocking their products en masse at discounted prices. "Their concern is partly about being in the wrong environment, which is very valid," explains Rao. "You have to create a Neiman Marcus experience online complete with customer care and relationship building."

To convince manufacturers to sign up, Naficy and Rao had to assure them that Eve.com would respect their expensive branding campaigns, would buy products only directly from them, and, most important, would never, ever discount products. The first taker was Vincent Longo, a New York–based makeup artist for supermodels and celebrities who sells his own line of cosmetics. After a cold call from Rao followed by a few months of negotiation, he signed on. "I was attracted to the concept of selling online because I had nothing to lose," says Longo. "I talked to my retailers and they all agreed that this would be a way to attract new customers to their stores. Also, I get to extend my brand."

Longo's endorsement encouraged other vendors of trendy cosmetic lines to join as well, creating a snowball effect that led to agreements with more than 200 makeup and fragrance brands, including well-established ones such as Calvin Klein and NARS. Many brands on the site have signed one- to two-year contracts in which Eve.com is their exclusive online retailer. In exchange, Eve.com builds individual boutiques for each manufacturer at no cost, scanning in thousands of product photos and writing individual product blurbs.

To keep both customers and suppliers happy, Eve.com developed first-rate customer service that offers the personal touch of one-to-one consultations. The management team has recruited a bevy of beauty consultants from behind department store cosmetics counters to answer customer questions by phone or online chat. Customers can email in their photos to get custom-tailored cosmetic and skin-care recommendations. They can also experiment with different looks by testing cosmetics on Eve.com staff members who function as virtual makeover models on the site.

THE BUSINESS MODEL

There's no question that there's money in makeup. In the United States, women spend $15 billion a year on cosmetics. Internet analysis firm Forrester Research forecasts that online sales of cosmetics will reach $1 billion by 2003, and chances are good that this figure will be met as more and more women start shopping online. Women are proving to be a formidable e-commerce force and are coming online at a faster pace than men. For example, the number of women on the Net jumped 32 percent from February to December 1999, outstripping the 20 percent growth rate for men during the same period, according to Nielsen/NetRatings.

Eve.com's strategy of focusing on high-end beauty products makes good business sense. Spending on prestige brands accounts for $5.5 billion of the $15 billion spent annually on makeup. And margins for high-end brands can reach up to and over 40 percent— far higher than those for mass-market cosmetics sold in drugstores. Since vendors won't sell to retailers that might dilute their brands by discounting prices, Eve.com's business is not vulnerable to the price competition that's widespread in other e-tailing sectors. Another plus: Cosmetics are lightweight and inexpensive to ship.

Even though women usually like to try cosmetics before buying them, Naficy and Rao are proving that these products can be effectively sold online. According to Naficy, 70 percent of women's cosmetics dollars are spent on replenishment purchases. "Most women already have a favorite lipstick and mascara so they just keep restocking on those," she explains. To capture a piece of the remaining 30 percent of the market, Eve.com, following the example set by cosmetic counter beauty consultants, offers plenty of makeup advice and free samples with every shipment.

The site's initial TV ad campaign made a big splash. Naficy and Rao collaborated with San Francisco ad agency Ingalls Moranville (the creator of Volkswagen's new Beetle campaign) to produce eye-catching ads in which red ladybugs and blue butterflies color women's faces and fingernails by landing on them. While these ads helped establish Eve.com's brand and create a buzz before the company's first holiday season, Naficy and Rao have since redirected more of their advertising budget to print ads in women's magazines—they've discovered that advertising in these targeted publications is a highly cost-effective way to build brand recognition.

Eve.com also advertises online to drive traffic to the site. It has inked exclusive merchant agreements with Women.com and Yahoo!, which means it's the only advertiser that appears on search result pages for keywords like *beauty* and *cosmetics*. The company also advertises on America Online.

LOOKING GOOD FOR THE FUTURE

Since Eve.com's first holiday season, traffic to the site has continued to ramp up fast. (At the time of this writing, the site was receiving more traffic than any of its competitors, according to both PC Data Online and Media Metrix.) But it does face challenges. First is the fact that Estée Lauder and L'Oréal, the two largest cosmetics manufacturers—accounting for more than half of the industry's sales—aren't selling through e-tailers and don't plan to for fear of alienating their brick-and-mortar retailers, the department stores. Nevertheless, Naficy believes the company will prosper and profit even if it doesn't win agreements with these brands. "Our customers are young and hip," she says. "They prefer harder-to-find trendy brands over those that are more prevalent in department stores and drugstores."

Secondly, Eve.com has to contend with the proliferation of beauty Websites, such as Beauty.com and Sephora.com, that are clamoring to sell online. Behind them are department stores, such as Macy's and Nordstrom, turning to the Internet as a new sales tool. But Eve.com's ability to secure exclusive deals with suppliers quickly has set it apart and is working to lock out rivals. While the presence of so many players makes consolidation in the cosmetics category inevitable, Forrester e-commerce analyst Evie Black Dykema thinks Eve.com will prevail. "The site has the most brands, and, more importantly, some of the *most desired* brands," she notes.

For their part, Naficy and Rao are keeping their cool in the competitive heat. They're looking toward expanding Eve.com beyond cosmetics to sell jewelry and eventually just about everything that's typically found on the first floor of department stores. "We used to be concerned about every little thing our competitors were doing," says Rao. "But competition is a fact of life. Now we're more focused on 'How do we get ahead?' than 'What are they doing?' We have a clear path—we know where we're going."

Varsha Rao's
TOP THREE LESSONS LEARNED

1. *"Persistence pays off,* especially in big business deals. Just keep showing interest in doing business with prospective partners and don't take no for an answer. 'No' sometimes just means 'No for now.'"

2. *"Listen to your customers and suppliers.* You'll never know everything, so reach out to your customers and vendors. They have a lot of knowledge to share. They've given us some of our best ideas."

3. *"Do something you enjoy.* Since there are no guarantees, you have to at least have fun."

Mariam Naficy's
TOP THREE LESSONS LEARNED

1. *"Hire the best.* Building the right team early paid off in many ways. Two of our first hires were our most influential—they opened doors and gave us credibility in the industry."

2. *"Get comfortable making decisions at Internet speed.* With competition breathing down your neck and customers demanding more ease and service from Internet sites, you have to adapt quickly."

3. *"Observe, but don't obsess over the competition.* We don't turn our business model around every time a competitor makes a change. If we did, we wouldn't get anything accomplished. Instead, we focus on our own business and try to make it the best it can be."

Eve.com: KEY STRATEGIC TAKE-AWAYS

- Problems and frustrations in daily life give rise to many a good business idea. When Naficy and Rao were working long hours as investment banking analysts, they didn't have time to go shopping. This frustration later turned into the inspiration for Eve.com.

- Build your network of contacts at every opportunity. Naficy and Rao expanded theirs and used it to get access to venture capitalists.

- If you have the opportunity, use a business incubator, especially if you're a first-time entrepreneur. In addition to office space and equipment, incubators provide invaluable access to advisers and other entrepreneurs. The time Naficy and Rao spent at idealab! allowed them to get intensive advice from Bill Gross and feedback from other entrepreneurs.

- If you're building an e-tail business, plan for the holiday crunch far in advance. For Eve.com, Christmas starts in the summer with strategizing to attract and prepare for the flood of customers that visit the site during the holiday shopping season.

- Multimillion-dollar ad campaigns aren't necessarily the most effective way to build Website traffic and a customer base. While Eve.com's successful TV ad campaign did get word out about the new brand, Naficy and Rao are directing more of their advertising budget to highly targeted print magazines because this has proved such an effective and less expensive way to attract new customers.

- When it comes to customer service, the little things count. In order to keep customers coming back, Eve.com gives out free samples with purchases, and supplies personalized gift and product advice.

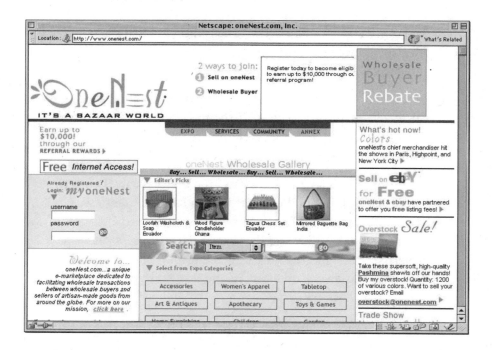

VITAL STATS

- Cofounder: Durreen Shahnaz, CEO
- URL: www.onenest.com
- Stock: Private
- Founded: 1999
- Headquarters: New York

oneNest

Linking Disadvantaged Artisans to Global Markets

"As a woman from Bangladesh, a poor Muslim country, starting a business never seemed like an option for me. But I wanted to do something in life to make a difference for people with limited opportunities. That's how oneNest came into existence."

—Durreen Shahnaz

GETTING GOODS TO MARKET IN RURAL BANGLADESH

Durreen Shahnaz perspired as she trekked out to a remote village in the Bangladesh district of Tangail. It was an August day in 1991, and the subtropical sun was beating down hard. She was making the journey to visit a woman to whom she had recently lent $30 so she could buy a loom and thread to start a modest business weaving colorful fabric. Before lending her the money, Shahnaz had first taught the villager how to write her name so she could sign the loan papers. "We practiced with a stick on the ground," says Shahnaz. "You should have seen her face when she signed her name and got her loan. She was so proud." Just a few years later the woman had ten weavers, including her husband and his three other wives, working for her.

This was a typical day for Shahnaz, who was an international development manager for Grameen Bank at the time. Her mission was providing microloans to poor landless women in rural Bangladeshi villages so they could start small businesses, including creating handcrafted products such as pottery, textiles, and clothing. The revolutionary bank, started by a Bangladeshi economics professor frustrated by the ineffectiveness of traditional rural economic development programs, makes microloans of $30 to $70 to voluntarily formed small groups of poor women. Since they can't provide collateral, the borrowers form a social contract: If one of them defaults, they're all cut off from future loans. The effect of the bank has included raising the status of its borrowers, decreasing their dependence on their husbands, and improving their children's nutrition.

Shahnaz's experience with Grameen Bank left a deep impression on her. She was struck by the beautiful textiles and other handicrafts created by the highly skilled women and by their incredible poverty. "I saw what a big difference a small amount of credit made to the otherwise destitute lives of these women," she says, noting that 80 percent of Bangladesh's people live below the poverty line. "Grameen Bank never told them what to do with the money. A transformation would occur when they found out that all they needed to do was make more money out of it. Every person has an entrepreneurial spirit, given the opportunity."

While the bank's microloans were making a positive difference in the women's lives, Shahnaz saw one major shortcoming: The bank didn't help the artisans get their goods to market. "These village women don't travel far from their homes," she explains. "If a woman uses a loan to buy chickens, her sons take the eggs to market." Shahnaz was convinced that, beyond credit, what these women most needed was an infrastructure for distributing their products to local and Western buyers.

ONE WORLD, ONE COMMUNITY

Shahnaz's experience with Grameen Bank was at the heart of her inspiration for creating oneNest, a New York–based Internet startup she cofounded in 1999 that lets artisans sell their goods to wholesale buyers on the other side of the world. Now, the 32-year-old entrepreneur's company is chipping away at trade barriers and empowering individual producers, regardless of the size of their business, to sell their handcrafted products to a global market.

While oneNest has the altruistic mission of helping alleviate world poverty, the company also aims to make a profit. Although online charity sites such as the Hunger Site (www.hungersite.com) are increasing in popularity, Shahnaz believes her venture will have a much greater impact as a for-profit corporation than as a nonprofit. "If we can be successful financially, we won't be dependent on other people's money and will be able to help many more people more quickly," she says. The company earns its keep charging sellers small fees to list and sell their products, and charges wholesale buyers subscription fees to access the site's product catalogs. She expects the company to turn a profit as early as 2002.

So it's helpful that oneNest's market is enormous: Handmade and independently produced goods represent a $50 billion market annually, and that's just in the United States. Globally, the market is $400 billion. And since it's intensely fragmented geographically (there are more than 380 million independent producers worldwide), oneNest and other Internet upstarts that aim to aggregate it have a big opportunity.

FROM BANGLADESH TO SILICON ALLEY

How did Shahnaz get from her home town of Dhaka, Bangladesh, to starting a promising dotcom in New York's Silicon Alley? From a young age she had an independent streak that her parents nurtured. "When I was born, I was the fourth daughter in a family with no sons. My family was hoping for a boy," she recalls. "My father felt so bad that all my relatives wanted me to be a boy that he gave me extra attention and latitude." Her feminist mother also encouraged her to be her own person—something unusual for girls in Bangladesh's traditional Muslim culture.

Shahnaz went to a strict all-girls school run by Catholic nuns, and, due to the rise in nationalism at the time, was educated in Bengali rather than English. "In school, I was always getting into trouble for questioning why we were doing things a certain way," she says, laughing. But her high school years were less trying because her family moved to the Philippines when her father, a government official, represented the Indian subcontinent to the Asian Development Bank there. So Shahnaz attended an American-style Philippine high school that didn't penalize her for her independent nature. In an effort to improve her English, she set and met an ambitious goal: to be editor of the school newspaper by her senior year. "Every morning I'd memorize 20 new words," she remembers.

When it came time to apply to college, Shahnaz had her heart set on going to school in the United States, but her parents expected her to attend college in India like her older sisters. After many arguments with her parents, they agreed to let her go, on the condition that she attend a women's college. Shahnaz picked Smith and graduated with a double major in economics and government. Afterward, she worked at Morgan Stanley for two years, where she bucked Bangladeshi convention yet again by falling in love and marrying an investment banker and New Jersey native, even though her parents were attempting to arrange her marriage at the time.

After her stint on Wall Street, Shahnaz returned to Bangladesh to work for Grameen Bank. "When I went back, I was working with women who hadn't ever been to a city and were having babies at age 12 or 13," she says. "I realized that my experience going to the States for my education and working on Wall Street had been an amazing opportunity."

A year later she returned to the United States, this time for graduate school. She earned an MBA from Wharton and an MA in international economics from Johns Hopkins, building the skills she'd find herself drawing on as the founder of oneNest. After working as a consultant for the World Bank and the Mitchell Madison Group, and as a bond trader at Merrill Lynch, she took a director position at Hearst Magazines International, managing their new magazines. Her talents were quickly recognized and she was promoted to vice president of Asia operations, making her, at age 30, the youngest VP at Hearst.

LEAVING THE CORPORATE NEST

Although she was a shining success in her career, Shahnaz was yearning to start her own business. Despite apprehensions about abandoning her successful career and putting her professional reputation on the line, she felt the time was right to start her venture to provide people around the world with a ready market for their handicrafts using the Net. After all, she reasoned, the Internet was growing at a phenomenal rate overseas. So she took a deep breath and walked into the office of George Greene, her boss and president of Hearst Magazines International, to tell him about her dream. He didn't want Hearst to lose Shahnaz, but he was very supportive. "He said that if I felt strongly about it, I should start my business, otherwise I'd regret it," recalls Shahnaz, who invited him to join oneNest's board.

Shahnaz then looked for business partners who believed in her mission and could help turn her dream into a reality. She approached her friend and former next-door neighbor in Bangladesh, Mushter Moin, who was managing editor of IBM's corporate Website. She also spoke with Victor Morgan, a friend and colleague from Mitchell Madison. Both men were so inspired by Shahnaz's idea that they quit their jobs to join oneNest as cofounders (Moin is CIO, Morgan is COO). They also had enough faith in the business concept that they were willing to work without pay until the business received outside funding, and, with Shahnaz, they contributed a total of $100,000 in seed money to help launch the beta Website.

After that, it didn't take Shahnaz long to bring together a diverse international group of professionals, including members with roots in Laos, Cuba, India, and the Ukraine. Like the founders, the people she hired initially were committed enough to work for free until the business got funding. "They believed in oneNest's mission of assisting disadvantaged communities around the world," Shahnaz explains. "They all worked with the belief that the idea was strong enough that it would eventually attract financing."

HATCHING A NEST EGG

Shahnaz knew $100,000 wasn't enough to get very far even with the founders and staff working pro bono. So in October 1999, four months after the business was founded, she pitched it to angel investors she knew from her days in investment banking and publishing. She was encouraged by how eager they were to lend a helping hand. Just six weeks later she closed a seed round of $1 million, giving 12.5 percent of the company to investors in exchange. "It was great to see that investors believed in my dream and passion," she says. "Having said that, raising the first round of financing is always the toughest. For every person who invested, there were two who didn't."

With the infusion of capital, the 18-person team recruited artisans, completed the site's back-end systems, implemented a MySQL database, designed the site, and launched oneNest's cyberbazaar in February 2000. At launch, the site featured a global fusion of more than 1300 products from every continent, including fine art, decorative items, home furnishings, clothing, and jewelry. (Shahnaz expected the number of products to surpass 20,000 by the time you read this.) Before the team had even begun promoting or advertising their virtual marketplace, the site was receiving more than 20,000 pageviews per day.

On the oneNest site, independent producers with access to a computer and the Internet can maintain their own product catalogs showcasing items along with stories about their cultural roots. Because many artisans in third-world countries don't have access to computers, Shahnaz has partnered with myriad small ethical exporters and nonprofit organizations that work directly with artisans, encouraging them to sell products made by their members on oneNest. The company has secured partnerships with humanitarian organizations—including the Asia Society, CARE, and PEOPLink—that share its mission of empowering individual producers, promoting fair trade, helping the impoverished, and preserving cultural traditions.

And oneNest has implemented a number of programs to serve the needs of sellers. Through a partnership with iShip, the company provides them with online tools for pricing and tracking shipments. And through a partnership with iEscrow, the site offers online escrow services so buyers don't have to pay until they've received and approved their items. Realizing that building trust between buyers and sellers is key—especially with transactions across borders—Shahnaz and company implemented a rating system that allows buyers and sellers to post feedback about each other. This system is helping ensure that buyers pay in a timely way and that sellers pack and ship items with care. "We can't solve the world trade problem, but we're doing what we can to make it a little easier," says Shahnaz.

The site offers wholesale buyers calendars of craft fairs and exhibits internationally. Artisans can indicate which events they'll attend and what they'll be selling, in case buyers want to visit their booths. Also, oneNest allows buyers to provide specifications for made-to-order items. Using reverse auction functionality, artisans can bid on these custom projects.

GETTING ARTISANS TO FLOCK TO ONENEST

While oneNest had more than 300 sellers signed on when the site was launched, Shahnaz knew her greatest challenge would be getting the word out and encouraging more artisans and wholesale sellers to register. To tackle this issue, she's partnering with portal sites around the world to distribute its services to a broad international audience. Because many artisans don't have Internet access, oneNest offers free ISP services in the United States, Canada, and Latin America, in partnership with 1stUp.com and quepasa.com. And oneNest plans to extend similar services to more international locations and is assembling a global network of "scouters" to contact artisans producing unique items and introduce them to the site.

To further draw new members, Shahnaz has instituted a cash reward program that allows anyone to earn $2.50 each time someone they've referred to oneNest registers. What's more, they receive one dollar each time one of their referrals refers someone else, and 50 cents for every new member *that* person refers. Site users can apply their cash rewards to purchases of merchandise from oneNest sellers. "Through this pyramid payment model, oneNest endeavors to entice anyone and everyone to spread the word about the site and earn a few dollars," says Shahnaz. Similarly, a commission-sharing program is in the works for anyone who refers more than 10 artisans.

By working with humanitarian organizations and reducing the number of intermediaries in a transaction, oneNest enables individual producers to earn a higher share of the value of their products than they otherwise would. Artisans who sell direct to wholesalers via the site keep

100 percent of the wholesale price of their products (minus a small listing fee and commission). Those selling through intermediaries (exporters and nonprofit organizations) get less—anywhere from 10 to 95 percent of the wholesale price. Because oneNest offers artisans and artisan organizations an opportunity to sell to a wide range of trade buyers, artisans typically earn at least 50 percent more than they would through the traditional sales channels available to them.

THE BUSINESS MODEL

While Shahnaz's initial vision for oneNest was a site enabling individual producers to sell products directly to consumers as well as to wholesale buyers, the artisans using the site provided the company with important feedback: Packing and shipping individual items was prohibitively time-consuming. They far preferred bulk orders, which were more lucrative. So in an effort to better serve their needs, Shahnaz shifted oneNest's focus. Instead of enabling sales to consumers, she's concentrating on enabling sales to all types of wholesaler buyers, including department stores, boutiques, and galleries.

While oneNest's new strategy is now focused on transactions between individual producers and wholesalers, it doesn't stop there. Shahnaz aims to have the company become the leading B2B e-commerce site for all aspects of producing handmade goods. To help reach this goal, the company is facilitating transactions between individual producers and raw materials suppliers.

Because oneNest doesn't carry inventory—sellers are responsible for shipping their merchandise—the company's overhead is low and its business is scaling fast. OneNest's diversified revenue streams fall into three categories: listing fees, commissions, and subscription fees.

Listing Fees

OneNest charges sellers fees to showcase their products on the site. To give sellers a risk-free chance to try oneNest, selling via the site is free for the first month. After that, they pay $30 a month to list up to 25 items, $75 to list up to 75 items, and $300 to list up to 1000 items. The average wholesale price of an item on the site is approximately $75, which makes these fees manageable for sellers. For those who want to sell individual items direct to consumers, oneNest has a partnership with eBay whereby oneNest sellers can auction items from their oneNest catalog off at eBay with a single click. For these types of sales, oneNest receives a share of the listing and transaction commissions.

Commissions

On top of listing fees, oneNest earns a slice of each transaction. For sales of less than $1000 to wholesale buyers, oneNest earns a five percent commission. For larger sales, it earns three percent.

The site allows artisans to keep an online inventory of the raw materials they need and then matches these needs with raw materials vendors. For example, tote bags made from saris are a popular item on oneNest. Shahnaz has signed up several sari manufacturers to use oneNest to sell fabric to the artisans that make the totes. The company collects a five percent commission for sales of raw materials.

Subscription Fees

The company earns revenue by charging wholesale buyers subscription fees to access the independent sellers' online catalogs. Once oneNest has fully ramped up operations, these fees are expected to account for more than half of the company's revenues.

FLYING PAST THE COMPETITION

Websites such as eZiba.com, Novica, and world2market.com also enable artisans and independent producers in less developed countries to sell directly to consumers in the first world. And while eBay, Yahoo! Store, and Amazon's zShops don't target artisans per se or cater to a global audience, they represent sales venues used by some independent producers. But oneNest stands out as the only site (at least for now) that enables artisans to sell in bulk directly to wholesalers.

Shahnaz's immediate business goals include licensing oneNest's wholesale catalog software. For large retailers, the company is creating customized, cobranded catalog sites that enable wholesale buyers to browse and make purchases from oneNest's catalogs on their own intranets. She's also focused on adding more services to make selling easier for independent producers. In the works are alliances with shipping and fulfillment companies to create neighborhood-based, drop-ship programs so artisans can outsource shipping and focus on creating their products.

Shahnaz also plans to create versions of the oneNest site in other languages and expand its services to wireless devices. These moves are critical since many of the artisans oneNest seeks to serve are located in non-English-speaking countries and around the globe in regions without wired Internet connections.

Despite all she's accomplished as an entrepreneur, Shahnaz's greatest thrill is helping others, as she did when she worked at Grameen Bank. She loves seeing the difference oneNest is making in people's lives. "One of our artisans from India showed us her hand-embroidered bedsheets," she says. "They were beautiful pieces of work. Now she's selling them to an upscale department store through oneNest."

Durreen Shahnaz's
TOP THREE LESSONS LEARNED

1. *"Don't start a business unless you feel passionately about it* with your heart and soul. Your motivation needs to be something other than making money, because there isn't enough money to compensate you for the stress of launching a Web startup."

2. *"Sell, sell, sell.* As a founder, you're the chief evangelist. Ninety percent of your job is to sell the company—its idea, goals, and potential—not only to investors but also to staffers."

3 *"Get the blessing of your spouse or significant other* before you plunge in. Without it, moving forward will be difficult because a Web venture is all-consuming."

oneNest: KEY STRATEGIC TAKE-AWAYS

- As a founding entrepreneur, plan to spend a large portion of your time raising money. One thing that took Shahnaz by surprise was how time-consuming raising capital turned out to be.

- Work your network. Shahnaz turned to her former investment banking and publishing colleagues when she needed advisers and investors.

- Recruit a core team that's deeply committed to the mission of your business. "At the end of the day, what keeps people at their company is their belief in what it's doing," she says.

- Convey your company's image and branding at every opportunity. The name oneNest underscores that the world is a small place—that everyone shares the same "nest." In oneNest's logo, each letter has a different style. It's meant to celebrate the diversity of the people who sell on oneNest and the uniqueness of their products.

- Be flexible about your strategy—you may need to shift or completely transform your business focus as you go. When Shahnaz learned that oneNest's producers preferred selling wholesale, she switched from B2C to B2B.

- Get creative when it comes to attracting a critical mass to your site. Among the methods oneNest is using to recruit artisans are cash incentives and local scouts.

VITAL STATS

- Cofounder: Andrea Reisman, CEO with chief product tester, Jack
- URL: www.petopia.com
- Stock: Private
- Founded: 1999
- Headquarters: San Francisco

14

Petopia

A New Kind of Bricks-and-Clicks Strategy

"I've been in and around growing companies all my life, and for all their turmoil and toil, I absolutely, passionately, adore them. They test every aspect of your person—your values, persuasiveness, intelligence, endurance, and interpersonal skills. And, in the end, they teach you what you're made of."

—Andrea Reisman

A DOG-EAT-DOG BUSINESS

No one knows better than Andrea Reisman that e-commerce is a cutthroat business. She's the CEO of Petopia, a pet-supply store and online "utopia" for pet lovers in one of cyberspace's most competitive and crowded sectors. And she's pulling ahead: Since Petopia's official site launch in August 1999, traffic has grown to more than 1.5 million unique visitors per month, placing it among the top 100 most popular shopping Websites. During the 1999 holiday shopping season traffic went through the roof. "We'd been live for just three months, and never in our wildest dreams did we imagine we would be that successful that fast," marvels Reisman. "Our CTO [the architect for Gap.com, babyGap.com, and GapKids.com] said he'd never seen traffic scale at the rate we were scaling." And Petopia is proving that kibble and collars can be successfully merchandised online: the high percentage of site visitors who make purchases—a conversion rate of 10 percent during promotions—is unusually strong for an online retailer.

True to its name, Petopia features a wealth of pet care information from vets and animal experts, along with discussion forums. A directory of groomers, pet sitters, vets, and pet-friendly hotels is a popular feature. The focus on pets continues at the company's trendy, industrial South-of-Market headquarters, where canines roam the halls, wagging their tails and chewing on treats. It's no wonder they're having a good time—they have their own onsite doggy playground. But man's best friend isn't the only kind of critter that's happy its owner works at Petopia. The offices are home to a Chinese water dragon, and several employee-owned guinea pigs and rabbits play in a cage worthy of rodent kings. Some desks are cluttered with Habitrails; others sport small aquariums.

But despite the fun-loving, animal-friendly environment, everyone at Petopia knows that working in dog time is part and parcel of building a successful e-commerce business—fierce competition has made for a frantic pace. "In our first 10 months we grew from eight people to 200. We raised over $100 million and created partnerships with PETCO and NBC," says Reisman, opening the conference room door to let in her Wheaton terrier, Jack, the company's chief product tester. "Our world has changed a lot in a very short period of time."

HITTING THE GROUND RUNNING

Since she first came upon her winning business idea, Reisman, already a seasoned entrepreneur at age 31, has been living in a nonstop whirlwind of money raising, team building, and deal making. A pro at running retail businesses, she couldn't resist pursuing an e-commerce venture—especially one related to pets. "I'd been in and around retail startups my whole life and had always loved dogs, so the category really clicked for me," she says.

When she researched the idea, the upside was clear. According to the American Pet Products Manufacturers' Association, 61 percent of U.S. households have at least one pet, and 41 percent have more than one. What's more, 74 percent of pet owners say they treat their animal companions as full-fledged family members—38 percent even admit to talking to their pets on the phone or leaving them messages on the answering machine. And while U.S. pet owners spent only $299 million online on pet supplies in 1999, Forrester Research predicts that sales will balloon to $4.5 billion by the end of 2004. What's more, when Reisman began investigating her idea, there were no major pet supply retailers online.

With facts like these to back up the concept, Reisman wrote a business plan, invested her personal savings, and raised a small amount of money from EcomPark, a Toronto-based angel fund recommended by a neighbor. All told, she had $300,000 in seed money. She packed a carry-on bag and flew from her home in New York to Oakland, California, in February 1999 to see whether Central Garden and Pet, a pet supply distributor, would consider an exclusive partnership. But much to her alarm, the distributor revealed that several other budding pet dotcoms, some of which had venture capital backing, had already come by with the same proposition. Since the startups were so young, they all seemed identical to the distributor, who decided to forgo partnering with any of them.

SWITCHING INTO UNDERDOG MODE

Reisman had brought only three changes of clothes for the short trip and was sleeping on a friend's sofa, but now she knew she'd need to stay longer. "It's very hard to compete with real venture-backed companies with only seed money—I realized I needed to raise capital fast," she recalls. She contacted Robert Zipp, a Silicon Valley–based startup adviser recommended by a business school friend, who introduced her to some Sand Hill Road venture capitalists. She made a pitch to five firms— Bessemer Venture Partners, Institutional Venture Partners, Sequoia Capital, U.S. Venture Partners, and AtVentures (CMGI's venture arm)—and all of them invited her back.

At the time, the VCs were in the midst of a feeding frenzy over the pets category, which they perceived to be the last large consumer e-commerce area up for grabs. One top-tier firm that Reisman prefers not to name made her an "exploding offer" for $4 million dollars that would detonate the next day. She had just 24 hours to decide whether to sign a letter of intent that guaranteed the investment firm the lead position in the first round of funding. Although she didn't appreciate the use of this tactic to preempt other investors, she didn't know whether a better offer would come through, so she accepted it.

By now Reisman's four-day trip to California had turned into a six-week crash course in capital-raising courtship. Exhausted but excited, she flew home on a red-eye flight, packed up her apartment and Jack, and flew back the next day to set up shop. She found an apartment, subleased office space from another startup, and started hiring. The first hires—designers and engineers—got to work and began developing Petopia's site at lightning speed.

But then a potential disaster struck. The promised $4 million never materialized. The venture firm had gotten cold feet when Amazon.com invested big bucks in rival Pets.com and reneged on the deal, but failed to be up front about it with Reisman. "They just kept delaying our funding date," she says. "They weren't honorable enough to say 'You know what? We've changed our minds.'"

REFUSING TO ROLL OVER AND PLAY DEAD

Reisman was in a pickle. She now had rent and employees to pay, and she had already called the four other venture firms she'd been in discussions with and told them she'd accepted another offer. Humbly, she went back to all of them and explained the situation. Three indicated that they might invest if she partnered with PogoPet, another dotcom. After talks with PogoPet's founder, David Fraze, the two fledgling startups decided to join forces under the Petopia name, with Reisman as CEO and Fraze as CFO. But again the investors balked.

At her wits' end, Reisman made her pitch to one more highly regarded firm, Technology Crossover Ventures (TCV). She said she needed an investor that wasn't afraid to compete with Pets.com head on. Impressed by her honesty, drive, and persistence, the firm closed a $9 million first round in May 1999. "I remember a senior partner saying, 'This is a huge bet on you,'" she recalls. "On the one hand, I felt exhilarated. On the other, I was petrified."

"Raising our first round of funding was scrappy, bloody, and miserable," acknowledges Reisman. It was so brutal, in fact, that *Forbes* decided to profile the company in a feature story about the trials and tribulations startups face when raising capital in Silicon Valley. "We managed to make lemonade out of lemons because we got great press out of the story," she says. "And, in some small way, it put out a warning to the venture community that they shouldn't treat first-time entrepreneurs that way."

At this point pet food and supplies was *the* new hot consumer category online, at least in the minds of VCs. The very next day after Reisman closed her round with TCV, the firm called to inform her that it was already time to pursue the second round. The competitive roar was intense, and marketing Petopia loudly enough to be heard over the din wasn't going to be cheap. This time the funding process went smoothly. Reisman pitched the business to venture firm Europ@Web (the Internet investment arm of Group Arnault), and it closed a second round a few weeks later. All told, Reisman secured an astounding $79 million before the company's Website had even been launched.

A NEW BEST FRIEND

In mid-1999, PETCO, the nation's number-two brick-and-mortar pet supplies giant, decided it didn't want to miss out on the e-commerce revolution. As a traditional company, though, it couldn't absorb the losses of launching its own e-commerce initiative, so it hired investment bank Morgan Stanley to evaluate 12 pet e-tailers and recommend one. Petopia was approached along with the 11 other candidates and asked for a proposal. The deal and dotcom PETCO liked best would become its new e-commerce partner, reaping tremendous benefits and gaining a clear advantage over competitors. The winner? Petopia. "We had an honest respect for the assets PETCO was bringing to the table," says Reisman. "So we were able to propose a deal that reflected our understanding of who they were, and that was compelling to them."

Overnight the deal catapulted Petopia into an online pet supplies leader. The startup got a warehouse-and-distribution infrastructure and

a real-world retailing channel. PETCO got an e-commerce sales channel
as well as a 26 percent stake in Petopia. The deal was a clear win for
Reisman: The company has the exclusive right to sell PETCO's products online, but isn't restricted to them. "We leverage PETCO's buying
power and distribution infrastructure, and they benefit by owning a
piece of our equity," explains Reisman. With the PETCO deal sealed,
Petopia was launched in August 1999, six months after the first
employee was hired.

AN ENTREPRENEURIAL PEDIGREE

Despite the pressures of competing at Internet speed, Reisman is calm
and collected. And it's no wonder: the class of '97 Harvard Business
School grad has a strong entrepreneurial background. Her mother and
father are two of Canada's best-known, most successful entrepreneurs.
Her mother started a chain of superstores in Canada called Indigo Books,
Music, & More. Helping build this business, Reisman got firsthand experience with the ups and downs entrepreneurs face. Her father founded
Onyx Corp., a diversified holding company that trades on the Toronto
Stock Exchange. Given that starting companies runs in her family, it's no
surprise that the first job she took after graduating from Dartmouth was
with the startup Cott Corporation, where she was quickly promoted to
run the company's $100 million beverage division.

Petopia's investors have been bowled over by Reisman's ability to execute fast. "The speed with which Andrea is growing Petopia makes it easily one of the fastest growing companies we've ever been associated
with," says Michael Linnert, general partner at Technology Crossover
Ventures, one of Petopia's investors. "She's extremely intelligent, has a
powerful vision, and is a great leader." And the company's investors
aren't the only ones who are rolling over for Reisman. In December
1999, *Forbes* chose her as one of eight people on their list of "Technology
Leaders of Tomorrow."

Despite her success, Reisman still turns to her mom and dad for
advice. "They understand that some days the sky's the limit and other
days the sky's falling," she says, adding that she also swaps insights and

advice with her well-connected business school classmates and her boyfriend Matt Johnson, founder of the textbook sales Internet startup BigWords.com.

BATTLE OF THE BRANDS

With so many pet supply e-tailers vying to lead the pack, Reisman's business savvy and experience are constantly being put to use. Pet e-tailers are spending furiously on national ad campaigns to imprint their brands in the American collective conscious. The problem? All the players have similar names; eight have the word *pet* in them. "Even the Pets.com sock-puppet campaign raised awareness of the industry in general, rather than an individual brand," says Forrester analyst Carrie Johnson.

But when it comes to the branding battle, Reisman has an advantage: She's building awareness of the Petopia name through kiosks in PETCO's 500 retail stores. She's also distinguishing her brand message from those of competitors by emphasizing the bond people have with animals. "Their site makes it clear that they are pet lovers; they're not just out to sell things," notes Johnson.

Reisman is advertising Petopia through both online and offline channels. The company has a weekly pet-care cable television show through a strategic alliance with NBC and ValueVision's SnapTV home-shopping network. Reisman also signed a $2 million deal with AOL to make Petopia an anchor tenant in its pet-shopping category and advertise on AOL properties. And she's inked advertising deals with Yahoo!, Excite@Home, iVillage, and others. Reisman's become very savvy about structuring ad deals. After noticing that online ad performance for some Web properties tended to drop off after the first month or two, she began incorporating 30-day-out clauses in advertising partnership agreements.

Petopia's branding campaign is showing positive signs of progress. Even though the site launched after Pets.com and Petsmart.com, its name recognition is high: In late 1999, PC Data Online ranked the site as a top-20 U.S. Web retailer among home Web users, and NextCard rated it the fastest-growing e-commerce business.

THE BUSINESS MODEL

Reisman was on to something big when she zeroed in on pets as a great consumer category. In the United States, pet supplies are a $23 billion industry, a market that's bigger than music and toys. Cat litter alone is a billion-dollar-a-year business. Worldwide, pet supplies are a $51 billion market that's growing 15 percent per year. Moreover, pet owners aren't especially price sensitive when it comes to pampering Fido—more than half of America's dog and cat owners regularly buy their pets gifts. High-end pet gifts—an additional market Petopia is pursuing—represent another $8 billion annually.

Petopia's sales channels are far more diversified than the run-of-the-mill pet e-tailer. "I really believe that the consumer of today and tomorrow is totally channel agnostic," says Reisman. "They just want to shop in whichever way is most convenient for them at the time." Customers can reach Petopia through the Website, kiosks in PETCO stores, the cable television show, or *In the Company of Dogs*, a mail-order catalog acquired in January 2000.

Approximately 40 percent of Petopia's revenue—which reached $3.5 million in the company's first year of operation— comes from pet food. One of Reisman's many smart marketing ideas is the Bottomless Bowl Subscription Service. Intended for time-crunched people who can't make it to the pet store or simply don't want to schlep a 40-pound bag of dog food home, this program allows a customer to specify the type and amount of food (or other recurring pet supply) needed, and have it shipped at regular intervals. This creates a predictable revenue stream for the company, and customers appreciate the convenience. "Dogs and cats eat the same amount every day," says Reisman. "Our business isn't particularly affected by seasonality or economic cycles." Reisman has also established a successful affiliate program that allows anyone with a Website to sell Petopia's products and earn up to a 10 percent commission and a five dollar referral fee for each new customer.

Petopia's commitment to its furry, feathered, and scaly friends isn't limited to making money by selling products, however. The company has altruistic goals as well: It has partnered with the ASPCA and Petfinder.com to encourage visitors to the Petopia site to consider adopting pets from shelters to decrease the need for euthanasia. The site also promotes spay and neuter programs.

WHO'LL BE PICK OF THE LITTER?

With the race for the online pet market so crowded, many Internet business analysts and investors are predicting a shakeout. "Not all players will survive," says Forrester's Johnson. "Some will be eaten by bigger fish." The sector's top three leaders include Petopia, pure play Web company Pets.com, and Petsmart.com, an online joint venture of brick-and-mortar chain Petsmart and idealab!, an Internet startup incubator. Although Pets.com was first to go public and is backed by e-commerce Goliath Amazon.com, Reisman views Petsmart.com as her chief rival, noting that it has a clicks-and-mortar strategy similar to Petopia's.

Analysts agree that the eventual winners will be businesses that have partnered with traditional companies for warehouse-and-distribution infrastructure. Shipping a bag of cat litter across the country isn't very profitable, but if you can ship it from a local distribution center, the shipping charges come way down. Petopia's partnership with PETCO is one of the key factors that, over time, will set Petopia a breed apart from pure play e-tail competitors like Pets.com.

Reisman makes no bones about the fact that she intends to take the company public as soon as she can—the company filed for its IPO in March 2000. Although she'd prefer to have more time to refine business operations before going public, she says the external pressures created by the heated competition in her niche won't allow for it. "Being a private company is a luxury, and one I wish we could afford for a long time," she says. "You have huge flexibility. A lot of people think of the IPO as the holy grail, but I don't see it that way at all. It's not an end game, it's just a financing event." But to secure a position that's heads and tails ahead of the rest, Reisman will need the currency of stock created through an IPO to make acquisitions that will further fuel Petopia's rapid expansion.

Reisman sees herself as a "serial entrepreneur," which isn't surprising for someone who knew by age 10 that she was destined for business school. She certainly has the stamina and energy to build multiple businesses—she routinely works 70-hour weeks and has twice completed the Boston Marathon. She envisions creating a series of businesses that delight customers. "Technology for its own sake isn't remotely interesting to me, but I really love the retail market," she confesses. "There's a good chance I'll start another Internet business, but whether online or off, it will be consumer oriented."

For now, Reisman is focused on the more immediate challenges of scaling her business faster than the competition, marketing her brand, and coming up with new, innovative ways of appealing to pet lovers. With her business smarts and keen customer focus, there's little doubt she has what it takes to make Petopia a top dog of pet supply e-tailing.

Andrea Reisman's
TOP THREE LESSONS LEARNED

1. *"Only work with people you trust.* That includes partners, investors, employees, bankers, accountants, agencies, and lawyers . . . everyone!"

2. *"Expect a roller coaster.* Your success won't be measured by your ability to avoid the downs, but rather by your ability to absorb the mercurial nature of the entrepreneurial experience while projecting confidence and calm."

3. *"Share the company's equity generously with your team members.* If your company succeeds, there will be plenty of reward for everyone. If it fails, having saved a few percent won't help you."

Petopia: KEY STRATEGIC TAKE-AWAYS

- Invest some seed money in your own business if you can. Why? According to Reisman, "It communicates a willingness to put your money where your mouth is. It doesn't have to be a lot of money, but it has to be something that's significant to you."

- If your business isn't funded and you're located where competition for office space is stiff, consider subleasing instead of renting your own space. This way you won't need to compete for space with already-funded businesses, which landlords prefer.

- Don't assume that signing a term sheet means you'll get funded. "VCs are so competitive for deals that things have been flip-flopped," observes Reisman. "First, they put down a term sheet to lock you up and buy themselves some time, and then they do due diligence on the company and category."

- Partner for what you need rather than building it from scratch. Petopia was only able to grow big fast enough to keep up with competitors by partnering with PETCO.

- Consider whether multiple distribution channels—including brick-and-mortar ones—work best for your category. For Petopia, a combination of sales channels is a good fit.

- Analyze your customer segments and fine-tune your business to focus on the most profitable ones. "If the customer is expensive to acquire and only buys items on sale, they're not the type you want to target," says Reisman.

VITAL STATS

- Founder: Felicia Lindau, CEO
- URL: www.sparks.com
- Stock: Private
- Founded: 1998
- Headquarters: San Francisco

15

Sparks.com

Creating a New E-Tailing Category

> *"I always knew I wanted to have my own business. I studied marketing and business in college and have always felt like an entrepreneur waiting to happen."*
>
> —Felicia Lindau

A HOT STARTUP

Sparks.com is on fire. The company, founded by Felicia Lindau, envisions a not-too-distant future in which it's the cyberstore where all netizens stop to buy paper greeting cards. Having already achieved "category killer" status by creating a brand-new type of Web business, the site offers a selection of more than 13,000 competitively priced cards from hundreds of quality card publishers. If you're looking for a card with a certain image or specific to an occasion, the search engine and navigation make it easy to quickly find the perfect one.

If you don't have time to pen your message, add a stamp, and mail the card yourself, a Sparks.com scribe can do it for a dollar. You can upload your existing desktop or Web-based address book from Microsoft Outlook, Palm software, Yahoo!, or Excite. If you enter your list of important birthdays, Sparks.com will keep you at your social best, emailing you reminder notes like "Alexandra's birthday is Friday." And, if you find a card you'll want to send eventually, you can store it, too, which makes it easy to order it when you're ready.

If you need to send a gift in a pinch, Sparks.com can help there as well. You can pick up flowers or choose a gift certificate from more than

50 major retailers, including The Gap, Barnes and Noble, and Wine.com. Lindau is betting that time-strapped consumers won't be able to resist the site's convenience and will embrace a brave new cyberworld in which the cards we send are not necessarily cards we've ever touched ourselves.

A SPARK OF INSPIRATION

From whence did the seed for such a revolutionary business idea come? In July 1997, Lindau was working as an account supervisor at the advertising agency Foote, Cone, and Belding, where she helped launch the Excite and Amazon.com brands. Her Internet-speed career left her no time to shop for a gift for her mom's birthday. At the time, her mother was having a pier built on a lake at the family's Texas ranch where Lindau's father, who died in 1988, is buried. After a quick click over to Amazon.com, Lindau found an ideal gift: a beautiful coffee-table book about piers.

Lindau was impressed with her Amazon.com shopping experience. "I was able to find something so personally valuable," she reflects. "I could have searched for months offline for that book and never found it."

Driving home from work late that same summer night, Lindau was congratulating herself about the great gift she'd purchased when she realized she hadn't bought a card. The drugstores had closed, and paper cards weren't available on Amazon.com. There was no way she'd be able to send one in time. But happily, this moment of frustration led to inspiration. "Intense and sudden inspiration," says Lindau.

Her inspiration was so overwhelming that she had to pull off the road right then and there as the entire vision for Sparks.com flashed before her eyes. "My head felt like it was about to explode with all the possibilities. My whole body heated up," she recalls. "I grabbed a piece of scrap paper from my messy car floor and starting mapping out the whole idea. I'd say that 90 percent of our present business model came to me in that one instant."

This was the genesis of Sparks.com—and a new consumer e-commerce category. What happened next typifies the sturm und drang of launching a hot new Web startup—marketing hurdles, technical challenges, and marathon bouts of pitching to VCs.

GETTING THE BUSINESS OFF THE GROUND

Inspired by her vision, Lindau was raring to launch the business. She was 31 at the time and had already racked up 11 years of experience as an advertising and marketing professional with an Internet-heavy résumé that would give any Silicon Valley headhunter goose bumps. Her experience in technology marketing, and as a dutiful card and gift buyer for family and friends, made her certain that the Sparks.com concept was the right opportunity, and that she was the person to seize it.

After taking a UC Berkeley night class on how to write a business plan and raise money, she crafted a plan full of relevant data, which she knew like the back of her hand as a result of her work on the Amazon.com account, and then she fearlessly quit her job. "I was so impassioned by my idea that I was more afraid *not to do* the business than *to do* it," she says.

Lindau enlisted friends who were excited to sign up for the high-risk, high-reward opportunity that Sparks.com offered. Lindau called Jason Monberg, a longtime friend who was a lead engineer at CKS, an interactive design agency. Although she'd called to get his advice about the technical costs of launching Sparks.com, she was amazed when he volunteered that he was ready and willing to abandon his fast-track career and join forces. Lindau jumped at the chance to bring him on board as cofounder and CTO. She knew his technical talents were top notch because she'd seen them in action—they'd worked together several years earlier as founding members of the Interactive Group at Anderson and Lembke advertising.

So Lindau and Monberg incorporated the company in May 1998 and began developing the Website, back-end systems, and marketing plan. Lindau hired her sister to head up customer service, as well as a card buyer to establish relationships with card publishers. With Monberg focused on the technical details, Lindau was free to work her marketing wizardry.

CALLING ON FRIENDS, FAMILY, AND . . . BENCHMARK

That fateful spring, Lindau approached her friends and family members to find out whether they knew of potential investors or were interested in investing themselves. Her progress was swift: By June 1998 her mother, a friend's father, and a software supplier who wanted to land Sparks.com's business had contributed a total of $250,000. Next she hired a contract CFO to help her raise funding, since she had few, if any, contacts in the capital community.

She and her temporary CFO identified the best venture capital sources and began pitching to them relentlessly. "We must have sent the business plan to 100 angels and VCs," she estimates. "I must have made 100 calls a day."

Lindau recalls that she did encounter some overt gender bias while seeking funding. "One VC advised me to get a 'front man,' and then went so far as to fax me the résumés of potential candidates," says the CEO. Determined to carry Sparks.com until the business secured funding from institutional investors, she took out a loan against her house. Finally, after six months, a prospective Sparks.com partner introduced her to Kevin Harvey at Benchmark Capital, who in turn introduced her to Bob Kagle, who, seeing a bright future for gift-related portals, decided to invest. Together, Benchmark and Venture Strategy Group closed a $3.5 million first round of financing for Lindau's new company.

After all that, what's Lindau's take on the funding process? "Getting funded was tedious and exhausting, but I'm glad it wasn't any easier," she says. "I learned so much during that time, and I honed the business model and pitch so well that it continues to serve me now."

WAREHOUSE CHIC

With their first round of funding secured, Lindau and Monberg set up the company's headquarters in San Francisco's industrial India Basin district and began staffing up. All aspects of Sparks.com's business coexist in one 15,000-square-foot, yawning warehouse. Employee desks, which are fashioned out of doors and sawhorses, are at one end of the floor. Rack after rack of greeting cards are at the other. Packing and shipping is in one corner, while gift boxes of chocolates are stored in a large closet.

The atmosphere is playful and bustling. The company's 60-plus employees can slide down a fire pole from a makeshift loft that was added to provide more space for desks. Dogs are welcome (Lindau brings in her Samoyed, Sputnik) and employees brainstorm from the comfort of neon orange, yellow, and green beanbag chairs. When employees look up from their monitors, they see a large mural of faces representing Sparks.com's customers and their reactions when receiving the perfect card: surprised, happy, laughing, touched.

Building a Website with an intuitive user interface and first-rate customer experience is tricky enough, but accurately shipping thousands of cards each day to the correct recipient from the correct sender is a major hurdle. But under Monberg's technical leadership, the company was able to tackle these challenges and launch the site on December 10, 1998.

Sparks.com's back-end systems allow customers to easily perform complex tasks, like sending the same card to several people. The site's proprietary search engine allows for fine, detailed keyword searches that make sifting through thousands of cards easy. "Our secret sauce is data entry," says Lindau. "Our database captures a million different shades of gray about the tone and style of our cards. Several hundred data points are entered for each one." Enter the keywords *ocean* and *romance*, for example, and the site produces images of half a dozen romantic cards that incorporate the word *ocean* or an ocean scene.

So what inspired the Sparks.com name? At first Lindau wanted to name the company *Jot* to highlight the site's convenience, but the name didn't go over well in focus group tests. Testers preferred a name that emphasized developing better relationships. So Lindau chose Sparks.com, which refers to the "spark" between people when they connect emotionally. "I must have been going through an 'sp' phase," she says. "I named Sputnik around the same time."

REWRITING THE RULES

From the beginning, Lindau strove to make card buying easy. We all know that buying cards the old-fashioned way is a time-consuming exercise in frustration. The average brick-and-mortar drugstore provides only 300 to 600 cards, which are meant to appeal to the widest number of people and often come from just one major publisher. Browsing for the right card can take eons, and you may not even find a suitable one.

So Lindau has rewritten the rules of card shopping. The company's huge selection puts drugstore card racks to shame. And Sparks.com never closes—you can buy a card day or night. The company is distinguishing itself is through immaculate customer service. The site guarantees same-day mailing, and employees wear surgical gloves when they handle cards to prevent smudges and fingerprints. The company's many scribes are selected for their fine penmanship. Lindau hopes Sparks.com's focus on delighting customers—a point where many e-tailers flounder—will help ensure its long-term success.

FANNING THE FIRE

In June 1999, with Sparks.com's order volume growing at a clip of 30 percent per month and profitability projected for 2003, Benchmark, Venture Strategy Group, and two other firms invested a $12 million second round of funding. With this second round, investors got a 50 percent stake in the company for their money.

Sparks.com is using the cash to ramp up the business as quickly as possible to keep up with its swelling customer demand. (The company was selling more cards per day in December 1999 than it sold during the entire 1998 holiday shopping season.) They've recruited an executive staff and are hiring new employees as quickly as they can find qualified applicants—no small task given the Bay Area's shortage of technical talent.

What marketing and promotion techniques is Sparks.com using to get the word out? A whole lot of everything: television, radio, newspaper advertising, online advertising, direct mail, and email. Because women make 90 percent of card purchases, Sparks.com's online ad campaign targets sites—such as MarthaStewart.com and WeddingChannel.com—that are heavily trafficked by women.

Sparks.com has had great success with its affiliate marketing program initiated in April 1999. By early 2000 the company had more than

10,000 affiliates. The affiliate program, which is promoted on the Sparks.com site, lets anyone with a Website earn money by selling Sparks.com's cards and gifts. Affiliates earn a one-dollar commission for every item they sell. "We've been very diligent in seeking out a wide range of affiliates to act as ambassadors for Sparks.com," says Lindau. "Launching our affiliate program was like opening thousands of retail stores."

The company has also had success with its guerrilla marketing tactics. It employs "card girls" who walk around crowded public areas, such as San Francisco's Union Square, before holidays, wearing huge hats outlandishly decorated with the holiday's theme and carrying modified 1950s-style cigarette cases filled with free Sparks.com-branded cards that they hand out to passersby. In the early days of Sparks.com, Lindau, her husband, a friend, and Sparks.com's public relations director donned the "card girl" hats themselves and staked out the *Today Show*. They handed out cards and coupons to the throng of people standing outside New York's Rockefeller Center, where the show is filmed. It was their great luck that on the day they stormed the crowd, the show featured a segment on dotcom advertising stunts. Lindau got a shot on the show with the Sparks.com logo prominently displayed on her huge hat and a crowd of people standing around her waving paper greeting cards.

It should come as no surprise that one of the company's favorite guerrilla marketing tactics is sending out cards. When someone at the company hears about an influential person doing something to make a positive difference in the world, they'll send them a card with a note about it. "This simple act has accomplished a lot for the company, from generating press coverage to initiating our first contact with one of our board members," says Lindau.

So, how does Lindau keep on top of the latest e-commerce trends and marketing tactics to ensure that Sparks.com's competitive edge is razor sharp? She networks a lot and finds that the best insight and advice come from the CEOs and founders of other dotcoms. "We're all learning the same lessons at the same time, and have a lot of data to share and compare," she explains.

THE BUSINESS MODEL

Selling greeting cards online may not sound like the stuff from which Net fortunes are made. The ticket price per item is miserably low. But the greeting card market is huge: Americans send more than 7.4 billion cards each year, spending $7.6 billion on them.

Greeting cards are a high margin business: The retail price of cards can be as much as 65 percent higher than the bulk wholesale price. What's more, the average greeting card consumer is a repeat customer who buys 30 to 40 cards each year—which means each new Sparks.com customer has a high average lifetime value. And unlike products such as cars and computers, which are bought infrequently, cards are like books or CDs, something most people buy again and again. In fact, 11 percent of Sparks.com's customers buy multiple times each month. Plus, cards are lightweight and easy to ship—an important factor for e-tailing businesses.

Sparks.com isn't solely focused on cards either. It's going after a slice of the $40-billion-per-year gift market. Their gift selection is currently limited to flowers and gift certificates (which the company buys for 85 to 95 cents on the dollar), but Sparks.com is aggressively pursuing many other gift retailing opportunities and will move into personalized gift marketing. With gifts, the company's estimated total market is greater than $50 billion.

ALONE IN THE COMPETITIVE LANDSCAPE

Sparks.com has the luxury of having few direct competitors. Most online greeting card sites offer electronic, not paper, cards. These sites, like Egreetings.com and Blue Mountain Arts, attract huge amounts of traffic because electronic cards are free.

Sending paper cards is still considered more personal and thoughtful than emailing an electronic greeting, which can be perceived by many as an unwanted time waster. While Sparks.com doesn't view e-card businesses as direct competitors, new upstarts like Snailgram.com are entering the paper card game.

And Lindau is keeping close tabs on the top card sellers offline, such as Hallmark, which together with American Greetings holds an 80 percent share of the greeting card market. But while Hallmark has initiated some e-commerce efforts related to gifts, they haven't embraced the Internet as a way to market individual cards to consumers in a very personalized way. For example, during the holidays in 1999, Hallmark.com sold only box sets of cards. "We have no plans to sell individual cards online," says a Hallmark spokeswoman. "We view our online effort as a way to extend our brand and as a retail channel for boxed cards and gifts." One likely reason is that brick-and-mortar greeting card giants would face big channel conflicts with retailers if they were to sell their cards direct to consumers online.

To work around this problem, American Greetings has actually partnered with Sparks.com, which sells paper cards from American Greetings along with cards from hundreds of different card publishers through AmericanGreetings.com, and handles all order fulfillment. With this exclusive arrangement signed, sealed, and delivered, Sparks.com has a huge new sales channel. As part of the alliance, Sparks.com also offers American Greetings' electronic cards over its own site.

Apparently, some executives from traditional greeting card companies are literally taken by Sparks.com. For instance, Thomas Johnston, a Hallmark executive and 17-year industry veteran, joined Sparks.com's board of directors.

The one competitor Lindau does worry about is—you guessed it—Amazon.com. "They're rolling out all the departments of a Wal-Mart, but haven't hit cards yet," she explains. Amazon.com, however, could also prove to be more friend than foe. There's no reason that Sparks.com wouldn't be an attractive partner or acquisition for the e-tail giant down the road.

WHAT'S IN THE CARDS?

Lindau has ambitious plans to increase the site's reach through partnership and sponsorship opportunities. A sign of what's to come: Sparks.com partnered with iVillage in late 1999 in a deal that made

Sparks.com the exclusive paper greeting card provider within the iVillage shopping network. The deal allows Sparks.com to market its cards to iVillage's predominantly female user base through sponsorship placements and advertising. Sparks.com also advertises through Snap, Excite, Ask Jeeves, and EarthLink, among others, and has several e-commerce partnerships in the works.

Although Sparks.com is currently focused on developing its service in the United States, it's also already shipping 10 to 15 percent of its orders internationally. Dealing with international e-commerce issues is a can of worms, unfortunately. There are customs and trade challenges, as well as technical ones such as designing Sparks.com to accommodate all types of international address forms. But Lindau says the company will clear these hurdles in due time.

Lindau and Monberg share the vision of growing Sparks.com into a brand and business that will continue to flourish a century from now. In a fast-moving sector where planning beyond the next few months is next to impossible, this degree of long-term thinking is a refreshing anomaly. Who knows? With Sparks.com's first mover status, blazing success, and lack of significant competitors, achieving permanent status as a top e-tailer could be in the cards.

Felicia Lindau's
TOP THREE LESSONS LEARNED

1. *"Don't be afraid to make mistakes.* Things are bumpy along the road, but you need those bumps in order to learn."

2. *"Collaborative decision making is critical.* Achieving employee support is more cumbersome than making a straight decision, but it pays to give everyone ownership. Then plans are executed with more heart and a higher degree of care."

3. *"Execution is harder than discovering opportunity by a factor of 10.* Discovering a winning business idea is a rush, but executing on that idea requires a tremendous amount of energy and full commitment."

Sparks.com: KEY STRATEGIC TAKE-AWAYS

- Use affiliate marketing. Sparks.com's program has extended its reach to more than 10,000 Websites, and this number is growing every day. The company uses LinkShare (www.linkshare.com), a provider of affiliate marketing services to administer its program. LinkShare tracks sales by affiliates and sends them their commission checks on behalf of Sparks.com.

- Seek out your peers in a noncompetitive Internet space for the best strategic and tactical advice. In the Internet space, you won't find many older, wiser mentors.

- Focus on employee retention. Lindau says her employees frequently receive cold calls from recruiters trying to hire them away. With the technology labor market so hot, it's critical that your business makes keeping employees a priority. Institute a company culture that's fun and empowers workers.

- Don't wait too long to hire senior staff. If you have the capital resources, bring them on board early in the game to help solidify the core team and fuel the company's growth.

- Weigh the consequences of outsourcing aspects of your site's development. The firms you outsource to may not share your objectives. Sparks.com learned to outsource development very judiciously. "Design and development firms want to complete the project as quickly as possible with the smallest investment satisfying the most narrowly defined goals of the project," says Lindau.

- Provide merchandise and content tailored to the individual customer. In Sparks.com's new baby channel, for example, a customer buying a congratulations card for a new dad can also be offered a gift certificate for babyGap. Take advantage of nuanced cross-selling opportunities.

VITAL STATS

- Cofounder: Veronica Allende Serra, chairwoman
- URLs: www.supervertical.com.br www.superbid.com.br
- Stock: Private
- Founded: 1999
- Headquarters: São Paulo, Brazil

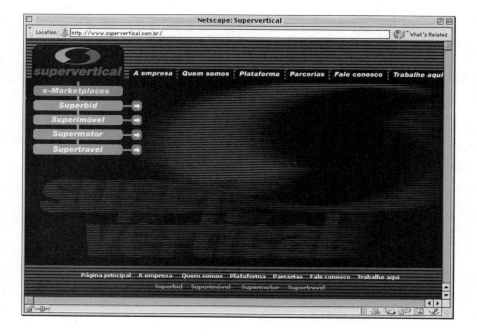

16

SuperVertical

E-Markets for Latin America

*"Believing in a vision, putting all my energy into it, and seeing
it work out is the most rewarding thing to me."*

—Veronica Allende Serra

BRAZIL'S DIGITAL POWERHOUSE

Although you've probably never heard her name, Veronica Allende Serra
has helped launch more than a dozen Internet companies as an adviser,
investor, and, more recently, a founding entrepreneur. Only 31 years old,
she's one of the most well connected among Latin America's Internet
elite. To hear Serra talk, you'd think she was a Silicon Valley native. Her
latest endeavor: SuperVertical, a 50-plus-employee company that's growing fast as it rolls out vertical online marketplaces in Brazil and other
Latin American countries.

SuperVertical's digital marketplaces connect buyers and sellers in
specific industries—computers, travel, and office equipment, for
instance—allowing them to easily transact online. A word on jargon: In
the evolving lingua franca of e-business, digital marketplaces go by several names, including *e-markets*, *online trading communities*, and *Net
markets*. Think of them as eBays for B2B commerce—places where
many business sellers and buyers exchange goods and services. The market Serra is initially targeting—businesses and consumers in Brazil—is
a big one. According to a study by the Boston Consulting Group and Visa,

Brazil accounted for a staggering 88 percent of Latin America's consumer e-commerce spending in 1999.

With free Internet access a widespread trend among local ISPs, Internet use in this part of the world is exploding. "Latin America is the next virtual frontier," predicts Serra, noting that people in Latin America, especially Brazil, are increasingly turning to the Internet to do research, find entertainment and travel information, shop, and catch up with friends through email and online chat. The numbers confirm the Brazilian phenomenon. Brazil accounts for nearly half of Latin America's online population, which was 13.3 million in 2000 and is expected to rocket to 29.6 million by 2004.

While Serra is confident that there are huge opportunities for Internet entrepreneurs in Latin America, she concedes that starting a business in Brazil also has its challenges: "Things in the U.S. are easier because there's more infrastructure. For example, if we want telephone lines, it takes over a month to get them. In the U.S., it takes just a couple of days."

THE BIRTH OF SUPERBID

The seed for Superbid, the company Serra cofounded in 1999 that would later become SuperVertical, was first planted at a birthday party when she bumped into some old high school friends—Rodrigo and Ronaldo Sodré Santoro. The brothers were auctioneers at one of Brazil's most highly regarded auction houses. Inspired by the success of eBay, they wanted to create an online version of their brick-and-mortar auction business. But to get the business off the ground, they needed top-notch partners with connections to the Internet and financial communities.

Enter Serra. Born in Santiago to a Brazilian father and Chilean mother, she's lived in several different countries and speaks fluent Portuguese, Spanish, English, French, and Italian. After graduating from Harvard Business School in 1997 (which she attended on a full scholarship), she served as a vice president at the investment firm Leucadia National Corp., where she analyzed investments in Latin America,

Europe, and Asia. After two years at Leucadia, she joined International Real Returns (IRR), a private equity fund where she was a partner overseeing Latin American investments. She was also acting as an adviser on Brazilian strategic alliances to the Argentina-based Internet startup Patagon.com, the first online stock brokerage and finance portal in South America. Her mix of Net know-how and financial savvy made her just the type of partner the Santoros needed.

Intrigued by their idea for an online auction house, she invited them to her home to talk. When her husband, Alex Bourgeois, joined the conversation, he was excited about the concept as well. After brainstorming about the idea of a consumer-to-consumer auction site, Serra suggested that there might be much broader auction markets to tap: those of business-to-consumer and business-to-business. With her finger on the pulse of new e-commerce directions, she could see an auction market that would enable all types of Brazilian suppliers to sell their inventory at a discount directly to consumers and other businesses. "I thought people would be uncomfortable buying used items over the Web," she explains. "And the margins for new items are higher."

So, in October 1999, she and Bourgeois joined forces with the Santoros to create Superbid, Brazil's first B2C and B2B auction Website. "At some point, the four of us were sitting in front of the fireplace at my house and we just said, 'Okay. Let's do it,'" says Serra.

Serra got to work researching the market and writing the business plan, and the four cofounders set up shop in a small office in Serra and Bourgeois's home. Serra, who had savings from her investing success, and the other cofounders put up a combined $500,000 to get Superbid off to a running start. "We all put in as much as we could, with the understanding that we'd even things out once our first round of funding came in," she says.

TECHNICAL TALENT AND BIG-NAME PARTNERS

The four founders knew they couldn't achieve their dream without top-notch technical talent, so they contacted two whizzes who had been instrumental in shaping and running J.P. Morgan's back-end securities trading infrastructure in Brazil and invited them to join Superbid, which they did. The core team moved quickly to partner with suppliers and create a Website with the technical mettle to handle a high volume of secure online transactions and payments. "Time-to-market was a high priority," says Serra, who wanted to be the first to stake a claim when she saw that Superbid's market was up for grabs. "There was a lot to do in a short amount of time. We needed to secure a large number of partnerships and implement a solid technology solution to make our concept fly."

The team's initial strategy was to focus on expensive, high-margin new products such as DVD players, home appliances, and computers. Serra approached brand-name multinational suppliers such as Apple, Canon, and IBM, as well as local companies selling airline tickets. She negotiated partnership arrangements whereby suppliers would auction or sell their products on the Superbid site and handle order fulfillment and delivery. For its part, Superbid would earn an average commission of five percent on items sold. Suppliers were eager to sign up since Superbid offered them the opportunity to sell direct to customers, allowing for higher profit margins, rather than going through traditional distribution channels, which, for these types of goods, are highly concentrated in Brazil.

UNIBANCO MAKES A BID

Concerns about fraud and misrepresented merchandise have made many Web users in Latin America wary about shopping over the Internet. Aware that businesses and consumers would shy away from Superbid if they weren't confident that payment processing was reliable and secure, Serra contacted Unibanco, Brazil's third-largest private bank, to see if they'd partner to function as the site's escrow officer and help develop the payment processing infrastructure. To reassure buyers, Serra envisioned having Unibanco hold each payment made via Superbid until the purchased item was delivered. "We decided we didn't want to be an eBay," says Serra. "We wanted Superbid to handle clearing and didn't want buyers and sellers finalizing deals. By clearing transactions, we were assured of getting our commisions."

This decision was a smart one. Unibanco was so intrigued by the Superbid concept that it decided to become a strategic partner and invested to the tune of $2 million. Having Unibanco on board was the stamp of approval Superbid needed to make Brazil's security-conscious consumers more comfortable with the idea of buying online. With this investment, the founding team started hiring, recruiting developers heavily from Brazil's top technical university, Universidade de Minas Gerais. The company initially rented a 500-square-foot office, but grew so fast that it had to move to an office 10 times the size just a couple of months later.

LET THE AUCTIONS BEGIN

The Superbid site was launched in April 2000, just six months after the business was founded—amazingly quick considering all the partnerships Serra had to make with suppliers, and the technical infrastructure that needed to be developed by the engineering team. "We couldn't believe how far we had come," says Serra. "More than 1000 people came to our launch party."

It didn't take long for word to spread about the great deals to be had at Superbid. Discounts on overstocked or clearance products bought on the site sometimes run as high as 80 percent. Buyers can make purchases as individuals or join buying groups to reap even greater cost savings. Through its partnership with Unibanco, Superbid offers a secure payment system that accepts credit cards and money transfers.

Here's how the process works: If, for example, a medium-size law firm in São Paulo orders 30 Toshiba notebook computers through Superbid, the law firm sends payment to Unibanco, which holds onto the money until the law firm receives the 30 computers. Unibanco then transfers the payment to the computer supplier minus a percentage retained for Superbid as a commission for its involvement in the transaction.

When it comes to customer service, Serra's taking steps to make sure the site is tops. Customers receive most products two to seven days after purchase, and they can track their shipments over the Website. Plus, they can access customer support anytime day or night, online or by phone. The result of all these features has been traffic and customers: Just weeks after the launch, the Superbid site was logging more than 80,000 pageviews per day.

The site serves the needs of its suppliers and business customers as well as it serves those of consumers. At Superbid, businesses can sell items either at a set price or via auction or reverse auction. (Reverse auctions, popularized by Priceline.com, allow buyers to indicate how much they're willing to pay for an item, and let sellers bid on their business.) The site's technology platform, based on an Oracle database and TIBCO middleware, integrates with suppliers' enterprise resource planning and back-office systems, which enables suppliers to access inventory management tools via Superbid.

GOING ONCE, GOING TWICE, GOING VERTICAL

After the launch, Serra and Bourgeois were surprised to see that the vast majority of Superbid's buyers were businesses, not consumers. "Most of the buyers were small companies that would buy 100 desktops or 200 monitors in bulk," says Serra. Also unexpected were numerous requests from the site's brand-name suppliers for an Internet solution they could use to purchase items from their own suppliers and business partners.

"Because Superbid's infrastructure integrates all the way back to the suppliers' warehouses and allows for group buying, auctions, reverse auctions, and direct sales, we *had already created* a B2B marketplace platform without realizing it," explains Serra. "Our platform, our alliance with Unibanco, and what we had achieved with Superbid was so unique that we had to use it for other opportunities."

With this new understanding, Serra and company reoriented their strategy. Instead of concentrating solely on auctions, their goal became creating digital marketplaces for specific industries. To accommodate all these marketplace portals, which would function as separate businesses, the founders incorporated SuperVertical, a holding company for a variety of vertical marketplace subsidiaries. Superbid became the computer and electronics marketplace under SuperVertical's umbrella, rather than the be-all and end-all of their business. Marcelo Marinis became Superbid's CEO, and Serra, who had been CEO, took the role of chairwoman of SuperVertical, overseeing business development, strategy, and fund-raising for all the vertical industries the company is pursuing.

This ambitious new direction puts SuperVertical in a whole new league. Rolling out vertical markets for cars and real estate is at the top of Serra's list. "Unibanco and other banks have large inventories of repossessed cars and property foreclosures that they need to sell quickly," she says. "Currently, it's really expensive to sell them and get word out to potential buyers. You can reach a lot more people online." Other markets on Serra's radar include travel, textiles, home appliances, and raw materials.

THE BUSINESS MODEL

Because SuperVertical doesn't stock any inventory itself, its operating costs are low. Beyond commissions, the company earns revenue by licensing its technology. It charges high-volume suppliers monthly licensing fees of $10,000 to $15,000 to sell products simultaneously through Superbid and their own Websites using Superbid's infrastructure. This gives suppliers a new e-commerce revenue stream as well as access to information about their online customers. SuperVertical captures detailed information about bid activity and sales, which suppliers can use to test prices and gauge demand for specific products. For example, if customers repeatedly bid on high-end speakers but only up to a particular price, this can tip the supplier off to the fact that there's demand for a less expensive, similar product.

An additional revenue stream for SuperVertical is ad sales. The company sells banner and box advertising space on its sites, as well as sponsorships in specific e-commerce categories. And, when Super-Vertical creates an e-commerce area on a supplier's site, it earns a share (usually 50 percent) of any advertising revenue generated.

While there are other auction sites in Brazil and the rest of Latin America (DeRemate.com and MercadoLibre.com, for example), they tend to focus on consumer-to-consumer transactions, and as a result can't easily guarantee payment or delivery. Superbid was among the first sites in Latin America to integrate and automate seamless online transactions. "After a customer wins an auction or clicks to purchase a product, there's a stream of communication between the bank (which functions as a clearing agent), the supplier, the delivery company, the call center, and the customer," Serra says.

Because the B2B e-commerce market in Latin America is so attractive, rivals are springing up fast. Among the most noteworthy are IndustriaLatina.com, Mercantil.com, and BtoBen (an incubator for online vertical markets), as well as U.S. companies moving into the region. But Serra is confident that her team's early start, state-of-the-art technology, and partnerships will keep the company a step ahead of its competition. "You need to have the right alliances in place to create successful marketplaces," she says. "Through our partnerships we have access to both buyers and sellers."

How is the company getting word out to consumers and businesses about Superbid and SuperVertical's other marketplaces? For starters, it advertises to its existing customer base via email and traditional direct mail. It also piggybacks on Unibanco's marketing efforts by including promotional material in their mailings to their seven million customers. SuperVertical currently spends the bulk of its advertising budget on offline ads—billboards, radio, cable TV, and print—but as more and more Brazilians come online, Serra plans to shift more of the company's advertising budget to online media. SuperVertical also markets Superbid through Latin American portal sites such as Terra and Zeek!.

SERIAL ENTREPRENEURSHIP BRAZILIAN STYLE

In addition to overseeing business development and strategy for Super-Vertical, Serra also makes time to invest in and advise Latin American Internet startups—she enjoys applying her entrepreneurial creativity to a number of different businesses at once. At the time of this writing, she was serving on the boards of four Latin American Internet companies and two nonprofits (Fundação Estudar, an education foundation, and Endeavor.org, an organization helping emerging-market countries take advantage of entrepreneurial activity).

As a woman entrepreneur and investor in Brazil does Serra feel that her gender has held her back? "There's no doubt that the venture capital and business communities in Latin America are male dominated," she acknowledges. "But I don't really care if people have prejudices at first—they get over them once we start working together."

As for her smarts and entrepreneurial creativity, no doubt some of it comes from the example set by her successful parents. Her mother, a ballet dancer with a Ph.D. in psychology, teaches movement theory at Brazil's Universidade de Campinas. Her father, who also has a Ph.D. (his is in economics), is Brazil's Minister of Health. Her parents saw to it that her education was first-rate. "Education is the legacy my parents felt they could leave me," she says. "Anything that's material can always be taken away from you. But if you have a solid education, you're like a cat—you'll always land on your feet."

Veronica Allende Serra's
TOP THREE LESSONS LEARNED

1. *"Don't give up too early.* Come up with a vision and strategy, and stick to it even if you're in an extremely competitive environment."

2. *"Great people are the most scarce and valuable resource.* Recruiting a top team capable of moving fast and accomplishing challenging tasks is key. Keeping this group motivated and focused is a must."

3. *"It's very important to have strategic investors on board* who will advise you about the direction of the company, provide industry insight, and lend credibility for future rounds of financing."

SuperVertical: KEY STRATEGIC TAKE-AWAYS

- Use your network. Serra regularly taps her business school and investment connections, which have helped put her in the limelight as one of Brazil's most successful Internet entrepreneurs and investors.

- Quickly react in response to your customers and to changes in the marketplace. When Serra and company saw that the bulk of purchases on Superbid were being made by other businesses, they shifted their focus to B2B e-markets.

- Choose your business and strategic partners carefully with the big picture in mind. SuperVertical's partnership with Unibanco has given consumers confidence in the company and helped them overcome concerns about purchasing online.

- When you see a market opportunity, move fast. Whenever a market is attractive, you can be sure there will be plenty of competition. While SuperVertical was one of the first B2B e-market companies in Latin America, it will need to continue executing fast to stay ahead. "The window of opportunity we have won't be open for long," says Serra. "I know that time can change the game."

- Reassure customers every step of the way. SuperVertical allows customers to purchase in whatever way they're most comfortable, whether by credit card or money transfer. The company also focuses on providing high caliber 24/7 customer support.

Part
IV

E-BUSINESS APPLICATIONS AND WEB TECHNOLOGY VENTURES

VITAL STATS

- Founder: Deidre Paknad, president
- URL: www.covia.com
- Stock: Private
- Founded: 1996
- Headquarters: Mountain View, CA

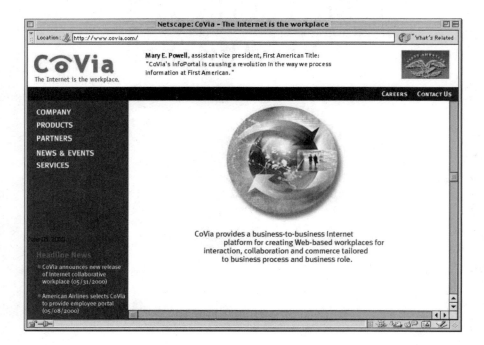

Netscape: CoVia - The Internet is the workplace

Location: http://www.covia.com/ — What's Related

C⊙Via
The Internet is the workplace.

Mary E. Powell, assistant vice president, First American Title: "CoVia's InfoPortal is causing a revolution in the way we process information at First American."

CAREERS CONTACT US

COMPANY
PRODUCTS
PARTNERS
NEWS & EVENTS
SERVICES

June 05 2000

Headline News

- CoVia announces new release of Internet collaborative workplace (05/31/2000)
- American Airlines selects CoVia to provide employee portal (05/08/2000)

CoVia provides a business-to-business Internet platform for creating Web-based workplaces for interaction, collaboration and commerce tailored to business process and business role.

17

CoVia

Turning the Internet into the Workplace

*"Above all, create a great product. Some people think you just
need a great advertising campaign, but it's your product that
makes your customers and your business a success."*

—Deidre Paknad

THE TIME IS NOW

The round steel clock on the wall above Deidre Paknad's desk doesn't
have numbers on its face. Instead, the word *now* appears everywhere a
number should be—both a Zen-like reminder of the present moment
and a jarring metaphor for work at Net speed where everything needs to
get done immediately. "It's a gift from my staff," explains the 37-year-
old entrepreneur.

As founder and president of CoVia, a Mountain View company that
creates Web-based workplaces for virtual collaboration, Paknad is accustomed to both "being here now" and working in an environment where
time has accelerated. The company, founded in 1996, creates secure, private portals where businesses and their customers, partners, and
employees can collaborate on the Web. The technology is revolutionizing
the way people work together: In a world where teams are increasingly
geographically dispersed, CoVia offers a single Web location where they
can communicate, collaborate, and coordinate efforts.

"The way people use the Internet today isn't how they're going to use
it tomorrow," predicts Paknad. "Today it's used for news, weather, shop-

213

ping, and as a brochure. But the big potential of the Internet is break-ing productivity barriers." Indeed, Net-savvy corporations with complex business relationships and distributed work forces are catching on. They're recognizing that Web-based workplaces provide a personalized way to communicate with customers and makes team collaboration eas-ier, reducing the time it takes to complete projects and close sales. After all, if a proposal needs to be reviewed by five different people who work in three different countries and at two different companies, doing this over the Web reduces the need for phone calls, faxing, and FedExing, and rad-ically streamlines the process. Given these benefits, demand for CoVia's product is growing fast: During 2000, revenues more than doubled, exceeding $5 million.

FROM STAY-AT-HOME MOM TO HOME-BASED ENTREPRENEUR

The idea for CoVia came to Paknad while she took two years off from a 10-year career in marketing and sales after the birth of her daughter, Zoë, now seven. It was during this treasured time as a full-time mom that Pak-nad's entrepreneurial juices started flowing. "This time gave me the head-room to think clearly, imagine, be creative, and jump off a cliff," recalls Paknad, stacks of books, including *Maximum Achievement*, *Burn Rate*, and *Creating the Digital Future*, piled high on the credenza behind her.

At that time, her husband, Daryoush Paknad, was working at Adobe Systems, where he was helping develop portable document format (PDF), a digital file format that preserves all the fonts, formatting, color, and graphics of any document, regardless of the application and platform used to create it. When Deidre heard about the extent of PDF's capabili-ties, she was fascinated and started brainstorming new possibilities. "I thought the technology combined with the Web had enormous poten-tial to radically accelerate the way businesses communicated both with customers and internally," she says.

But she also believed that applying the technology in this way was an idea ahead of its time. "Most companies lacked the internal expertise to take advantage of the opportunity," she says. "If I'd gone out in 1996 and started talking to businesses about Web-based applications for delivering information to their customers, my business would have bled to death."

Even though the market wasn't ready for her forward-looking ideas, she couldn't put her entrepreneurial impulse on hold. So she started a home-based Web-production business flexible enough to let her care for Zoë at the same time. In 1996 she launched a Website for her newly hatched business, which she named Glyphica. From the start the site gave the business a global reach, and she had little trouble landing clients. "Most of my early customers were located on the East Coast, and some were from as far away as Hong Kong," she remembers. "It took me just three weeks to get a $140,000 contract. During phone calls I'd say 'we' as if the company had multiple people, but it was really just me, my daughter, and her nanny."

Soon the work was coming in faster than Paknad could keep up with it, so she hired nine students to help produce content. "I had five workstations in one bedroom, three in a small office off the kitchen, and one on the kitchen table," she says. It soon became clear that Glyphica wasn't really a home business after all, so three months after hiring the first employee, she moved it to a 450-square-foot office in Palo Alto, California.

Paknad wasn't fazed by the risk of striking out on her own. She and Daryoush had saved a financial cushion from their corporate careers. But she did worry about her employability. "If the company didn't get off the ground, I would've had to return to the job market with a time gap on my résumé and a business that had flopped," says Paknad, a UC Santa Cruz alum and the only member of her family to graduate from college.

A RADICAL METAMORPHOSIS

Two years after hanging out a virtual shingle, Paknad's business creating Websites and content for companies was thriving—she was up to 15 full-time employees and just as many contractors, and had been able to grow the business solely through operating profits. "Our customers routinely financed our growth because they paid in advance," she explains.

She soon became aware of a recurring theme: Her clients were mostly corporate sales and marketing professionals who wanted to leverage the power of the Web but didn't know how to create and publish HTML-based content and didn't want to spend time learning how. She realized the time was ripe to realize her vision of creating Web-based software that would enable these types of clients to easily publish and share documents on the Web themselves—something that would be far more powerful than doing it for them on a piecework basis.

Paknad set out to fill this unmet need in early 1998, transforming Glyphica from a small Web services business into CoVia, an Internet application startup with massive growth potential. "Our software business grew from my understanding of customers' real issues," she explains. "They wanted to be able to communicate and share documents over the Web as easily as they stuffed envelopes—and this was a problem that Daryoush and I fully understood how to solve." Excited by the company's new focus and eager to fulfill a longstanding dream of building a software business with his wife, Daryoush left his job (he was now at Netscape) to join Deidre as cofounder and VP of engineering.

But shifting gears to software development meant that the wife-husband team needed cash—and lots of it. Software developers don't come cheap, nor does marketing a technology product. Paknad decided her best bet was to approach her existing business clients, one of which was Adobe, to seek investments. She knew Adobe's venture capital arm, Adobe Ventures, had invested in a slew of successful Net companies, including Netscape, Vignette, and Siebel Systems. So she gave them a call.

John Warnock, Adobe's CEO and chairman, was intrigued when he heard her idea—after all, it leveraged PDF, one of Adobe's core technologies. So Adobe Ventures invested, funding Glyphica's first round of $1.5 million in June 1998. "The Adobe Ventures team included a mix of people from both Adobe and Hambrecht & Quist [another Glyphica customer], so I had access to several key advisers who were also clients when developing my new business plan and growing the company," she explains. With this infusion, Paknad hired a team of top-notch software developers who, under Daryoush's leadership, got to work developing the product.

OPENING ENTERPRISE PORTALS

By October 1998 the product was ready. Dubbed InfoPortal, it allows any-one in a company to easily publish material on a corporate intranet or extranet. The product consists of a suite of Web applications and server software that can interface with enterprise database systems. Since the Web browser is the client, the InfoPortal platform is easy and cost-effective to deploy (there's no client software to install)—something that's critical in an age of dispersed work forces.

The timing of the release couldn't have been better—InfoPortal hit the market just as "enterprise portals" were becoming the latest e-business craze. Today, the majority of large companies already have or plan to implement enterprise portal solutions. "Nineteen ninety-nine was the year of tire kicking," says Gene Phifer, VP and research director at the Gartner Group, a technology research firm. "Year 2000 and beyond will see enterprise-wide deployment. The outlook for this market is excellent."

So what, exactly, is an enterprise portal anyway? In a nutshell, it's a Web interface that provides personalized access to corporate information and lets you access and manage documents and workflow based on your role in an organization. Like a My Yahoo! for corporate information, an enterprise portal allows employees to set up custom password-protected views of their corporate intranet that present only the information they're interested in seeing. These B2E (business-to-employee) portals allow workers to meld information from internal company databases, such as 401(k) plan data, vacation accrual, and health insurance details, with Internet information, such as weather, stock quotes, and news, at a sin-gle point of access. They also let employees easily create and publish doc-uments for business partners and customers on the company's extranet without having to know a thing about HTML or Web publishing. For com-panies whose employees and partners suffer from information overload, an enterprise portal is just what the doctor ordered. "Enterprises are implementing portals to increase employee productivity and tackle the twin problems of 'info glut' and 'info famine'—they want to save employ-ees from drowning in information that's irrelevant," says Phifer.

InfoPortal is ideal for corporations with information that needs to be shared but isn't in HTML. To publish a document to an intranet or extranet, all users need to do is drag and drop the file from their computer desktop to the intranet or extranet area where they want to post it. The file is instantly posted so others can access it. What's more, users can choose to convert a document to PDF when posting so it can be easily accessed by anyone, no matter what platform of software programs they use.

The technology is a boon for corporate Webmasters who have been bogged down by the tedious labor of converting manuals, marketing collateral, and reports to HTML. In pre-enterprise-portal days, employees wanting to publish to their corporate intranet typically gave their document to the Webmaster, who put it at the end of a long queue of items to be converted to HTML and published. Employees sometimes had to wait weeks for their information to be posted. In shifting publishing power to the content creator, CoVia makes this frustrating wait unnecessary and keeps overtaxed Webmasters from crying uncle.

THE WORKPLACE OF THE FUTURE IS VIRTUAL

Paknad began by marketing InfoPortal to information technology (I.T.) departments wanting to enable employees to publish to their company's intranet or extranet. But this was just the tip of the iceberg. The product could also be used to create secure, virtual workplaces for geographically dispersed customers and business teams, allowing all aspects of collaboration to be managed and tracked in one place—nothing short of revolutionary.

By early 2000 she launched a marketing campaign to reach four groups that stood to benefit the most: small businesses, sales professionals, knowledge workers, and human resources organizations. Soon small businesses were renting the product through the Websites of well-known companies (such as Adobe, SAP, and Dell, among others) to create their own virtual workplaces using their browser. And sales professionals were using it to interact with customers securely over the Web. Instead of spending a lot of time disseminating marketing material to customers, salespeople can now create custom, private sites where potential customers can access marketing materials and review proposals and contracts. The net effect has been to radically shorten the time it takes to close sales.

Knowledge workers, design and publishing professionals, and product development teams also began using the product to collaborate virtually on projects. Freelancers, in-house staff, and business partners can all participate in product development through their browsers. And since all files are automatically indexed, versioned, and made searchable, finding and reusing them is easy. Team members can also access shared contacts, a shared project calendar, and even upload project contacts into their Palm Pilots or other personal digital assistants.

CUSTOMERS ARE CLAMORING

Because virtual workplaces shorten the time it takes to complete a project, publish to the Web, or close a sale, CoVia has an easy sell. "Demand for our technologies is increasing exponentially," says Paknad. Indeed, it didn't take her long to build a list of more than 75 business clients, including big-name partners such as Adobe, Intuit, and SAP, which extend the technology to their own huge customer bases, as well as business customers deploying the technology internally, such as E*Trade, First American Financial, and Wells Fargo. And customers aren't the only ones who have recognized the revolutionary potential of CoVia's technology. In April 2000 the company was nominated for the prestigious Computerworld Smithsonian Award for the second year in a row, becoming part of a historical record of the world's most innovative technology applications.

While Paknad landed CoVia's first round of funding easily (Adobe Ventures was the only investor she approached), the second round gave her a full taste of pounding the pavement along Sand Hill Road. "I talked to 30 investors and three said yes," she recalls. "Ironically, instead of celebrating, I mourned the fact that 27 said no." But she only needed one willing investor and was in the enviable position of having three. In December 1999 she closed an $8 million round led by Viridian Capital, a VC fund that invests in women-led companies.

Now CoVia is located in an 18,000-square-foot office in the heart of Silicon Valley. "We'll outgrow the building within six months," says Paknad. There's little doubt she'll need more space soon: the company's workforce tripled to 130 between spring 1999 and spring 2000, and she's using the latest influx of cash to recruit a crew of senior execs and sales and development managers. In early 2000 she hired a CFO, general counsel, and even a top-notch CEO (all are women) to help manage CoVia's growth.

THE BUSINESS MODEL

CoVia is grabbing its piece of the ballooning market for e-business software tools, which the Delphi Group forecasts will reach nearly $40 billion in 2002. The trick for Paknad is getting word out to customers about InfoPortal and making the technology as ubiquitous as possible. And she's come up with an innovative business model for tackling the challenge. Instead of marketing InfoPortal to one customer at a time, she's focused on selling it to huge businesses that already have millions of loyal customers. And here's the brilliant part of her plan: CoVia's big-business clients can use InfoPortal internally and allow *their* customers to use it too.

Because some of these big-business clients fear losing their customers to newer dotcoms, they have an incentive to market CoVia's products to their customer bases to provide them with Web-based collaboration applications they might otherwise turn elsewhere for. CoVia's large clients act as application service providers (ASPs), renting the InfoPortal suite of applications to their customers as a special service. This gives CoVia's large clients a new revenue stream and another means of extending their brands to their customers since CoVia brands InfoPortal's applications with the companies' look and feel, including logos. But they're branded with CoVia's logo too, giving the startup phenomenal reach.

This multilevel deployment strategy is a big win for the company, creating multiple revenue streams. Each time CoVia signs up a new large partner company, it gains millions of potential new customers for its virtual workplaces in one fell swoop. The company licenses its technology for $250,000 to $500,000 to partners and also shares in the ongoing monthly subscription fees *their* customers pay. Typically, CoVia's deals bring in between $500,000 to $1 million in the first year, and more in subsequent years as more users subscribe.

What's Paknad's secret to successfully landing big-name partners? She personally networks with decision makers at potential client companies, and makes sure her existing customers are happy with CoVia's product so that they recommend it to others. "If you show somebody a terrific technology they can use, you're very likely to win a new customer," she says. "Our products have to be great enough to make our customers say so in the marketplace."

THE NEXT FRONTIER

Although CoVia was one of the first companies to enter its corner of the market, it's not standing there by itself. Other startups have stormed the scene, including Autonomy (now public), Plumtree Software, Epicentric, and HotOffice.com. But CoVia has a unique advantage over its rivals. Instead of offering a portal solution solely to individual businesses or spending millions on advertising to aggregate traffic at a Website offering collaboration tools, CoVia is going where users already are. Paknad's strategy of quickly signing up large partners and then extending services to their customers is a competitive advantage that's enabling the company to amass an enormous user base. "The first mover advantage is only as good as the speed with which you can consolidate it," she says. "Through our partnerships, more than 40 million subscribers currently access our tools via the Web. Our technology allows us to take advantage of leveraged distribution that is unlike anything our competitors offer." Fast emerging as a leader in its market, CoVia is targeting profitability for 2003.

Paknad is also bringing virtual workplaces beyond desktop Web browsers. The company has partnered with AvantGo to enable users of

Palm Pilots, Windows CE devices, and mobile phones to access InfoPortal's applications wirelessly. "With the wireless market exploding, mobile collaboration is the next frontier," says Paknad. "This is especially true in Europe, where mobile Internet use is widespread."

Despite the fact that Paknad had to move CoVia out of her home when Zoë was young, she makes spending time with her daughter a priority. She often brings Zoë to work in the early evenings and lets her visit the handful of employees who've known her since she was a baby. "What I hope is that her perception of her access to the business world will always make her feel welcome and like an equal participant in it," says Paknad, glancing at Zoë's carefully crafted letters on her white board. The seven-year-old has clearly been at home in this high-tech environment for years. When asked at age three if she needed help after her computer crashed, Zoë replied, "No, I just need to reboot."

Deidre Paknad's TOP THREE LESSONS LEARNED

1. *"There's no such thing as a free lunch.* Despite the myth that capital grows on trees and you can start a business and become a millionaire the same year, it's incredibly hard work and takes a significant toll on you. Building value takes a lot of soul."

2. *"It's lonely.* As a first-time CEO, I was unprepared for the isolation and weight that you occasionally feel in the role. For me, spending time with other CEOs eases the loneliness that comes with the territory."

3. *"People make it all worthwhile.* I can't count the number of times I've been moved by the emotional investment, energy, and contributions of the people within my company."

CoVia: KEY STRATEGIC TAKE-AWAYS

- Don't give up on your idea even if you think it's a year or two ahead of its time. Paknad bided her time with a Web-production business until she felt that the market was ready for corporate portals and virtual workplaces.

- Consider all the potential applications of your business concept or technology. Paknad originally marketed InfoPortal solely as an enterprise portal solution, but expanded to marketing versions for other types of customers—salespeople, small businesses, and product development and design teams.

- Nurture your company culture from the start. "If you're lucky, you can create a kind of social glue early on that's the result of shared challenge, success, hard work, and reciprocity," says Paknad.

- When building your initial team, look for people who are highly entrepreneurial. "They'll be far more interested in doing whatever it takes to grow a business into something substantial," notes Paknad.

- Look for innovative ways to get the word out about your business and its products or services. CoVia developed an original business model to disseminate the company's brand and product at multiple levels in the market: to large corporate partners as well as their customer bases.

VITAL STATS

- Paula Jagemann, president and CEO
- URLs: www.eci2.com
  www.onlineofficesupplies.com
  www.ios2.com
- Stock: Private
- Founded: 1998
- Headquarters: Vienna, VA

Netscape: eCommerce Industries, Inc.

Location: http://www.eci2.com/   What's Related

eci² ™
eCommerce Industries, Inc.

Home   Contact Us   Site Map

ECI2 Press Releases

- Acquisitions Press Release - May 11,2000
- OPDXchange Press Release - May 11,2000

OPDXchange ™
About OPDXchange
FAQs
Press Release
Contact Us

opDNA ™
About opDNA

Company
├ About ECI²
└ Press Releases

Acquisitions
├ DDMS
└ UBC

Subsidiaries
├ IOS²
└ OOSC

eCommerce Industries

From E-Tail to E-Business Solutions

"I could have retired on my stock options after the company where I worked for two years went public. But that's just not me. I'm temperamentally unable to give up working."

—Paula Jagemann

GIVING NOTICE

Paula Jagemann was a little nervous as she walked down the hallway to her boss's office. It was May 1998 and she was finally going to tell him about her startup company, Online Office Supplies Company, which she'd been building on the side. Its Website would launch in three months. He was shocked and in disbelief. "We're in the most exciting industry on earth and you want to sell paper and pencils?" he asked incredulously.

Her boss, John Sidgmore, is vice chairman of MCI WorldCom and, at the time, was CEO of UUNet, the world's largest Internet service provider. Now he's also chairman of Jagemann's new venture, eCommerce Industries (called ECI² for short) and helped finance her company with $2.5 million from his own pocket. "This was more blind faith in Paula than anything else," he says, explaining his decision. "But it was also the opportunity to automate an old, traditional market." And on the Internet, this market was wide open.

NOT SEXY, BUT VERY SELLABLE

Paper and pencils may not be glamorous but, according to financial analysts, they're expected to sell well online. The office products industry is worth an estimated $225 billion and growing. Surprisingly, superstores such as Office Max, Office Depot, and Staples control only 33 percent of the total market. And analysts say online sales of office products will grow from $2.9 billion in 1999 to more than $65 billion by 2003, making this the fifth-largest B2B online market.

Office supplies are part of the first wave of e-commerce for the business-to-business and small-business markets. On the Internet, buyers can track order histories, get real-time pricing and product information, and comparison shop. Office supplies are a natural fit for the Web: Most items are small and lightweight, they don't require handling or inspection, people need them repeatedly, and most buyers know what they want before they shop. Moreover, the current process for ordering them is labor-intensive, involving phone calls, faxes, and outdated thick paper catalogs.

Jagemann's original concept was simple: Take the hassle out of buying office products by offering volume discounts and secure credit-card transactions, guaranteeing overnight delivery and providing a quick-order list for the 100 most commonly ordered products. The Web storefront features a price-comparison chart and a search engine that lets customers search by name, manufacturer, category, SKU (stock keeping unit), or part number. What makes the site stand out is what lies under the hood—an engine that's scalable enough to support 100,000 orders a day.

A TOPSY-TURVY LIFE

Jagemann is no stranger to challenges. Born in Manchester, England, in 1966, she was the only daughter among four children. Her family moved to Tehran, Iran, when she was nine, but when they took a vacation to the New Jersey shore, the shah was overthrown and the American embassy was overtaken, leaving her family's assets frozen. They remained in New Jersey but their home life deteriorated—her father became an alcoholic and drug addict who eventually ran out on the family, leaving them with no money. Jagemann's mother had to hold down two jobs. "She's definitely my inspiration, she worked her butt off," says the entrepreneur. Still, Jagemann had to scrap her plans to attend college. She took a job with her mother in the reservations department at Trump's Castle in Atlantic City, where she quickly worked her way up to a managerial position.

She met her future husband, Joseph Jagemann, on a trip to Virginia, and in 1987 moved to Maryland to live with his family. She was hired as an executive assistant at Telephone Industry Consultants (Telic). There, she met John Sidgmore, Telic's new president, who became the most influential person in her life. He recruited Jagemann as his assistant and started giving her increasingly substantial things to do. For starters, she was put in charge of the $1 million corporate travel budget. "He made me feel challenged and appreciated," she says. At Sidgmore's suggestion, she enrolled as a part-time economics major at Hood College and he paid her tuition. She left to attend college full-time in 1991, but Sidgmore, who had then gone on to become CEO of UUNet, needed his right-hand woman. Offering her 72,000 stock options, he lured her back to head up public relations.

Jagemann soon became an integral, powerful member of UUNet's team. For example, when reviewing a contract to provide connectivity for the Microsoft network in 1995, she caught a loophole that would have cost UUNet millions because it would have had UUNet building a worldwide network rather than the U.S. system the two parties had discussed. By the time UUNet went public that year, Jagemann was the company's director of investor relations, a position that gave her a class-one education about company valuations and accounting figures while working on UUNet's filing with Goldman Sachs.

Jagemann was nonchalant about the outcome of the IPO. "I grew up poor, so risk is in my blood," she says. But having worked on the filing, she had a gut feeling that the IPO would be a success. She talked her mom into investing her entire retirement nest egg in the IPO. Luckily, Wall Street acted favorably toward UUNet. The stock opened at $14 and doubled to $28 by the end of the first day. Jagemann's shares, originally priced at seven cents each, were now worth millions. Instant wealth didn't radically alter Jagemann's lifestyle, but she did pay off her mother's mortgage and started college funds for her nephews and nieces. The biggest splurge: buying a BMW and one of the first Porsche Boxsters.

DOING DOUBLE DUTY

Half a million of that bounty also went to fund Jagemann's first venture, Online Office Supplies Company. She credits her brother-in-law, an office products salesman, for giving her the idea by griping that his company wasn't selling online. When she saw that few other companies were doing so either, Jagemann leaped into action. She started by working on a business model with Goldman Sachs analysts she knew from UUNet's IPO preparation. "From their research, I found that this was a market that was totally overlooked," she says.

Jagemann stayed on at her job at UUNet while starting up Online Office Supplies Company. This double life had its advantages. For one, her position gave her access to highly skilled technical colleagues, several of whom she persuaded to build her company's new e-commerce engine "in exchange for pizza and beer." It also allowed her to host her company's systems on UUNet's first-class servers at a discount. On the advice of her expert colleagues, she brought in a Web development firm to create a B2B site with built-in purchasing requirements, custom catalogs, and reporting features. The firm developed the initial site at cost ($500,000) because it had previously developed sites for UUNet; otherwise, the price tag would have been in the millions.

Thanks to her role as Sidgmore's assistant and director of investor relations, Jagemann was able to call half a dozen high-tech CEOs and, within 20 minutes, gather a board of Silicon Valley high-fliers with a combined net worth of nearly $2 billion. They included Sidgmore; Sky Dayton, founder of EarthLink; Mory Ejabat, CEO of Zhone Communications and formerly CEO of Ascend; and Dan Rosen, general manager of new technology at Microsoft, who helped put UUNet on the map by convincing none other than Bill Gates to invest in the ISP. Ejabat gave her a $4 million-a-year deal for Ascend's office supplies business; Rosen introduced her to Microsoft people; and Dayton put her in touch with the right contacts at EarthLink. On top of this, she handled UUNet's office-supplies purchases, which came to $70,000 each month.

Combined, these advantages helped her convince United Stationers, a $3.8 billion wholesaler, to handle fulfillment for her venture. According to Jagemann, it wouldn't have been easy to attract their interest otherwise. "I went from a random cold caller to having instant credibility," she explains.

COMPETITION IN ALL CORNERS

As an early mover into the office supplies e-tail space, Jagemann's prospects looked good. She had low overhead, no need for fulfillment operations, no paper catalogs, and no sales tax—all of which she expected to translate into lower prices and higher margins. No office products retailer—online or off—could claim dominance over the highly fragmented market.

Jagemann's original hope was to be the Amazon.com of office supplies. But the office supplies market in 1998 was vastly different from the market Amazon entered in 1995, when none of the brick-and-mortar book retailers even had Websites. By contrast, when Jagemann started her venture, OfficeMax was already selling its products online. It didn't take long before other established players such as Staples and Office Depot were investing millions in their own Web efforts. With brand names, billions of dollars in sales, and established distribution networks that fulfill thousands of orders a day via their own fleet of trucks, these companies proved formidable adversaries.

The superstores weren't Jagemann's only competitors either. Contract stationers such as Boise Cascade, BT Office Products, and U.S. Office Products quickly bolstered their procurement systems with technology from Ariba and Commerce One to help large corporations streamline their purchasing processes. At the same time, dozens of other Internet entrepreneurs launched office supply e-tail efforts. Among the most visible was AtYourOffice.com, which beat Online Office Supplies Company's Website to market by a month.

SHIFTING GEAR

Jagemann hardly stood idle while a pack of rivals circled. Like many Internet CEOs, she encountered one of the basic tenets of e-commerce: Be prepared to fix your business model, even before it breaks. So when the market changed course, she did too. In November 1998, United Stationers approached her and asked to license her technology to independent dealers, helping them to sell products on the Web. Initially she balked, thinking, "It would mean a lot of money, but I don't want to enable our competitors." But she presented the proposal to Sidgmore, and within minutes they had worked out a solution. While the margins on office products are in the single digits, the margins on technology are much higher.

Shifting gear would be complicated, however. The most lucrative approach was to license the technology both to United Stationers' independent dealers and to dotcom companies such as Egghead.com that wanted to add office products to their mix. The problem: These two customer sets represented competing sales channels, each of which received different pricing from United Stationers. "We needed to guarantee the dealers that pricing information would remain in the hands of a noncompetitive entity," explains Jagemann.

So Jagemann and Sidgmore created two distinct companies—Online Office Supplies Company and Internet Office Solutions and Services (or IOS^2), each with its own CEO and executive staff and each targeting a different sales channel. They launched a parent company for them, which they named eCommerce Industries (or ECI^2). "It was so easy for us to come to that model because it's exactly what UUNet does," says Jagemann, explaining that UUNet sells its infrastructure technology to Net and technology companies such as AOL, Microsoft, and EarthLink, which use it to serve their customers. Online Office Supplies Company continues to sell its products directly to businesses, but on the side. Its newly created sister company, IOS^2, sells the award-winning back-end e-commerce technology used to power Online Office Supplies Company's transactions. "We've always thought of ourselves more as an Internet company than an office supplies company," says Jagemann.

THE BUSINESS MODEL

Some of the first clients to be wooed by the IOS[2] infrastructure technology were accounting firm Arthur Andersen and dotcom companies such as Medibuy.com and Inc.com. "We put a button on their site that takes them to a custom, private-label office-products catalog that contains the items their organization buys," explains Jagemann. "We ship the supplies and handle customer service, and they don't have to lift a finger."

Through its arrangement with United Stationers, Online Office Supplies Company has exclusive rights to sell United Stationers' 35,000 products online. This means Online Office Supplies has the advantage of range of distribution, product selection, and speed of delivery. "Everything is drop-shipped for us by United Stationers so we never have to take possession of the goods," says Jagemann. "You remove an awful lot of costs." Online Office Supplies Company earns margins of 10 to 20 percent on most items sold compared with single-digit margins for traditional office product suppliers.

In that same deal, IOS[2] became the exclusive technology provider for United Stationers' independent dealers—approximately 15,000 mom-and-pop distributors. That means setting them up to sell online. IOS[2] technology can be custom-tailored to any specific set of business rules. For example, it can automatically keep employees from exceeding their budgets or buying Mont Blanc pens when a simple Bic will do. "They can also include their own specialized products and mix and match with supplies from our catalog," says Jagemann. "We make it simple for them."

IOS[2] licenses its technology for a monthly fee and charges a small per-order transaction fee on top of that. Dealers pay a one-time set-up fee and can choose to pay either a higher transaction fee with a lower licensing fee or a lower transaction fee with a higher licensing charge.

ECI[2] earns the bulk of its revenue through licensing its online catalog and e-commerce technology. The rest comes from commissions earned on office supply sales.

A ROSY FUTURE

With ECI^2 shifting into e-commerce back-end technology solutions, Sidgmore and Jagemann rounded up an additional $56 million in venture capital in two rounds from Accel Partners, New Enterprise Associates in Reston, Virginia, an early UUNet investor, as well as from private investors. But ECI^2 wasn't hurting for cash. "I could have funded this company myself for a couple of years," says Jagemann. "We took the money solely because it gives you the initial blessing on Wall Street. It primes you for that great step of an IPO." Jagemann used the money to lease 20,000 square feet of office space in Tysons Corner, Virginia—she knows she'll need the space because ECI^2, while only at 80 employees now, is hiring furiously. Even in this tight market for high-tech talent, hiring has been incredibly easy because of the company's promising outlook. In fact, many of Jagemann's friends as well as her husband are employees.

Jagemann is expanding Online Office Supplies Company to offer furniture, logoed products such as pens and promotional items, and computers. To strengthen ECI^2 offerings, she used $20 million in cash and stock to acquire Data Management Systems, a provider of infrastructure software to the office supplies and furniture industries, and United Business Computers, a company specializing in back-end systems for wholesalers. The company has beefed up its customer service to 24-hour support and features multilingual operators, which will come in handy during the company's next big push—global expansion. Fulfillment services were just launched in the United Kingdom through a local office supplies distributor there, and the company is building sites for independent dealers so they can sell online. Client bases are also being built in Canada, France, Germany, and Scandinavia.

The company's new investors asked Jagemann to quit her day job at UUNet where, incredibly, she continued to work as Sidgmore's executive assistant all the time she was building her business. She left reluctantly in December 1999. Nevertheless, she still has some ties. "I still do stuff for him like helping to create presentations," she says.

Now Jagemann can devote her 80-hour workweeks solely to ECI^2. Having finally finished her college education with a BA in economics in May 1999, she has vowed to take a little more time to stop and smell the roses. She's trying to work out more, read a few more novels, and ride the horse her husband gave her last year. She's also trying her hand at journalism—Jagemann pens a biweekly Web column for Oxygen Media and donates her $30,000 annual fee to cystic fibrosis charities (both her niece and nephew have the disease). Jagemann wants to have children in a few years, and her husband has offered to stay home and take care of them, so she can continue full speed ahead in the business world since she enjoys it so much.

Jagemann is determined to make the most of her first venture. She's aiming for Goldman Sachs to take ECI^2 public by the time you read this. She's diligently recruiting the staff and executive management needed in order to free up her time to lead and promote the company. At the rate things are going, profitability should be right around the corner. While the company brought in $1.5 million in revenues in 1999, Jagemann's expecting it to be in the black as early as 2001.

Jagemann believes the Internet is an ideal arena for women pursuing their business dreams. "The Internet has happened so fast that 50 to 100 years of embedded glass ceilings simply don't exist," she says, noting that in the office supplies industry, which is far more traditional, she's one of few women. "Being a woman in the office supplies world is certainly different, but being the technologist who's going to revive and catapult this medieval industry forward, well, I've got to say, it's pretty neat."

Paula Jagemann's
TOP THREE LESSONS LEARNED

1. *"Don't be daunted by the competition.* Never think that just because there's an incumbent, you might as well give up. Who thought in the beginning that we could take on Office Max and Staples? If you have a solution or an advantage that could make an industry better, use it."

2. *"Don't get too emotional about equity.* It was hard to see my stake go from 80 percent to 50 percent. If we go public, that will drop into the teens. It's hard to let your baby go, but remember that in the stock market, the value of your remaining stake can skyrocket."

3. *"Keep alert about new technology.* Don't rely on your CIO for all the information or refer to anyone else as the visionary. Be on top of what's going on. I read every trade magazine for new innovations in an ongoing quest to use the best of that technology to make my business better."

ECI²: KEY STRATEGIC TAKE-AWAYS

- Mentors, advisers, and investors may be much closer at hand than you think. Jagemann is an inspiring example of an entrepreneur who was able to enlist the help of her immediate colleagues and coworkers.

- Keep your eyes peeled for overlooked business opportunities. When Jagemann started her company, most big-name office supply stores hadn't begun selling online.

- Don't overlook simple business ideas. As Jagemann has proven, an idea doesn't have to be whizbang to be a moneymaker.

- Be prepared to change your business model. When the competition from brand-name retailers such as Office Max and Staples proved stiff, Jagemann began selling e-commerce technology solutions.

- Find creative ways to avoid channel conflicts. United Stationers' dealers didn't want Online Office Supplies Company, which they considered a competitor, gaining access to its pricing model for different sales channels. Jagemann was able to avoid a conflict of interest by implementing her technology infrastructure business as a new initiative under a new company separate from Online Office Supplies.

- If you're a woman entrepreneur, use the status to your advantage. Many state and federal government agencies give special consideration to minority- and women-owned businesses for contracts and deals, as Jagemann discovered when she was contacting potential clients.

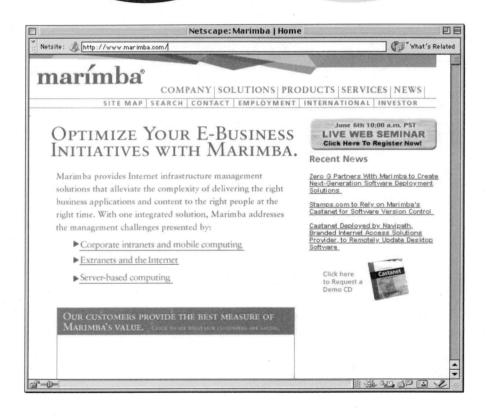

VITAL STATS

- Cofounder: Kim Polese, chairwoman and chief strategy officer
- URL: www.marimba.com
- Stock: MRBA
- Founded: 1996
- Headquarters: Mountain View, CA

Netscape: Marimba | Home

Netsite: http://www.marimba.com/ — What's Related

marímba®

COMPANY | SOLUTIONS | PRODUCTS | SERVICES | NEWS |

SITE MAP | SEARCH | CONTACT | EMPLOYMENT | INTERNATIONAL | INVESTOR

OPTIMIZE YOUR E-BUSINESS INITIATIVES WITH MARIMBA.

Marimba provides Internet infrastructure management solutions that alleviate the complexity of delivering the right business applications and content to the right people at the right time. With one integrated solution, Marimba addresses the management challenges presented by:

- ▶ Corporate intranets and mobile computing
- ▶ Extranets and the Internet
- ▶ Server-based computing

June 6th 10:00 a.m. PST
LIVE WEB SEMINAR
Click Here To Register Now!

Recent News

Zero G Partners With Marimba to Create Next-Generation Software Deployment Solutions

Stamps.com to Rely on Marimba's Castanet for Software Version Control

Castanet Deployed by Navipath, Branded Internet Access Solutions Provider, to Remotely Update Desktop Software

Click here to Request a Demo CD

OUR CUSTOMERS PROVIDE THE BEST MEASURE OF MARIMBA'S VALUE. CLICK TO SEE WHAT OUR CUSTOMERS ARE SAYING.

19

Marimba

Letting Software and Data Flow Across the Net

"I always loved the idea of being an entrepreneur, of driving your own destiny, being in charge of your own future, and creating something without a lot of boundaries."

—Kim Polese

JUMPIN' JAVA

For Kim Polese, Christmas 1995 was unlike any other. Instead of trimming the tree and opening gifts with her family in her hometown of Berkeley, California, she was spending her five days off in a nonstop brainstorming session with Sami Shaio, Jonathan Payne, and Arthur van Hoff, three of her engineering coworkers from the Sun Microsystems Java team. At Sun, Polese and these three talented software developers had experienced what many would consider a life-defining success: They were instrumental in developing and promoting Java, the platform-independent programming environment and language that offered developers an alternative to the stranglehold held by the Windows platform.

Polese, who holds a BA in biophysics from UC Berkeley, worked at Sun for seven years, where she became the product marketing manager for a secret project known as Oak—the programming platform she would later name Java when it was ready for release in spring 1995. Java was a natural fit with the Web—it could be embedded into HTML, adding small interactive applications ("applets") that could be downloaded to browsers along with Web pages. It could also be used to create robust desktop programs that could run on any computer platform.

Coinciding with the Internet explosion, Java spread like wildfire. The Internet was in desperate need of a way to create cross-platform applications that could be delivered across networks, and Java came to the rescue, generating intense media hype as well as tremendous excitement and quick adoption in the developer community. By the end of 1995 it was the hottest programming language around. No previous computer language had ever spread as fast and furiously. When Java was only 900 days old, there were already 900,000 active Java programmers. (By way of comparison, C++ had only 100,000 active programmers when it was 10 years old.)

With the near overnight proliferation of Java, Polese and her co-conspirators at Sun started joking that they should start a company together, but the jesting soon turned serious. Polese knew that Java would generate plenty of new companies, and figured that if there was ever a right time to combine her love of technology with her desire to be an entrepreneur, it was now.

So her goal during the five-day brainstorming session with Marimba's other future founders was to figure out whether the group had a good enough idea on which to build a business. By the end of their working holiday they'd outlined a preliminary plan for a software product that would enable companies to automatically update and deliver software applications and information to people's desktops across the Net—without hogging bandwidth. "Our vision was that the Internet should be like a utility—like water or electricity," explains Polese. "When you flip on a light switch, the light just automatically comes on and you don't have to wait for it to download across a network, configure dip switches, or deal with the technology. We wanted to do the same thing with the Internet. But instead of water or electricity, software and information were what needed to flow automatically." Convinced that they had a great idea and a big business opportunity, they decided to go for it.

Now Polese is chairwoman and chief strategy officer of Marimba, a growing, public, 200-plus-employee, Internet infrastructure company that sells its technology (which she refers to unglamorously as "plumbing") to Fortune 1000 companies. Marimba boasts a strong corporate customer base and steadily climbing revenues too: between 1998 and 1999, revenues grew 84 percent, topping $31 million.

Polese is one of the first women in Silicon Valley to found and lead an Internet technology business from idea all the way through a successful IPO—and she served as CEO from the business's inception to mid-2000. This distinction won her reams of recognition and has made her a high-profile entrepreneur: *Time* magazine named her one of the "Top 25 Most Influential People in America," *Red Herring* picked her as a "Top 20 Entrepreneur," and *Upside* included her in its "Upside Elite 100" listing of technology industry movers and shakers.

MAKING A CLEAN BREAK

Mustering the courage to disembark from mothership Sun came easily to Polese, who had dreamed of starting her own company since she was a kid. "Even if we crashed and burned after six months, I would have learned so much by then about the whole process of starting a company, getting financing, and writing a business plan that I knew it would be worth it even if the whole thing failed miserably," she says. Realizing that in releasing Java she'd achieved the most personally fulfilling thing she could at Sun, and that she no longer needed to be there to ensure that Java saw the light of day, she felt it was the right time to make a move.

But before jumping ship, she and her partners went to top-notch Silicon Valley law firm Gunderson Dettmer. The founders knew they'd certainly make some waves when they simultaneously resigned from Sun's Java team, and they wanted to be sure they wouldn't be wrongly accused of stealing intellectual property. Besides assuring the founders that their break from Sun would be clean, the firm gave them valuable advice on incorporation, navigating the world of venture capital, and patent issues. "They gave us all sorts of advice that we absolutely needed on issues we wouldn't have known about it if we hadn't enlisted them," says Polese.

They rented cheap office space in Palo Alto—the defunct storage room of a stationary store that had closed—got loaner computers, stocked the fridge with beer, and hunkered down. While Polese's cofounders began developing the product, she got to work turning the mock business plan into a real one and filing for a patent. Polese, who is also a ballet and jazz dancer, took breaks from work only for dance classes. When they needed breaks from long hours of writing code, Shaio, Payne, and van Hoff, all three musicians, turned from their computer keyboards to their guitar fret boards and drum sets.

For the first six months after leaving Sun, Polese and her cofounders were the entire company. Each kicked in $15,000 to bootstrap the business, lived off of their personal savings, and worked under a shroud of secrecy for fear of prematurely exposing their concept to would-be competitors. "Even though our office space was pretty funky, I think self-funding was the right way to go because we were able to build value into the company during the first six months and not give away equity," explains Polese.

The press speculated to no end about what these four former key members of the Java team were up to, and their secrecy just amplified the buzz. Venture capitalists pricked up their ears too. Java was all the rage, and VCs were dying to know what this startup was doing and get in on the action first.

UNVEILING A JAZZY PROTOTYPE

By the end of 1996 the founders had built a prototype of their product and signed up their initial beta customers. They were ready to unveil it and raise funding to refine and market it. The musical foursome dubbed the company Marimba and punnily named their flagship product Castanet. "I like names that are easy to spell, remember, and pronounce, and reflect the energy of the company and the people behind it," says Polese. "When I chose 'Java,' it was the same thing—a name that kind of captured people's imaginations."

Based on Java, Castanet provides an efficient mechanism for getting software, software updates, and information from point A to point B over the Net securely. And here's the neat part: Castanet sends only data that has *changed*, thereby conserving bandwidth. Moreover, the product compresses the data, further minimizing the impact on the network. Software downloads can be interrupted and then pick up where they left off. End users download a piece of client software called a *tuner* and on the server side, businesses install a *transmitter* that lets them dispatch software and information to any subset of users with the Castanet tuner regardless of their device or computer platform. As long as users are connected to the Internet, the software or information is automatically updated when revisions are made to it on the server side.

Castanet has helped companies reduce information technology (I.T.) expenditures, since they can use it to remotely install and update software sitting on employees' desktop PCs, as well as to distribute software to suppliers, customers, and business partners. The product relieves sys admins of the tedious task of visiting employees one at a time, CD-ROM in hand, to manually install or update office suite software, email clients, and the like. It also saves employees the hassle of having to download upgrades and patches from the Net. What's more, Castanet enables companies to tailor applications and information to specific groups of users.

Marimba's first customers were companies trying to deliver sophisticated applets through the browser and struggling because downloading them across the Net was taking so long. Problems were compounded because these companies usually didn't know which type of browser and version each end user would have. Bear Stearns was one of the first companies to license Castanet. It had a large bond-trading applet it was delivering to brokerages, but every time someone wanted to trade a bond, they'd have to wait for the applet to download. Using Castanet, the company was able to eliminate the problem: They let the part of the application that rarely changed reside on users' desktops, while the rest of it updated itself automatically throughout the day, allowing brokers to monitor trades in real time and giving Bear Stearns the ability to update the application remotely.

Because of the tremendous visibility the founders generated by leaving the Java team en masse, they had the unusual luxury of being able to pick and choose from among the best venture capital firms. They made appointments with several VCs that had already contacted them while they were creating the Castanet prototype. "We had a solid business plan and a very comprehensive presentation that really articulated what the company was doing," explains Polese. "When we went out and talked with investors, we were very clear about the company's mission and why it was going to become a big business." Their focus and vision shined through, and, in August 1996, Kleiner Perkins invested $4 million from its Java Fund in the startup, making Marimba the first company to receive money from the new fund.

After the founders had raised the first round, Polese brought in some very experienced executive recruiters to help staff the management team. They began looking for the best people they could possibly find. And hiring the best at the beginning turned into a self-fulfilling prophecy. Their high-caliber first employees attracted more of the same. "One of the most important things you can do in building a company is overhire," advises Polese. "At the very beginning, hire better and more people than you think you need. This is the team of people that will really dictate whether or not your company is successful."

A BRIEF HISTORY OF PUSH

Around the time Castanet was released, the media began hyping a concept called *push* as the new big wave in Internet business. Push was an extraordinarily broad category that referred to any technology or company enabling users to subscribe to information automatically sent to their computers via the Internet without their having to ask for it. Marimba was lumped into the push category along with many other diverse companies, such as BackWeb and PointCast. With the sudden trendiness of push, Polese's phone started ringing off the hook—companies around the world wanted to know how they could do push too.

Microsoft and Netscape joined the fray, offering competing push products (the Active Desktop and Netscape Netcaster, respectively) that allowed content providers to automatically deliver selected information to people's desktops. Ultimately, though, the push concept became most closely associated with PointCast. The company shoved a glut of news and information (like sports scores and stock quotes) across the Internet, flooding computer screen savers with continually updated information.

As the hype about push grew to a feverish pitch, Marimba and Polese became overnight high-tech stars. Marimba became one of the media's favorite poster children for push. At the height of the mania in early 1997, PointCast turned its nose up at an outrageously high $450 million buyout offer from Rupert Murdoch. But then, just as suddenly as push had made headlines, its popularity fell apart. Network administrators started noticing that PointCast was clogging up their corporate networks; as more and more employees installed the screen saver on their desktops, the flood of data soon turned to a congested trickle.

With this turn of events, push, and PointCast in particular, became synonymous with network nightmares. Companies associated with the category, including Marimba, fell out of favor (ironic, given that Polese believes Marimba's technology could have actually solved PointCast's problem). PointCast eventually ended its search for a buyer in 1999, selling itself for a paltry $7 million.

PLAYING THE MARKET . . . TO THE TUNE OF $1.4 BILLION

Despite all the hype swirling around them about the swift rise and sudden "death" of push (and by extension, Marimba), Polese and company stayed focused on signing up new customers and building a solid business. Kleiner Perkins led a second $15 million round of funding for the startup in 1997, and by early 1999, Marimba had filed its red herring, the initial prospectus a company must file with the SEC before going public. By that time, *Internet infrastructure* existed as a term in the technology lexicon and as a market category, and Marimba found itself with a new label that more accurately reflected its quadrant of the Net sector.

Marimba's IPO was a smashing success that demonstrated just how exaggerated rumors of the company's demise were and vindicated its strategy of enabling companies to deliver software across the Net. Institutional investors' enthusiasm for Marimba was high. Morgan Stanley, the company's IPO underwriter, bumped up the offering price not once, but twice. Marimba went public at $20 per share, raising $68 million after expenses. The stock closed at $61 on its first day of trading, giving the company a $1.4 billion market cap and making the cofounders' 13 percent stakes worth $182 million each.

Even though Marimba's revenues were growing steadily each quarter and marching toward profitability, there was an outside misperception, fueled by the media, that the company had initially been a phenomenal success, then somehow failed, and then, with the IPO, had been reborn. "Going public allowed us to open up the books and show people just how well and consistently we've been performing," says Polese. "But I still encounter people who say, 'You did a great job at turning that company around.' And I tell them, 'I never turned the company around. We've been building it all along.'"

THE BUSINESS MODEL

Marimba is carving out its piece of the booming multibillion-dollar market for Internet infrastructure technologies, a sector of the Net economy that's still in its infancy. And it's no longer a one-product company. Keeping with the musical naming scheme, it also has a product called Timbale that distributes files, software, and data to servers rather than desktop machines. To boost the performance speed of their Websites, companies are increasingly distributing their servers geographically in order to locate them close to end users—the shorter the distance a packet has to travel across the Internet, the faster it reaches them. Timbale enables companies with "server farms"—dozens or even hundreds of distributed Web servers—to automatically replicate, synchronize, and distribute data across them.

Marimba's niche promises to be increasingly important as more corporations move to managing software distribution and servers remotely. The company uses both licensing and subscription pricing models in selling its products: Castanet is licensed to customers who pay a fee that depends on the number of desktops and mobile devices that will receive software and data. (Because Marimba targets large companies, the price for Castanet is typically around a quarter of a million dollars.)

For Timbale, the price depends on the number of servers to be managed using the product. Marimba also sells its products on a subscription basis to ASPs (application service providers) and ISPs, which rent them to their customers. Marimba earns approximately three-fourths of its revenue through product sales. The company earns the remainder from maintenance and support.

STRIKING A CHORD WITH CUSTOMERS

What marketing strategies does Marimba use to attract customers? Many. To generate sales prospects, the company advertises in Internet and computer networking trade publications such as *InfoWorld* and *Information Week*, and tailors its ads to corporate technology decision makers such as CIOs and I.T. managers.

Marimba also has a strong presence at I.T. trade shows such as the Gartner Group I.T. Expos, ASP Summits, and Enterprise Management Summit. According to Polese, this has been a more effective strategy than going to larger, broader trade shows like Comdex. "These vertically oriented shows let us establish a better dialogue with attendees and specifically target the products and solutions we showcase," she says. Besides trade shows, Marimba puts on technology seminars to educate potential customers about how the Internet can help them better manage software and information distribution.

All of these marketing strategies are paying off. Marimba boasts hundreds of corporate customers, including many Fortune 1000 companies such as Home Depot, Charles Schwab, Intuit, Nasdaq, and Chrysler. Home Depot uses Castanet nightly to send updated databases of inventory and pricing information to its 800-plus stores. Other customers, such as Intuit, use it as an add-on to their existing software products so they can update them remotely, automatically delivering patches to users. One key sign of Marimba's success with its customers is its ability to generate repeat business: More than 50 percent of the company's licensing contracts are with repeat customers.

Marimba isn't without competition, however. Other players include BackWeb, Novadigm, and Sterling Software. But Castanet has commanded a leading position, and Timbale is quickly being adopted by ASPs, ISPs, and other companies that need to manage many servers. Polese is confident that Marimba's early start, first-rate technology, and broad corporate customer base give it a leg up on rivals. "We've only just scratched the surface of where we can ultimately go as a company," she says. "Our challenge now is scaling quickly enough to keep up with all the opportunity in the market."

A COMPUTER GAME NAMED ELIZA

How did Polese get turned on to computers in the first place? As a kid she spent a lot of time playing at Berkeley's Lawrence Hall of Science, a museum with hands-on technology exhibits for children. "There was a really fun game called Eliza, which was, as it turns out, one of the first significant AI [artificial intelligence] programs," she says. "That was my first interaction with computers, and it was fun." When she was an undergrad in college, Polese passed this enthusiasm on to kids by teaching basic programming at the very same museum.

But Polese worries that more women and girls don't associate technology with fun. Even in the Internet sector, where women are starting consumer e-commerce companies in large numbers, she notes that they aren't as involved with the technology side of the Net. To help address this imbalance, she serves as an advisory board member for Women in Technology International (www.witi.org) and speaks at industry events and conferences to encourage more women to pursue careers and assume leadership roles in technology.

"There's no reason women should feel like they're unable to or don't have the background to work in technology," she says. "Many men don't have the background, but they go and do it anyway. There's such a learning curve in this industry that it's better to just get on board and start getting used to it instead of worrying that you don't know enough."

Kim Polese's
TOP THREE LESSONS LEARNED

1. *"Hire up.* Hire better people than you think you need. And never hire friends over experience."

2. *"Form your own network.* Don't look for one perfect mentor. Make connections with smart people throughout your industry. Attend industry conferences and events, and strike up conversations with people."

3. *"Be a sponge.* Don't be afraid of what you don't know. Go out and learn it. Be open, curious, and inquisitive. All the smartest people are."

Marimba: KEY STRATEGIC TAKE-AWAYS

- If, while working at a company, you get a business idea that's even remotely related, seek legal counsel before you quit. Most venture capitalists and high-tech law firms strongly advise that you leave your current employer before you begin writing your business plan to avoid the possibility of intellectual property lawsuits.

- Consider using an experienced recruiter to staff up. Finding great employees can be tremendously time-consuming. Early on, Polese enlisted an executive recruiter specializing in pre-IPO startups to court the right management team.

- First and foremost, ensure that your customers are successful using your technology, product, or service. Marimba provides specific examples of customer successes to educate prospective customers about the benefits of using the company's products. Polese has found this to be a more effective way to sell Marimba's products than initially emphasizing specific product features.

- If your company catches a wave of media hype, don't take press coverage personally. While Polese was dismayed by the media's fixation on her as a female technology CEO, the press has nevertheless helped get the word out about the company.

- Focus on building a business for the long term. Many Net entrepreneurs want to take their companies public or sell them as quickly as possible and cash out, but this is counterproductive to creating a quality business that will last. Polese believes that a commitment to the long-term view is vital for building a strong, sustainable business.

VITAL STATS

- Founder: Vani Kola, CEO
- URL: www.rightworks.com
- Stock: Private
- Founded: 1996
- Headquarters: San Jose, CA

Netscape: RightWorks – Power Procurement

Location: http://www.rightworks.com/index_n.html   What's Related

**B2B EXCHANGE SOFTWARE
FOR POWERING DIGITAL MARKETPLACES**

RightWorks

HOME
COMPANY
PRODUCT
MARKET PRESENCE
NEWS
PRESS RELEASES
EVENTS
CAREERS
CONTACT US

THE FUTURE OF DIGITAL MARKETPLACES STARTS HERE.

As companies throughout the world race to bring their businesses to the Internet, RightWorks is quickly emerging as the leading provider of software for powering the B2B exchanges that are changing the way companies do business. The recent announcement of ICG's acquisition of a majority stake in RightWorks--which now values privately held RightWorks at $1.25 billion--is yet another indicator that RightWorks has both the vision and the technology to help power the next wave in the Internet economy: digital marketplaces. Click here for the full story

BREAKING NEWS

RightWorks Expands Network of Suppliers with TPN Register

Breakaway Solutions and RightWorks Team with HigherMarkets to Create First Higher Education E-Marketplace

ICG Commerce Teams Up With RightWorks and CommerceQuest

RightWorks and Aspect Sign

FEATURED HIGHLIGHTS

RightWorks Selects webMethods for Seamless Integration with Leading Enterpri Systems webMethods B2B Provides Business-To-Business Integration (B2B/) S to Increase Productivity and Supply Chain Efficiencies for FacilityPro.com and O Leading B2B Marketplaces

RightWorks Emerges as the Standard Infrastructure of Choice for Powering Digit Marketplaces Breakaway Solutions, Tradeum, a VerticalNet Inc. Company, and CommerceQuest Select RightWorks as Core Enabling Technology

RightWorks and ec-Content, Inc. Partner to Simplify Content Management for Ne Marketplaces Partnership Streamlines Access to Broad Range of Quality, Search Catalog Content

RightWorks, ec-Content partner on b-to-b offerings--The combined offerings of RightWorks and ec-Content will help trading exchanges assist participants in the product-discovery and negotiations processes.

20

RightWorks

Powering Procurement on the Net

"I have a lot of confidence in my ability to succeed at things that I have never attempted. I like to take quantum leaps."
—Vani Kola

THE B2B BLIZZARD

Vani Kola has amazing intuition. As early as 1995—a year before Yahoo! went public, when the commercial Internet was still in its infancy—the 36-year-old entrepreneur and mother of two young daughters foresaw the e-business phenomenon that's now whirling through the world of corporate enterprises. Today she's at the helm of RightWorks, a well-capitalized Internet software company that's making it as easy for corporate employees to buy a Palm Pilot as it is for you to buy a book or CD from Amazon.com.

Moving corporate procurement procedures to the Web is no small task, especially considering the bureaucratic maze most purchase requisitions must navigate before they're finally approved. But the effort required to get online can be worth it. After implementing an "e-procurement" solution, companies can quickly save huge amounts of money. In fact, automating order-flow systems can improve the bottom line by an estimated 5 to 10 percent.

But Kola isn't stopping with Web-enabling corporate procurement processes. She has her sights set on a market that extends far beyond automating paper-based purchasing: She's going after a slice of the business-to-business exchange market, which is exploding as corporate America migrates to e-business. RightWorks, an e-procurement leader, is deploying its Web-based software (also named RightWorks) for *online B2B marketplaces* that assemble business buyers and suppliers in a plethora of vertical markets (think metals, paper, chemicals). With this new form of business intermediary fueling the B2B revolution, Kola has expanded her company's focus to include automating procurement for e-commerce further up the supply chain, making RightWorks the first Web technology company to automate raw materials purchasing.

When you step off the elevator into RightWorks' space-station-like, doughnut-shaped fourth-floor offices, you can see an internal courtyard, complete with babbling fountain, or a view of downtown San Jose's palm-tree-studded cityscape. But the company's employees are too busy refining and marketing RightWorks' application to enjoy the view. With the rise of digital marketplaces, Kola and company are pursuing a whole new breed of customer. And RightWorks' application can already be found under the hood of leading e-markets.

PLOTTING HER COURSE AT THE LOCAL LIBRARY

In 1995, Kola was working as an engineering project manager at Consilium, a company that creates software applications to automate computer-chip and other complex manufacturing processes. After overseeing the development and successful launch of new software to streamline record-keeping for pharmaceutical manufacturing, she was ready for a new challenge. "I'd been working in software development for seven years and had gained the engineering management experience I wanted," says the India-born entrepreneur perched on a chair in her office, where her six-year-old daughter's bright paintings of horses and houses adorn the walls. She considered three options: going to Stanford Business School, moving to another company to get more experience, or starting her own business. Ultimately, her entrepreneurial curiosity got the best of her. "I had all these ideas so I decided to strike out on my own," she says.

It's not surprising that Kola jumped seemingly effortlessly into launching her own technology business. Throughout her life she's been full of spunk and derring-do. Case in point: As a young woman, she shocked her parents with the news that she wanted to major in engineering. "Women in my family don't necessarily go to college and they don't often go to engineering college," she explains with a bright smile. "But when I know I want something, I can convince, cajole, and charm until I get it, or if that doesn't work, I just go out and do it anyway." And that's exactly what she did, graduating with honors in electrical engineering from India's Osmania University and then earning an MSEE from Arizona State.

When it came to starting her own business, Kola was equally gutsy. She quit her job and made a list of 10 business ideas, all in the B2B space. "My instincts were that the B2B impact of the Internet would be enormous, and very few people were talking about this trend back in 1995," recalls Kola, whose work at Consilium had attuned her to the ways technology can simplify business processes. To narrow her list of ideas, Kola headed to the Sunnyvale Public Library, which houses a wealth of resources for Silicon Valley entrepreneurs. She did preliminary research and got information on how to write a business plan.

One of the hardest things Kola had to do was scratch ideas off her list. "I wanted to work on them all," she says. "The hardest part of being an entrepreneur is focusing." After whittling down the ideas to five, she began bouncing them off future potential customers and anyone else who was willing to hear them. She listened carefully to people's feedback, and then crossed off four more ideas. She decided that the one with the best chance for success was procurement automation. "That's where the deepest problems were and that's where the value message was strongest," she says.

AN ANGEL AND A COCKTAIL PARTY

After drafting a business plan and dubbing her company-to-be MediaKola, the spirited entrepreneur dove into raising seed money. She knew she wouldn't be able to get the business off the ground without some funding from the get-go. Creating the Web-based e-procurement solution she envisioned would require a major software development effort and the help of top-notch Silicon Valley programmers.

Kola started her search for seed capital by contacting successful entrepreneurs, many of whom were also angel investors, to tell them about her idea and get their advice. "Getting funded when you're just starting out is very difficult," admits Kola, who was pregnant part of the time she was looking for angel funding. "Investors have to bet on you as a person since there's little else to go on, especially if you have no prior experience building a company." One prospective angel even told her he wasn't comfortable investing in a pregnant entrepreneur, but this annoying encounter only strengthened her determination.

One of the first people who placed his bets on Kola was Dr. Suhas Patil, the founder of Cirrus Logic, an integrated circuit manufacturer. Kola met him through the networking organization The IndUS Entrepreneurs (TiE; www.tie.org) and, with her characteristic pluck and enthusiasm, told him all about her business. Patil was so impressed by her persistence and entrepreneurial passion that he invested $500,000 in seed capital along with five other wealthy Indian entrepreneurs in June 1996.

With seed funding secured, Kola rented a small office in downtown San Jose and got to work recruiting an all-star team through her network of colleagues and friends. "A great team is the most important thing for a business," she says. "Your idea will succeed or fail based on the people you select. Employees with a need to win and a drive to succeed make the difference between a team you can count on in good times and bad, and a team that falls apart."

What's the best place to recruit Silicon Valley technical talent? If you ask Kola, she'll tell you to try a cocktail party or check next door. She hired a NASA engineering manager she met at a cocktail party, as well as a neighbor who happened to also be a talented programmer. She also snatched up a user-interface specialist she met through a mutual friend. "Looking back, I'm amazed that I was able to recruit these people," she marvels. "I had minimal funding and they all accepted salary cuts to come pursue this crazy dream with me."

LAUNCHING THE FIRST PRODUCT, BIRTHING A SECOND BABY

Together the team created RightWorks' software product and launched it in the spring of 1998, just weeks after Kola's second daughter was born.

Just two days after the delivery, Kola was back at work helping her team get ready for the launch. Next up for Kola was a demanding press analyst tour to demo the company's product, with her newborn in tow. They visited five or six different cities in just a few days. "I brought my four-week-old daughter and mother with me," says Kola, whose stamina can run circles around that of any high-powered Silicon Valley exec. "My mom was very supportive and helped with childcare when I was busy demo-ing."

But Kola's talents extend beyond juggling product demos and baby feedings. She also has a flair for creative marketing. In one early guerrilla marketing tactic, Kola created an oversized direct-mail piece proclaiming the benefits of RightWorks' product and featuring a picture of herself mounted on foam core. It was too big to toss in an office wastebasket, so each recipient would at least have to take a look before deciding what to do with it. She personalized it with recipients' names and mailed it to Fortune 500 CEOs, generating a flurry of responses. "Michael Dell even emailed me to say 'Good luck. I like what you're doing,'" she recalls.

The first potential customer to show interest was Fujitsu, which wanted to improve efficiency by enabling self-service, Web-based purchasing for employees. Unfortunately, it turned out that RightWorks' software was incompatible with another system in use at Fujitsu. Undeterred, Kola returned six weeks later with a new version of RightWorks that interfaced perfectly with Fujitsu's internal systems. Fujitsu was the first, but it wasn't the only company quick to see the benefit of using the RightWorks product: Applied Materials and E-Tek Dynamics signed up shortly afterward.

"We're seeing CEO panic," says Ian Williams, vice president of marketing at RightWorks. "They know they must transform their companies into e-businesses, but they don't know what that means or where to start." RightWorks' clear value proposition is helping quell this panic and continuing to land the company big-name customers such as Wells Fargo and SGI, who pay upward of $500,000 for the RightWorks' e-procurement solution.

Thanks to Kola's vision, employees at RightWorks' client companies can use their Web browsers to access a custom-tailored catalog of products offered by multiple suppliers. After someone makes a purchase, the requisition is routed automatically through the approval chain via email, and then on to the supplier for fulfillment. Vendors can update the catalog themselves, and corporate purchasing departments can analyze buying trends with a few clicks of the mouse. The net effect is reduced paperwork, a streamlined process, and fewer unauthorized employee purchases.

MONEY TO GROW ON

After the team had successfully implemented RightWorks for its first few customers, Kola began pitching to institutional investors in hopes of landing enough money to expand. After discussions with a handful of carefully selected venture capitalists, she secured a $5 million round from Sequoia Capital in 1998. In retrospect, she wishes she'd sought institutional funding earlier to help jump-start her business. "I could have gotten the same investment at the same valuation a year earlier, but I didn't realize it at the time," she says. "The speed of growing a business has accelerated. Bootstrapped companies have too tough a time moving as quickly as their well-funded competitors. It took a long time to build businesses like HP, Apple, and Microsoft—they were putzing around in their garages for years. But now, the way to build a technology business is to be extremely well-capitalized."

Getting institutional funding at this and later stages was downright easy for Kola. "After we had proven our success in the marketplace, investors started a feeding frenzy and money was offered by several sources," she says. By January 2000 the company had amassed more than $33 million from Lehman Brothers, Sequoia Capital, i2 Technologies (one of RightWorks' partners), and other private investors. Just months later Kola was making headlines: She sold about half of her company's equity to Internet Capital Group (ICG), an investor in B2B companies, for $22 million in cash and about $635 million in stock—a deal that placed the company's value at an extraordinary $1.25 billion and represented the largest investment ever made by ICG at the time.

What's Kola's advice for other entrepreneurs seeking institutional funding? "The initial valuation investors give your company is relative. Don't get too hung up on the number. Instead, consider whether you and your team will own a small piece of a big pie or a big piece of a small pie," she says. "Choose your VCs carefully. They'll play key roles in helping you build a successful business and will become key partners."

THE BUSINESS MODEL

Unlike Web sites that depend on large traffic streams to make money, RightWorks' revenue comes from selling its Web-based software. While, as a privately held company, RightWorks doesn't disclose its revenue numbers, it uses different pricing models depending on how its application is used and focuses on deals of more than $500,000.

RightWorks sells its product to three main types of business customers:

Online Marketplaces

Companies using RightWorks software to run e-procurement for online B2B marketplaces pay an up-front flat fee of $500,000 to $5 million. The size of the fee depends on the volume of transactions the exchange estimates for the first year it uses the product. After the first year, RightWorks earns a slice of all transactions, which guarantees it an ongoing revenue stream and allows it to participate in the success of the digital marketplaces it serves.

Application Service Providers

ASPs (companies that host Web-based applications customers pay to use) can purchase RightWorks software and offer it as a service to their customers. The price an ASP pays depends on either the anticipated transaction volume or the number of customers who use the service.

Corporate Intranet Customers

Companies pay a per-user licensing fee to use RightWorks' e-procurement software on their corporate intranets. Corporate customers can either host the RightWorks solution themselves or outsource hosting through RightWorks.

COOPETITION IS THE NAME OF THE GAME

The frequency with which competitors turn into partners in the Web space has made *coopetition* the e-business buzzword of the day. Online exchanges such as Commerce One, which RightWorks once considered a competitor, are now becoming customers and allies as they turn to partnering for e-procurement solutions instead of building their own. "Through our partnership with Commerce One, businesses that want to participate in Commerce One's marketplace use RightWorks' platform for procurement," Kola explains. "And, conversely, businesses that use our platform can populate their online catalogs with products from Commerce One's exchange." VerticalNet—another early B2B exchange leader with more than 60 industry-specific vertical portals (Net jargon enthusiasts prefer the more concise *vortals*)—is another example of an online exchange that's implementing RightWorks' solution to streamline procurement.

While B2B exchanges are proving to be a lucrative new market focus for RightWorks, Kola's company is nevertheless facing fierce competition. Mountain View–based Ariba, whose stock skyrocketed after its IPO in May 1999, also offers Web-based procurement as part of its B2B e-commerce platform. Other competitors include e-business solution giants Oracle and SAP (the leading enterprise resource planning vendor), as well as smaller companies that are moving into this area.

Current competition aside, the key challenge facing Kola is growing RightWorks as quickly as possible so it can secure its place as the leading e-procurement solution provider. To this end the company is rapidly expanding. It has turned up the heat on its marketing efforts and has begun selling its product in Europe. And its San Jose headquarters are bursting at the seams with the growing number of new employees.

SHOOTING FOR THE MOON . . . OR IS IT MARS?

Kola is steering the company toward an IPO to raise additional capital resources to gain an even larger footprint in the market. "We have the opportunity to land this ship on the moon or Mars," she says. "Where we land depends on how well we tune the engines, how well we pilot the ship, and the quality of the crew." With its hotshot partners, ongoing revenue streams, growing customer base, and billion-dollar-plus valuation, Right-Works seems to be turbocharged for space travel.

What does the future hold in store for Kola? Although she's completely focused on leading RightWorks, she daydreams about spending more time with her two young daughters and someday starting a nonprofit organization dedicated to helping young women and underprivileged children expand their career choices. She also wants to devote more time to advising other entrepreneurs, especially women. And it's certainly a good time for this.

According to Deepka Lalwani, founder of the Silicon Valley–based nonprofit organization Indian Business and Professional Women (www.ibpw.org), the number of female Indian and other entrepreneurs has grown tremendously over the past few years. "These days, it seems like every third woman attending our events is starting her own company," observes Lalwani. Kola is happy to count herself among the growing number of Indian-American women entrepreneurs. "Indian girls need more role models," she says. "If my success makes me a role model for them, as well as other women and entrepreneurs in general, I'm proud to be a part of that." Kola has certainly inspired at least one girl so far: her six-year old daughter, who's already dreaming about being an engineer and entrepreneur like her mom when she grows up.

Vani Kola's
TOP THREE LESSONS LEARNED

1. *"Never give up.* You have to fundamentally believe in yourself and your idea when others won't."

2. *"Network, network, network.* Long-term relationships are very important. Accept offers of help and advice graciously."

3. *"Give back and uphold what you believe in.* As the founder and the soul of a company, be a leader. This means building an identity based on integrity."

RightWorks: KEY STRATEGIC TAKE-AWAYS

- When evaluating multiple business ideas, consider where the pain is. Many technology pundits and VCs say that "it's easier to sell painkillers than vitamins." In other words, pursue a business idea that solves a serious problem. Kola picked e-procurement because that's where she saw the biggest gains for future customers.

- Be constantly on the lookout for new emerging markets. With the rapid growth of B2B exchanges, Kola shifted her emphasis from intranet-based corporate purchasing to enabling procurement for online marketplaces such as i2's TradeMatrix.com.

- Don't wait too long to secure institutional funding, which can help your company grow quickly. In hindsight, Kola believes she should have sought institutional funding before developing RightWorks' product.

- Go after the best insitutional investors—those who can provide solid advice, connections, experience, and business know-how in addition to money. "I had the option to bring in Sequoia Capital at a much lower valuation or bring in some second-tier investment firms at a higher valuation," says Kola. "I believed Right-Works' long-term success depended on having first-tier investors and convinced my board to go with Sequoia."

- Be willing to take risks. You might fail, but it will also increase your chances for success. RightWorks made some risky decisions when it shifted its strategic focus to the emerging digital exchange market and rearchitected its technology accordingly.

- Focus on sales and marketing from the start. In RightWorks' initial phase, the team was completely focused on developing their product, not on marketing it. Kola believes that marketing Right-Works sooner, even before its initial product launch, would have helped create buzz that would have made the sales effort easier.

Appendix A
Resources for Entrepreneurs

There are literally thousands of organizations, Websites, magazines, and books that provide practical help to entrepreneurs. Some of the most relevant and unique resources for Internet entrepreneurs (especially women) are listed here.

ORGANIZATIONS

Association of Internet Professionals (AIP)
www.association.org

AIP is a worldwide community for Internet professionals that serves as a networking forum for anyone working in the Internet space.

Endeavor
www.endeavor.org

This nonprofit organization's mission is to be the leading supporter of entrepreneurship in Latin American emerging markets. With offices in Chile, Argentina, and Brazil, it helps entrepreneurs get seed and VC financing, sign strategic alliances, find proper management, and make contact with key people they need to access so that their ventures succeed.

The Forum for Women Entrepreneurs (FWE)
www.fwe.org

FWE is an organization for women building and leading high-growth technology companies. It offers innovative programs, access to funding sources, and a supportive and knowledgeable online community.

GirlGeeks
www.girlgeeks.com

This is a career and mentoring Website for women in computing, I.T., and the Internet. It reaches an international audience of women who want to further their technical understanding, skills, and careers through close community interaction with top women role models and mentors.

GraceNet
www.gracenet.net

This free membership organization based in the San Francisco Bay Area is dedicated to promoting the contribution of women in technology.

Indian Business and Professional Women (IBPW)
www.ibpw.org

IBPW is a Silicon Valley support network for professional women. Through seminars and workshops, it promotes education, leadership, and self-development. These events are open to women and men of Indian and non-Indian origin.

The IndUS Entrepreneurs
www.tie.org

A Silicon Valley nonprofit established to foster entrepreneurship in the South Asian American community through networking and mentoring, IndUS offers regular meetings with discussions and speakers that focus on topics relevant to all entrepreneurs.

The Interactive Media Trade Association
www.mdg.org

This San Francisco–based nonprofit offers members networking and business development opportunities. A number of its programs, such as *VC one-on-one*, are aimed at entrepreneurs.

Round Zero
www.roundzero.com

Round Zero offers a forum where Silicon Valley professionals can exchange entrepreneurial experiences and discuss technology trends. It aims to foster entrepreneurship through its members' collective knowledge and broad network.

Software Development Forum
www.sdforum.org

SDF is a Silicon Valley forum that lets software and Internet professionals learn and network. It offers more than 20 events per month, many of them addressing issues faced by entrepreneurs and startups.

Webgrrls International
www.webgrrls.com

This organization provides a forum for women in new media and technology to network, exchange job and business leads, learn about new technologies, and mentor each other. With chapters in cities around the world, Webgrrls provides both online and offline resources for women at all levels of Internet use and technological interest.

Women in Multimedia (WiM)
www.wim.org

A nonprofit organization, WiM provides support and resources to women involved in new media and Internet careers and examines the social implications of emerging technologies.

Women in Technology International (WITI)
www.witi.org

WITI is dedicated to increasing the number of women in executive roles in technology, helping women become more financially independent and technology-literate, and encouraging young women to choose careers in science and technology.

The Women's Technology Cluster
www.womenstechcluster.org

This San Francisco–based organization is the first high-tech incubator designed to help women entrepreneurs launch and fund successful Internet and I.T. businesses. It provides office space, equipment, and training to its member companies.

WEBSITES FOR ENTREPRENEURS

Advancing Women
www.advancingwomen.com

This site offers many special sections for businesswomen. The Business Center, Biz Tools, and Web Women areas focus on entrepreneurs and women in technology.

Dotcomdivas.net
www.dotcomdivas.net

Join this free online forum for women Internet entrepreneurs and benefit from the knowledge, resources, and information shared by members. To join the site's list, send a blank email to dotcomdivas-subscribe@egroups.com.

EntreWorld
www.entreworld.org

This online directory scours the Web and provides only the most relevant entrepreneurial content. Especially useful are the Starting Your Business, Growing Your Business, and Supporting Entrepreneurship areas of the site.

Idea Café
www.ideacafe.com

This Website includes a wide variety of resources for small business entrepreneurs, including access to online experts and advice on everything from choosing a business name to determining how much money you need to get going.

SBA's Office of Women's Business Ownership
www.sbaonline.sba.gov/womeninbusiness

This government agency provides programs and information for women entrepreneurs, including training, counseling, and mentoring services to help women start and expand their businesses.

Silicon Valley Bank eSource
www.esource.svb.com

Silicon Valley Bank's Website for entrepreneurs offers infrastructure services for high-tech startups, practical advice, technology news, and event listings.

SiliconValley.com
www.sv.com

This technology news site run by the *San Jose Mercury News* includes local, national, and international technology news. It's a one-stop location to get the latest skinny on what's happening in the technology business arena.

Wall Street Journal Startup site
www.startup.wsj.com

Updated daily, this *Wall Street Journal* Website is a must-see for all entrepreneurs. The Startup Toolkit section offers a multitude of resources to help you get your company off the ground and funded.

FUNDING RESOURCES

Artemis Ventures
www.artemisventures.com/resources.html

The Website of this venture capital fund includes many "how tos" for entrepreneurs. Find out how to avoid the seven deadly sins of entrepreneurs, how to create a killer business plan, and how to build a stellar executive team.

Capital Across America
www.capitalacrossamerica.org/wbo.htm

This small business investment company (SBIC), licensed by the SBA, was founded to provide women business owners with capital. It also offers women entrepreneurs advice and resources.

Capital Connection
www.capital-connection.com

This financing site for entrepreneurs provides useful tools and information to help startups find capital sources. See the Resources for Women Entrepreneurs section at www.capital-connection.com/womensvc.html.

Garage.com
www.garage.com
Through its investor network, Garage.com helps entrepreneurs obtain seed capital. It also provides mentoring resources to entrepreneurs to help reduce the time it takes to get their startups funded.

Money Tree
www.mercurycenter.com/svtech/companies/moneytree/
Wondering which startups are getting funded? And how much money they've received? The Money Tree Survey by PricewaterhouseCoopers, conducted quarterly, shows the equity investments made in private U.S. companies by the venture capital community by region and industry.

National Venture Capital Association
www.nvca.org
Need an overview of how the VC process works? This site provides one. It also provides venture capital funding statistics and links to resources for entrepreneurs and venture capitalists.

Springboard 2000
www.springboard2000.org
Ready to make your investor pitch? This is the Website for the Springboard 2000 venture capital forums, which connect investors and women founders seeking funding. Be sure to check out the Learning Center, which offers links to women-focused venture capital and entrepreneurial resources.

VentureOne
www.ventureone.com
This venture capital research firm has a Website that offers information on connecting startups to venture capital. Be sure to visit its Entrepreneur Resources sections as well as its Industry Data section, which provides quarterly statistics of the amount of venture capital invested by industry as well as funding trends.

Venture Wire
www.venturewire.com
Sign up for this free daily email newsletter to get the inside scoop on what businesses are getting funded, how much they receive, and the latest merger and acquisition activity.

vFinance
www.vfinance.com
At this site, you can search a database of angel investors and venture capitalists to find those who are a good match for your business plan. You can also submit

your plan to the site's network of investors and keep tabs on investments made by VCs.

Viridian Capital
www.viridiancapital.com

This venture capital firm focuses on investing in companies that are led, founded, or cofounded by women, and companies that sell products and services primarily to women. Like Capital Across America and the Women's Growth Capital Fund, it's an SBIC.

Women's Growth Capital Fund
www.wgcf.com

This fund invests in women-owned and managed businesses. Like Capital Across America, it's an SBIC licensed by the SBA.

MARKET RESEARCH RESOURCES

eMarketer
www.emarketer.com

This site offers statistics and commentary about Internet trends, as well as practical marketing advice for e-businesses.

Forrester Research
www.forrester.com

Forrester is an independent research firm that focuses on the future of technological change and its impact on businesses, consumers, and society. If you're researching a particular Internet market, there's likely to be a Forrester report with relevant data. A subscription to all its reports is pricey, but many briefings and reports are available for free on the Website.

Jupiter Communications
www.jup.com

This research firm provides clients with views of industry trends, forecasts, and best practices. Jupiter's research and advisory services, offered on a subscription basis, provide Internet business reports and data.

Media Metrix
www.mediametrix.com

This site ranks Websites by the number of unique visitors, reach, and other measures. You can view a list of the top 50 Web properties ranked by the number of monthly unique visitors for free. If you want more detailed information, there's a hefty subscription fee.

PC Data Online
www.pcdataonline.com
Similar to Media Metrix, PC Data Online provides Website rankings and demographic data about Website visitors. You can view a report showing the reach and number of unique visitors for the top 50 Websites for free (click on Public Reports). To see more detailed information, you'll need to pay a subscription fee.

MAGAZINES

Business 2.0
www.business2.com
This publication covers the Internet and technology business sectors, staying abreast of new industry trends.

Fast Company
www.fastcompany.com
Fast Company focuses on the best new practices that companies are putting in place as they address the needs of the new economy. The articles typically cover current issues affecting high-tech companies, as well as stories about the people and leaders in high tech.

The Industry Standard
www.thestandard.com
This weekly magazine covers the people, companies, and trends shaping the Internet economy.

Red Herring
www.redherring.com
This technology business magazine and Website centers on people starting, running, or investing in technology companies. You'll find stories about cutting-edge technologies, startups, and the latest happenings in the venture capital world.

Upside
www.upside.com
Providing an insider view of the world's leading technology companies, *Upside* features content geared toward high-tech entrepreneurs. Perusing its pages is a great way to spark new business ideas.

BOOKS

Crossing the Chasm: Marketing and Selling High-Tech Products to Mainstream Customers by Geoffrey A. Moore.
A business classic, this book describes the common traps high-tech startups encounter, and spells out how to avoid them.

Customers.com: How to Create a Profitable Business Strategy for the Internet and Beyond by Patricia B. Seybold.
Written by the leading e-business consultant who wrote the Foreword to this book, *Customers.com* shows how a customer-centric approach is critical to success in e-business. It's loaded with instructive case studies and sound advice.

The E-Myth Revisited: Why Most Small Businesses Don't Work and What to Do About It by Michael E. Gerber.
This classic outlines the key obstacles that cause many small businesses to fail and how to overcome them.

The Entrepreneurial Venture by William A. Sahlman et al.
Written by a group of Harvard Business School professors, this handbook for entrepreneurs provides practical advice as well as instructive case studies.

Financing the New Venture: A Complete Guide to Raising Capital from Venture Capitalists, Investment Bankers, Private Investors, and Other Sources by Mark H. Long.
This guide to financing explains the step-by-step process entrepreneurs should use to raise capital from angels and venture capitalists for a new venture.

High Tech Start Up: The Complete Handbook for Creating Successful New High Tech Companies by John L. Nesheim.
Incorporating a wide variety of case studies and examples, Nesheim explains the steps entrepreneurs typically take to start and grow a high-tech company. The book provides insight on the funding process and the stages a company goes through as it evolves.

Inside the Tornado: Marketing Strategies from Silicon Valley's Cutting Edge by Geoffrey A. Moore.
This follow-up to *Crossing the Chasm* explains how entrepreneurs in high tech can create and execute marketing strategies for the mass market. The book provides down-to-earth, practical theories and real-world case studies.

Pratt's Guide to Venture Capital Sources by Stanley E. Pratt.
This industry-standard reference book provides a comprehensive listing of venture capital sources in the United States. It's best to check this one out from the library—the cover price is $500-plus.

Rules for Revolutionaries: The Capitalist Manifesto for Creating and Marketing New Products and Services by Guy Kawasaki.
Written with Kawasaki's trademark flair, this book lays out strategies for beating the competition and successfully marketing a product in today's business world.

Appendix B
Net Biz Buzzwords

Affiliate marketing Multilevel marketing on the Web. The first affiliate marketing program was implemented by the mother of e-commerce companies, Amazon.com. Affiliate marketing programs allow anyone with a Website to earn commissions and referral fees by selling products for an e-commerce company.

Angel A sugar daddy of startups. An angel is a wealthy individual who invests in young private companies.

Applet A small Java program, such as a scrolling stock ticker, that runs within a Web page.

Application Program Interface (API) A set of functions that a computer program uses to interact with the operating system. Using Windows APIs, for example, a program can open files, dialog boxes, and windows associated with the Windows operating system.

Application Service Provider (ASP) A company that provides Web-based software, such as content management or accounting software, to business customers.

Bandwidth If you think of the Internet as plumbing, bandwidth is how fat a pipe is. It's the capacity of an Internet connection to transfer data. Its units are bits per second (bps) or kilobits per second (Kbps or simply K). Examples of high-bandwidth connections are T1 and T3 lines. 56K is a low-bandwidth connection. *Bandwidth* has also come to mean mental space or time (as in "I'd love to help you, but I don't have the bandwidth").

Banner Short for *banner advertisement,* it's the rectangular graphic at the top of most commercial Web pages. Banner ads are usually linked to the advertiser's Website.

Beta An early version of a Website or software program that's not yet ready for commercial release but available to selected people or companies so they can test it and report bugs.

Bootstrapping When you don't take outside funding from anyone to start your business. Entrepreneurs sometimes self-fund (i.e., bootstrap) their business's growth through personal savings and operating profits. Bootstrapping is a viable option for smaller companies, but usually doesn't make sense if you're in a high-growth business with a lot of competition. (Companies with VC funding can almost always squash their bootstrapped competitors.)

Browser Client software such as Netscape Navigator and Microsoft Explorer that allows you to surf the Web.

Brick-and-mortar A real-world (as opposed to a Web-based) business. This term came into use with the rise of e-commerce.

Business-to-business (B2B) E-commerce between businesses. Examples of B2B companies are Ariba (creator of software to enable B2B e-commerce), Vertical-Net (a site that connects business buyers and sellers in different industries), and RightWorks (maker of Web-based procurement software).

Business-to-consumer (B2C) Consumer-oriented e-commerce. Examples of B2C companies are Amazon.com, Eve.com, and Petopia.com.

Client In the context of the Web, the client is an HTML browser such as Netscape Navigator or Microsoft Explorer. More generally, a client is a program that initiates communication across a network. The program that waits to be contacted by the client is a server.

Consumer-to-consumer (C2C) E-commerce between individual consumers. A prime example of a C2C business is eBay.

Content The text, graphics, and other elements that are the primary information on a Web page. Many Web professionals consider content to be everything on a Web page except navigation and advertising.

Conversion rate The percentage of browsers who buy. If 100 people visit a Website during a certain time span and 10 of them make a purchase, the site has a 10 percent conversion rate.

CPM Cost per thousand page impressions. Advertising on the Web is priced based on the number of times an ad is viewed. For example, a $50 CPM means an advertiser pays $50 every thousand times the ad is served. The term *CPM* is a carryover from traditional media.

Destination Website A site you visit as an end in and of itself, not as a jumping-off place to other sites. Destination sites are most often a medley of content, community, and commerce. Examples of destination sites are iVillage, Fool.com, and ThirdAge.com.

E-tail Retail on the Web.

Extranet A part of the Internet that can be accessed by a company and designated users outside of the organization, such as employees working remotely and business partners. A firewall (a type of specialized software) protects an extranet from being accessed by unauthorized users.

Guerrilla marketing Creative, unconventional marketing tactics usually employed by startups lacking large marketing budgets. Guerrilla marketing tactics sometimes provide big bang for the buck.

Hit Accessing a file via the Web. Web pages are composed of multiple files—each graphic is its own file, and the text on a Web page is usually contained in a separate HTML file. When a Web page composed of several files loads in your browser, each file is counted as a hit. A Web page consisting of three images and the HTML file itself, for example, would count as four hits to the Web server hosting the page, but only one pageview.

HTML (Hypertext Markup Language) The language used for coding Web pages. An HTML file consists of text, which is displayed in a Web browser, and tags, which tell the browser how to format the text.

Impression An impression is the successful loading of an entire Web page in a browser (also known as a pageview).

Internet infrastructure Companies and technologies contributing to the Internet's underlying hardware and software.

Internet Service Provider (ISP) A company that provides access to the Internet for individuals and businesses. Popular ISPs are EarthLink and MCI WorldCom.

Intranet A part of the Internet that can be accessed only internally within a company or organization. A firewall, a type of specialized software, protects an intranet from being accessed by unauthorized users.

Keyword A word or group of words entered into a search engine.

Killer App A revolutionary software application. Web-based email is considered one of the Net's killer apps.

Mezzanine round The last round of funding a company receives from institutional investors before going public.

Pageview The successful loading of an entire Web page in a browser (also known as an impression).

Path-to-Profitability (P2P) The means by which a company achieves profitability. This bit of jargon has come into vogue as Net entrepreneurs and VCs have come around to the conclusion that burning cash can't last forever. The term underscores the greater emphasis now being placed on achieving profitability quickly.

Portal A site that provides an entrée to the Web at large. Portals are sites such as Yahoo!, Lycos, LookSmart, and AltaVista, which allow you to search or browse directories of Websites. They are jumping-off points to other places on the Web.

Reach An estimate of the percentage of Web-enabled machines that access a Website during a specified time period. Reach is a common metric that is used to measure success for a media-oriented site. A site that has a reach of seven percent for a specific month (which is stellar) means that seven percent of Web-enabled machines are estimated to have accessed the site that month. For a given month, extremely well-known sites such as Yahoo! and Amazon.com have reaches greater than 20 percent, whereas less well-known sites such as llbean.com and CareerMosaic.com have reaches under four percent. Media Metrix and PC Data Online, two Web tracking companies, publish estimates of reach.

Run of site Web advertising space for which an advertiser pays to have its banner placed anywhere on the site where there's available inventory. Run-of-site ad placements are much less expensive than targeted advertising.

Seed money The initial outside investment a startup receives to get off the ground. It's often provided by friends, family, and angel investors.

Series A, B, C, etc. In the venture capital world, investments in startups are made in separate funding rounds. Each round is usually larger than the previous one. The Series A round provides entrepreneurs with the money they need to start their business. Series B and Series C, as well as subsequent rounds, are used to grow the company.

Server In the context of the Web, a server stores Web files that browsers can access. More generally, when two programs communicate across a network, a server is the program that serves files when contacted by a client.

Sticky This term describes content or features that keep users coming back. Stock quotes, horoscopes, and Web-based email are examples of sticky features.

Venture capitalist (VC) A professional institutional investor who works at a firm that invests other people's money in private companies. Venture capitalists are often instrumental in getting high-tech startups off the ground.

Viral marketing Any Web marketing tactic that spreads a message like wildfire. It's often used to mean "word of mouth." Including a marketing message (such as "Try Yahoo! Messenger") at the bottom of all email messages is an example of an exceptionally effective viral marketing tactic used by providers of free Web-based email.

Vortal Shorthand for "vertical portal." It's a Website that provides an entrée to a specific industry, subject, or market online. Examples are sites such as Internet.com (an information and resource site about the Internet) and GoFish.com (an online marketplace for, you got it, seafood).

Index

Photo Credits

Chapter 1. Eugenie Diserio, Astronet: Photo by Andrew Stewarts

Chapter 4. Candice Carpenter, iVillage: Photo by Shonna Valeska

Chapter 6. Mary Furlong, ThirdAge Media: Photo by Evan Pilchik

Chapter 7. Katie Burke, Desktop.com: Photo by Kim Harrington

Chapter 8. Susan Strausberg, EDGAR Online: Photo by Videler Photography

Chapter 9. Janina Pawlowski, E-Loan: Photo by Robert Houser

Chapter 10. Rosalind Resnick, NetCreations: Photo by Jay Manis

Chapter 12. Varsha Rao and Mariam Naficy, Eve.com: Photo by Bob Adler

Chapter 13. Durreen Shahaz, oneNest: Photo by Robert Kraybill

Chapter 14. Andrea Reisman and Jack, Petopia: Photo by Eric Schumacher

Chapter 18. Paula Jagemann, eCommerce Industries: Photo by Stephen R. Brown

Chapter 20. Vani Kola, RightWorks: Photo by Tom Lewis Photography

About the Author

Elizabeth Carlassare is an Internet strategist and a coach for women in technology and women entrepreneurs, helping them reach their goals and craft the lives they want. She's also the creator of dotcomdivas.net, an online open forum for women Internet entrepreneurs. She's regularly interviewed by the press on the topic of women's entrepreneurship and the Internet.

Elizabeth has more than 10 years of experience at high-technology companies, including Adobe Systems, Intuit, SGI, and MyWebtivity (an Internet company she cofounded).

She holds a certificate in Web/IP Systems Engineering, an MS in Energy and Resources from UC Berkeley, and a BA in physics and French literature. She lives in Santa Cruz, California, with her partner, Jon, and cat, Bozo. Email her at elizabeth@dotcomdivas.net.